Further praise for *The Radical and the Republican*

"[A] fine new account of Lincoln's friendship with Frederick Douglass."   —Adam Gopnik, *The New Yorker*

"Extremely insightful. . . . *The Radical and the Republican* should be read by all people who wish to understand reform and the nature of change in the Civil War era and the two men who played such indispensable roles in emancipating not only the slaves but much of the country from the scourge of slavery."
                    —Phillip Shaw Paludan, *Civil War Book Review*

"An eye-opening and absorbing account of the relationship between Lincoln and Douglass."
                    —Chuck Leddy, *The Christian Science Monitor*

"Studded with telling quotes from both men and comes to conclusions that are often really far reaching."
                    —Michael P. Riccards, *Washington Times*

"Compelling. . . . A fresh and fascinating look at the lives of these two pivotal players during the Civil War. This book makes a substantial and singular contribution to the literature. . . . The author has taken a complicated tale and made it understandable and accessible to the reader without being patronizing."
                    —James A. Percoco, *Civil War News*

"A sharp analysis by Oakes of how Lincoln the politician and Douglass the reformer worked, separately and together, to abolish slavery in America. Oakes's narrative focuses on the fascinating symbiosis between these two highly public men . . . but it's

also a brilliant meditation on the timeless, crucial roles played by the radical and the politician to resolve any public issue."

"Oakes brilliantly follows the choreography by which Lincoln and Douglass, 'both uncommonly intelligent,' moved from a position of mutual incomprehension to one of mutual admiration and respect, one great man taking the measure of another great man." —Garry Wills, author of *Lincoln at Gettysburg*

"James Oakes has an uncanny feel for how American politics actually worked in the Civil War era. His beautifully carved gem of a book rescues Abraham Lincoln and Frederick Douglass from the smugness of posterity—and forcefully explains how radicalism and mainstream party politics converged to overthrow American slavery." —Sean Wilentz, Princeton University, author of *The Rise of American Democracy: Jefferson to Lincoln*

"James Oakes' absorbing story of two familiar American heroes—Frederick Douglass and Abraham Lincoln—resonates with new perceptions and insights. This is a great American tale told with a deft historical eye, painstaking analysis and a supple clarity of writing. *The Radical and the Republican* is a significant book that should be read by all Americans."

—Jean H. Baker, author of *Mary Todd Lincoln: A Biography*

"Here they are, with equal billing, two of America's master politicians, Frederick Douglass and Abraham Lincoln. They made history back in those quaint days when, occasionally, politicians acted with both character and courage. James Oates has given us a bracing book."

—William S. McFeely, author of *Frederick Douglass*

ALSO BY JAMES OAKES

Slavery and Freedom:
An Interpretation of the Old South

The Ruling Race:
A History of American Slaveholders

THE RADICAL AND THE REPUBLICAN

FREDERICK DOUGLASS,
ABRAHAM LINCOLN,
AND THE TRIUMPH OF
ANTISLAVERY POLITICS

James Oakes

W · W · Norton & Company

New York   London

For information about permission to reproduce selections from this book,
write to Permissions, W. W. Norton & Company, Inc., 500 Fifth Avenue,
New York, NY 10110

Manufacturing by RR Donnelley, Bloomsburg
Book design by Margaret Wagner
Production manager: Anna Oler

Library of Congress Cataloging-in-Publication Data

Oakes, James.
The radical and the Republican : Frederick Douglass, Abraham Lincoln, and the
triumph of antislavery politics / James Oakes. — 1st ed.
p. cm.
Includes bibliographical references and index.
ISBN-13: 978-0-393-06194-9 (hardcover)
ISBN-10: 0-393-06194-9 (hardcover)
1. Douglass, Frederick, 1818–1895. 2. Lincoln, Abraham, 1809–1865.
3. African American abolitionists—Biography. 4. Presidents—United States—
Biography. 5. Slavery—Political aspects—United States—History—19th cen-
tury. 6. Antislavery movements—United States—History—19th century. 7.
United States—Politics and government—1861–1865. 8. United States—
Politics and government—1857–1861. 9. United States—Race relations—
History—19th century. 10. Friendship—United States—Case studies. I. Title.
E449.D75015 2007
973.7'1140922—dc22   2006032215

ISBN 978-0-393-33065-6 pbk.

W. W. Norton & Company, Inc.
500 Fifth Avenue, New York, N.Y. 10110
www.wwnorton.com

W. W. Norton & Company Ltd.
Castle House, 75/76 Wells Street, London W1T 3QT

1 2 3 4 5 6 7 8 9 0

For our son,
DANIEL AGUSTÍN OAKES

CONTENTS

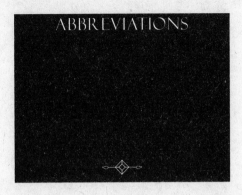

ABBREVIATIONS

CW   Roy P. Basler, ed., *The Collected Works of Abraham Lincoln* (New Brunswick, N.J., 1953–)

FDP   John W. Blassingame, John R. McKivigan, and Peter Hinks, eds., *The Frederick Douglass Papers* (New Haven, 1979–)

HI   Douglas L. Wilson and Rodney O. Davis, eds., *Herndon's Informants: Letters, Interviews, and Statements about Abraham Lincoln* (Urbana and Chicago, 1998).

Life & Writings   Philip S. Foner, ed., *The Life and Writings of Frederick Douglass* (New York, 1950–)

RW   Don E. Fehrenbacher and Virginia Fehrenbacher, compilers and eds., *Recollected Words of Abraham Lincoln* (Stanford, Calif., 1996)

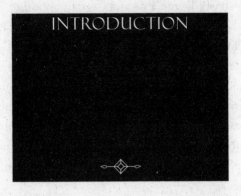

INTRODUCTION

The press reports were vicious. Lincoln had spoken recently in Springfield and on June 15, 1856, a leading Democratic Party newspaper, the *Illinois State Register*, denounced his speech as "niggerism." Lincoln had said nothing he had not said many times before. If anything the speech was already familiar to his listeners. Since the founding days of the Republic Congress had exercised the power to restrict slavery's expansion, Lincoln argued, and Congress should continue to do so—for the simple reason that slavery was wrong. But the Democrats, led by Illinois Senator Stephen A. Douglas, had no such moral qualms; they were content to allow the territories to decide for themselves whether or not to legalize slavery.

Lincoln's claim that slavery should be restricted because slavery was wrong struck Democrats as a flagrant appeal to radicalism. It was black abolitionist propaganda, the *Register* cried, adding that Lincoln's speech "has as dark a hue as that of Garrison or Fred Douglass."[1]

Frederick Douglass. It was enough for the *Register* to print the name with no further identification. Everyone knew who he was: an escaped slave, an infamous abolitionist, easily the most prominent black man in the United States. It was not the last time Illinois Democrats would fasten that name around Lincoln's neck.

Stephen Douglas did it all the time during his famous debates with Lincoln in 1858. In their second encounter, at Freeport in late August, Douglas the senator claimed that Douglass the abolitionist was one of Lincoln's closest advisers. When the crowd hooted at this, the senator pressed his point further. He claimed that on a previous visit to Freeport he had seen Frederick Douglass himself seated in a "magnificent" carriage and accompanied by two white women, a mother and her daughter, all of them being driven by another white man.

"What of it?" someone in the crowd shouted.

"All I have to say of it is this," Senator Douglas answered, "that if you, Black Republicans, think that the negro ought to be on a social equality with your wives and daughters, and ride in a carriage with your wife, whilst you drive the team, you have a perfect right to do so." Senator Douglas then passed along a rumor to the effect that "one of Fred. Douglass' kinsmen, another rich black negro, is now traveling in this part of the State making speeches for his friend Lincoln as the cham-

1. *CW*, vol. 2, p. 344.

pion of black men."[2] For an accomplished race-baiter like Stephen Douglas, there was no more effective weapon than linking his opponent with the name of Frederick Douglass.

So he did it again, during the debate at Charleston, Illinois, on September 18. The senator said that in 1854, while canvassing the northern part of the state, "I found Lincoln's ally, in the person of Fred. Douglass, THE NEGRO, preaching abolition doctrines, while Lincoln was discussing the same principles down here." He cited a more recent speech "made by Fred. Douglass . . . in which he conjures all the friends of negro equality and negro citizenship to rally as one man around Abraham Lincoln, the perfect embodiment of their principles."[3]

Anticipating the senator's relentless race-baiting, Lincoln asked his listeners during a Chicago speech to "discard all this quibbling" about "this race and that race and the other race being inferior." Senator Douglas could hardly let such a remark pass, so during the sixth debate, in Quincy, on October 13, he quoted it verbatim and then strung together the names of prominent abolitionists, asking rhetorically, "Did Lovejoy, or Lloyd Garrison, or Wendell Phillips, or Fred. Douglass, ever take higher abolition grounds than that?"[4] To hear the senator talk, Abraham Lincoln and Frederick Douglass were close friends and staunch allies.

It comes as something of a shock to see just how much vulgarity Stephen Douglas was prepared to inject into his exchanges with Abraham Lincoln. (It is almost as shocking to watch how far Lincoln was willing to descend in his unsuccessful efforts to capture the low ground from the distinguished sena-

2. Ibid., vol. 3, pp. 55–56.
3. Ibid., pp. 171–72.
4. Ibid., p. 263.

tor.) Were *these* the Lincoln-Douglas debates? One of the great highlights of American political discourse? Needless to say, the debates had their better moments, especially when Lincoln moved up rather than down, ascending to some of his finest, most poetic denunciations of human slavery. When Lincoln proclaimed that every man, black or white, had an inalienable right to the fruits of his own labor, Douglas was driven to distraction. Lacking a decent reply, the senator instinctively resorted to racist invective and carefully worded hints about the relationship between Abraham Lincoln and Frederick Douglass.

Sometimes the senator just made things up. He almost certainly had not seen Frederick Douglass in Freeport, much less riding in a carriage with two white women. Moreover, Lincoln was not an abolitionist. He and Douglass had never met. Lincoln surely knew who Frederick Douglass was, and by the fall of 1858 Frederick Douglass knew who Abraham Lincoln was, but the same would be true of anybody who read the newspapers. It would be reasonable, then, to dismiss the Illinois senator's strenuous efforts to connect Abraham Lincoln to Frederick Douglass as one more bit of racist pandering.

But Stephen Douglas was a smart man and an uncommonly shrewd politician. He knew what he was doing, and some of the things he said were not made up. Frederick Douglass had been in Chicago in 1854, "preaching abolition doctrines," although Lincoln was not preaching the same things downstate. And Douglass had given a speech in 1858 praising Lincoln, though not for his abolitionism, as the senator said, but for upholding the best principles of the Republican Party. Indeed, the senator's demagogic references to Frederick Douglass would have fallen flat if it were not at least plausible that the famed abolitionist was a close ally of Abraham Lincoln's. It *was* plausible because by the mid-1850s Lincoln the lifelong politician was rapidly becoming one of the nation's leading proponents of antislavery politics. Meanwhile Frederick Douglass, the lifelong abolitionist, had a few years earlier become a convert to antislavery politics. The politician and the abolitionist were converging, and with good reason. They stood together on the same side of an immense historical struggle, pitting those who hated slavery against those who did not. Stephen Douglas did not hate slavery, and he fought ferociously against those who did. From his perspective the differences between Abraham Lincoln and Frederick Douglass were trivial, and he trusted his constituents to agree. Many of the senator's listeners in 1858 therefore had no trouble believing that there was some connection between Abraham Lincoln and Frederick Douglass. Not because it was true, but because it might as well have been true.

The senator did have a point. What difference was there, he wondered, between a politician whose platform was based on his hatred of slavery and a radical reformer who devoted himself to slavery's abolition? One hundred and fifty years later it takes some work to grasp the distinction between antislavery politics and radical reform.

Abraham Lincoln understood the distinction, and so did Frederick Douglass. Although he never mentioned Douglass by name, from the time of his earliest public expressions of opposition to slavery Lincoln was sharply critical of the abolitionist movement to which Douglass faithfully belonged. He was still making the point when he ran for President in 1860, repeatedly insisting that he was not an abolitionist. For that very reason Douglass maintained a skeptical distance from Lincoln in 1860. Douglass had hopes for the Republican Party, but he didn't fully trust Lincoln. And it stayed that way for several years.

Douglass was alternately elated and unsparing about Lincoln's presidency. It took eighteen months for Abraham Lincoln to proclaim emancipation—too much time, in Frederick Douglass's view. But it took a long time for Frederick Douglass to appreciate the constraints that American democracy placed on antislavery politicians. During those years Douglass had a lot of rough things to say about Lincoln.

Douglass's criticism gradually subsided. He eventually came to think of Lincoln as both a good friend and a great man. For that to happen both of them had to change. Everyone knows that as the war years passed Abraham Lincoln grew in wisdom and judgment. More than that, Lincoln was radicalized by the war. He eventually took the radical position on emancipation, the radical position on black troops, and in the end he moved toward a radical position on equal rights. Lincoln overthrew his lifelong conviction that the Constitution protected slavery in the southern states when he found, tucked away in the war powers of the presidency, a legal justification for emancipation. He then committed himself to the enlistment of black soldiers, over-turning a long-standing prohibition on black troops in the U.S. Army and, not coincidentally, turning the southern world upside down. Lincoln even began to awaken from his lifelong insensitivity to racial injustice. He abandoned all talk of coloniz-ing blacks somewhere outside the United States, and late in his presidency he was urging politicians in Louisiana to consider allowing black men to vote. These were radical moves or, at the very least, moves in a radical direction. To a committed aboli-tionist like Frederick Douglass, the President's radical turn made Lincoln an increasingly appealing figure.

Douglass changed as well. As Lincoln was becoming a radi-cal, Douglass was becoming a Republican. Long before the Civil

War he had come to appreciate that militancy alone was not enough to bring about social change, that all his fiery speeches and ferocious editorials would amount to empty bellowing until they were translated into concrete policies by politicians with their hands on the levers of power. He also came to appreciate that in a democratic system politicians answered to a wider constituency than his narrow circle of abolitionist radicals. In the end Douglass realized how much skill, even genius it had taken for a politician like Lincoln to maneuver the northern electorate toward the same radical conclusions he himself had reached. In short, Douglass had come to appreciate the power of mainstream politics.

This was no sudden epiphany on Douglass's part. The arc of his entire biography propelled him toward the center of things. He began his life as a slave, an outsider by definition, someone with no political standing anywhere in the United States. Having escaped to New England, Douglass was free to enter public life, but he did so by joining a faction of radical abolitionists that condemned all political agitation against slavery. By the late 1840s Douglass had begun to glimpse the radical potential of electoral politics, but he remained contemptuous of the major parties and their leaders. In 1860 he came very close to endorsing the Republican candidate for President, only to back away. But by 1864, having met Lincoln and seen what he could do, Douglass abandoned his long-standing disdain for the compromises that were, and are, a necessary part of any genuinely democratic politics.

Here, then, is the story I want to tell: how Lincoln and Douglass converged at the most dramatic moment in American history. The story commands our attention in part because the two extraordinary personalities are fascinating on their own terms. But there is more to it than that. Lincoln and Douglass, seen together, reveal what can happen in American democracy when progressive reformers and savvy politicians make common cause.

Abraham Lincoln and Frederick Douglass are among the people I most admire in all of nineteenth-century American history. It frustrates me that it took so long for them to come together. So I've brought them together in this book, standing them side by side, so as to measure them in each other's light and see them from each other's perspective. Here are two men whose historical reputations rest chiefly on their mutual hatred of slavery. Why did it take so long for them to appreciate each other? What kept them apart, and what eventually drew them together? There are long and complicated answers to these questions, and they take up most of this book.

But there's a short answer as well. Lincoln was a politician and Douglass was a reformer, and the difference, as either of them might have said, was at some point irreconcilable. As a politician Lincoln liked to position himself as the conservative, moved by forces greater than any one man. As a reformer Douglass preferred to position himself on America's left flank; he would hold fast to the moral high ground no matter how great the forces arrayed against him. Lincoln's shrewdness as a politician could obscure the bedrock principles from which he never deviated. But just as often Douglass's high-mindedness obscured the political calculation that went into the construction and reconstruction of his antislavery arguments. So long as both men stood on their respective perches, so long as they found it necessary to present themselves as the conservative politician and the radical reformer, the differences between them would seem greater than they actually were.

Historians are impressed by the skill with which Lincoln

manufactured his image as the voice of moderation amid screeching extremes. We should be no less impressed by the skill with which Douglass constructed the image of the aggrieved citizen, unjustly excluded from equal participation in the republican experiment, first as a slave and then as a black man. Beneath all of Douglass's seeming dogmatism rested a perfectly reasonable question: Why should he or anyone else have to settle for something less than equal rights? That was Lincoln's question too, and if it made Douglass's radicalism more reasonable, it made Lincoln's pragmatism more radical. They were never as far apart as they seemed.

Ironically, northern Democrats were the first to suspect that what Abraham Lincoln and Frederick Douglass had in common was far more threatening than what divided them. In 1864, as Lincoln was running for reelection, Democrats revived the issue of the President's connection to Frederick Douglass, an issue they had first broached in Illinois nearly a decade earlier. Only this time the Democrats had solid evidence. In December 1863 Douglass had given a speech detailing a meeting he had with Lincoln at the White House a few months before. When Douglass's speech was published, the Democrats gobbled up the juiciest quotes and regurgitated them in a pamphlet entitled *Miscegenation Indorsed by the Republican Party*. The Democrats were especially delighted by Douglass's boast that President Lincoln had received him "just as you have seen one gentleman receives another!"[5] Republican strategists reacted in panic to the Democrats' race-baiting and asked Douglass not to campaign publicly for Lincoln's reelection.

5. *FDP*, ser. 1, vol. 3, p. 606.

Lincoln did not panic. At the very moment that Democrats were savaging the President for having met with a notorious black abolitionist, Lincoln invited Douglass back to the White House for a second meeting. Douglass had been impressed by Lincoln at their first encounter. After leaving the White House the second time, Douglass seemed smitten; he never repeated his harshest criticism against Abraham Lincoln. And he never left the Republican Party.

THE RADICAL
AND THE
REPUBLICAN

I

"I WON'T STOP UNTIL I REACH THE UNITED STATES SENATE"

◈

I found employment on the third day after my arrival in New Bedford, in stowing a sloop with a load of oil for the New York market. It was new, hard, and dirty work, even for a calker, but I went at it with a glad heart and a willing hand. I was now my own master—a tremendous fact—and the rapturous excitement with which I seized the job, may not easily be understood except by some one with an experience something like mine. The thoughts—"I can work; I can work for a living; I am not afraid of work; I have no Master Hugh to rob me of my earnings"—placed me in a state of independence, beyond seeking friendship or support of any man. That day's

work I considered the real starting point of something like
a new existence.

—*Frederick Douglass*

The senator from Illinois was right: Frederick Douglass was
watching his reelection campaign, though not from a carriage
accompanied by two white women. In a speech at Poughkeepsie,
New York, Douglass joked about the recent misfortunes of
Democratic Senator Stephen Douglas, who was at war with an
administration of his own party while waging a bitter reelection
campaign against a formidable opponent. I used to hope, Douglass
quipped, that the Illinois senator might one day bring real distinction to the name Douglas, but with the senator's career in ruins the
former slave would have to build a reputation of his own. The audience roared with laughter, but Douglass concluded his joke with a
more serious point. He would leave the Democratic senator "in the
hands of Mr. Lincoln" and his fellow Illinois Republicans, who
together have "nobly upheld" the highest principles of their party. It
was August 1858, and it was the first time Frederick Douglass took
notice of Abraham Lincoln.[1]

Douglass liked what he saw, especially the address Lincoln
had given at the outset of his campaign for the Senate. It was
Lincoln's famous "House Divided" speech, and Douglass quoted
it approvingly and at length. Lincoln pointed out that the best
efforts of leading politicians to quell the agitation over slavery
had failed. Indeed, they were doomed to fail, Lincoln warned,
because at stake was a historic struggle between liberty and slavery, a struggle that would not end until "a *crisis* shall have been
reached" and a victor emerged. If liberty was defeated slavery

1. *FDP*, ser. 1, vol. 3, p. 237.

would spread itself throughout the United States. If liberty was victorious slavery's expansion would be halted and "the public mind" calmed by the knowledge that slavery had been put back where it belonged, on the road to ultimate extinction. These were the only alternatives, Lincoln insisted, for slavery and freedom could no longer coexist within the same nation. "A house divided against itself cannot stand."[2]

"Well and wisely said," Frederick Douglass commented. "Liberty or Slavery must become the law of the land."[3] By 1858 Abraham Lincoln and Frederick Douglass were saying the same thing, preaching the same antislavery politics. Why was this surprising?

Because there was nothing obvious or inevitable about it. It took some time for Lincoln to reach the conclusion that slavery and freedom were locked in a war to the death. It is even more astonishing that Frederick Douglass had, for several years, made the same conclusion the central theme of his antislavery politics. Astonishing not because the struggle between liberty and slavery was such a daring theme, but because of how far Douglass had to come to articulate any form of antislavery politics. For he had been born and raised a slave in a nation where slaves were not supposed to have anything to do with politics, much less antislavery politics. This supposition went well beyond the obvious fact that slaves could not vote or hold office; the same was true of many others in antebellum America, most obviously women. Beyond the denial of voting and officeholding, the slave's political identity was perfectly extinguished. Unlike women, slaves had none of the rights that gave citizenship its political vitality. They could not speak, publish,

2. *CW*, vol. 2, p. 461.
3. *FDP*, ser. 1, vol. 3, p. 237.

or assemble in public. They could not join protest parades; they could not give speeches; they could not publish newspapers. Slaves were not even supposed to read newspapers. They were not to engage in politics. In the world he grew up in, Frederick Douglass's politics were supposed to have been obliterated.

But they were not. As a slave he taught himself to read by mastering *The Columbian Orator*, a children's schoolbook filled with the inspiring speeches of great politicians who sang the praises of liberty and the rights of man. As a teenager Frederick pored over newspapers gobbling up the details of congressional debates. He read about a congressman who had once been President, John Quincy Adams, and his courageous efforts to force the House of Representative to accept antislavery petitions. When he was only eighteen or nineteen years old his friends invited him to join the East Baltimore Mental Improvement Society, where they discussed the major political issues of the day. Decades later one of the society's members vividly recalled his friend's youthful ambition. "I have not forgotten a remark you made . . ." wrote William Lloyd, "in a Debate one night you told me you never meant to stop until you got into the United States Senate."[4] Slaves were not supposed to think such things. When he escaped to freedom in September 1838, Frederick Augustus Washington Bailey, soon to become Frederick Douglass, was already full of political ambition.

He was also filled with hatred for slavery, not just the fact that *he* was a slave but that *anybody* was. By his own account young Frederick began to hate slavery when he was six or seven years old. In the years to come he was sometimes treated well and

4. William E. Lloyd to Frederick Douglass, June 13, 1870, Douglass Papers, Library of Congress.

sometimes with brutality, but when Frederick thought about the difference between good and bad treatment he concluded that even the kindest master could not make slavery tolerable. He had seen slavery at its most violent and its most benign, yet all of it made his resentment grow. By the time he ran away, when he was twenty years old, the young man already knew what an "abolitionist" was and knew that he was one. From a very young age Frederick Douglass had dared imagine that one day he would be free, just as he dared imagine that he would one day be a senator.

These two urges—one for freedom and the other for political life—were hard to separate in Douglass's mind. He never forgot the encomiums to freedom that were printed in *The Columbian Orator*. He often recalled how delighted he had been to discover, while he was still a slave, that there were politicians in the North who spoke openly in favor of his freedom. He could not have imagined becoming a senator without also imagining his freedom. Had he escaped and gone directly from slavery in Maryland to upstate New York, Douglass's abolitionism and his interest in politics would have fused quickly and naturally into antislavery politics. A new Liberty Party, dedicated to the legal overthrow of slavery, had been formed in 1839 and 1840. Although political abolitionists disagreed among themselves about the best way to frame the new party's message, all agreed that the problem of slavery required a political solution. But many abolitionists objected to any political agitation whatsoever, and the disagreement split the antislavery movement along roughly geographical lines. Abolitionists in Ohio and New York were instrumental to the Liberty Party's founding. But Douglass went to New England, where the abolitionists he met harvested his hatred of slavery but tried to squelch his interest in politics. It worked for a few years. Before he could become an abolitionist, Douglass had to escape slavery. But before he could embrace antislavery politics, he would have to escape William Lloyd Garrison.

THE GARRISONIAN DETOUR

When I escaped from slavery, and was introduced to the Garrisonians, I adopted very many of their opinions, and defended them just as long as I deemed them true. I was young, had read but little, and naturally took some things on trust. Subsequent experience and reading have led me to examine for myself. This has brought me to other conclusions. When I was a child, I thought and spoke as a child.[5]

—*Frederick Douglass, 1860*

When Douglass escaped from slavery in Baltimore, Maryland, he went first to New York City, where sympathetic abolitionists encouraged him to move on to more friendly terrain—not to Rochester, New York, where he eventually ended up, but to New Bedford, Massachusetts. There Douglass quickly discovered William Lloyd Garrison's fiery antislavery paper, *The Liberator*. He became an avid reader. Garrison's organizational home, the New England Anti-Slavery Society, was particularly influential in that part of the country. Douglass began attending local antislavery meetings and testifying against slavery in nearby churches. In August 1841, three years after his escape, Douglass attended a conference of Garrisonian abolitionists on Nantucket Island. He stood up and talked about his life as a slave and the delegates were stunned. Inspired by Douglass's performance, Garrison himself

5. *Life & Writings*, vol. 2, pp. 479–80. For a slightly different text, see *FDP*, ser. 1, vol. 3, p. 365.

took the platform and turned the heat up even further. The Garrisonians invited Douglass to join their movement and he quickly agreed. He quit his job and took to the road, preaching against slavery the Garrisonian way. There were other ways of spreading the word, some of them more compatible with Douglass's way of thinking, but he had entered the movement through the Garrisonian portal, and it shaped the way Douglass initially framed his own antislavery message.

The Garrisonian argument against slavery was simple but devastating: Slavery degraded everyone and everything it touched. Because they were pacifists, the Garrisonians had few tactical options. They rejected force in the struggle against slavery. The government could not compel the South to emancipate its slaves, nor could the slaves themselves rise in violent rebellion against their masters. Instead the Garrisonians advocated "Moral Persuasion," which in practice meant denunciation. They were good at it. They denounced the churches, not only those that defended slavery but those that merely accepted slaveholders into their congregations. They denounced the Constitution because it recognized and protected slavery. Garrison himself called the Constitution a "pact with the devil." He burned a copy of it in public. A corrupt Constitution meant a corrupt political system, so the Garrisonians denounced politics. They especially denounced other abolitionists who adopted antislavery politics. Instead Garrisonians preferred what they called the nonvoting policy. And just as they would not pollute themselves by participating in a degraded political system, so they sought to insulate the nation from slavery's corrupting influence by calling on northern states to secede from the Union. "No Union with Slaveholders" was their motto. More than a few observers noted a discrepancy in Garrisonian abolitionism between its histrionic rhetoric and its remarkably passive plan of action.

For several years Frederick Douglass was, in his own words, a faithful disciple of William Lloyd Garrison. He agreed that it was the first duty of the free states to dissolve the union with the slave states. He condemned "the pro-slavery character" of the Constitution and adopted the "*non-voting principle*." He rejected politics. He would not vote. He would not support antislavery candidates. He even flirted with pacifism. In 1843 he got into a public disagreement with more militant blacks, such as Henry Highland Garnet, who encouraged slave insurrection. As a faithful Garrisonian Douglass instead worked to promote a moral revolution by persuading listeners and readers that slavery was hateful. As part of that effort he would publish his own autobiography.

Douglass wrote his *Narrative of the Life of Frederick Douglass, an American Slave* in 1845, at the height of his association with Garrison. Although filled with shocking personal anecdotes, the book set out its central theme in Garrisonian terms: Slavery degraded everyone and everything it touched. Douglass wrote of "the brutalizing effects of slavery upon both the slave and the slaveholder." It undermined the slave family, but it also distorted the relations within the slaveholders' family. It turned capable and intelligent slaves into thoughtless ciphers, but it also turned humane and decent whites into cruel and bitter overlords. Slavery made ignorance a virtue and literacy a crime. It degraded Christianity, transforming believers into sinners and churches into temples of Satan. It degraded the law by unleashing lawlessness on the plantations, where rape was not a crime and murder went unpunished. Everything slavery came into contact with became brutal and uncivilized.[6]

6. *FDP*, ser. 2, vol. 1, is the authoritative version of the *Narrative*.

This was a sweeping indictment of slavery, but it was also a curiously narrow one. The *Narrative* was focused intently on slavery's degrading cruelty and the unseemly hypocrisy of the churches. But Douglass made no appeal to the principles of the Declaration of Independence; he had nothing to say about slavery's violation of the principle of fundamental human equality or its denial of the universal right to liberty. Nor did he invoke political economy. Nowhere in the *Narrative* did Douglass claim that slavery distorted the southern economy, stifled individual initiative, or thwarted the virtues of self-discipline. He claimed that slavery corrupted the entire South but not that it threatened northern freedoms. Thus Douglass passed over a number of antislavery arguments that would have appealed to a broad base of northern voters. Of course, appealing to voters meant politics, and to a faithful Garrisonian, politics was a degraded enterprise beneath the dignity of a great moral movement.

But precisely how faithful a Garrisonian was Douglass? There were some signs, early on, that he was less than a perfect match for the movement that claimed him. He betrayed an un-Garrisonian respect for the Liberty Party, the abolitionist organization that virtually invented antislavery politics in the early 1840s. More tellingly, he was never a very convincing pacifist. Even when he argued against support for slave insurrections, Douglass tended to fall back on pragmatic as much as principled considerations. The masters had all the guns; the slaves would get themselves killed; the survivors would be worse off than before. Then there was the matter of Edward Covey, the notorious "negro breaker" Douglass had been sent to by his master. If there was a climactic scene in the 1845 *Narrative*, surely it was the bloody brawl between Covey and Douglass. The former slave wrote with evident pride about his decision to fight back against Covey's assaults. It was a turning point in his life, Douglass wrote, the moment when he had in his own mind ceased to be a slave. He recounted the story of the fight with the skill and gusto of a gifted sportswriter, compelling the reader to root for the underdog and cheer his victory. The Covey story makes no sense as a pacifist sermon. It does, however, fore-shadow Douglass's later support for revolutionary violence. By 1852 he was publicly declaring that the "only way to make the Fugitive Slave Law a dead letter is to make half a dozen or more dead kidnappers."[7] Fugitive slaves who killed their would-be cap-tors had every moral right to do so. By 1859 he was pronouncing John Brown a hero of the antislavery movement.

But fifteen years earlier Douglass had been a sincere and grateful follower of William Lloyd Garrison. "I stand in relation to him something like that of a child to a parent," Douglass admitted after his ties to Garrison had been fractured.[8] Still later he offered a biblical addendum: When he was a child, he had acted as a child, suggesting that he could not have remained a Garrisonian forever. Ironically, the thing that set in motion the events that led to Douglass's estrangement from his father figure was the publication of his most thoroughly Garrisonian tract. He had written the *Narrative* in part to persuade the skeptics who wondered if someone so articulate had ever really been a slave. The autobiography provided the names and details that would prove Douglass's story true, but in so doing it had exposed him as a runaway. To escape recapture Douglass fled to Great Britain shortly after the *Narrative* was published in 1845. Even as he was leaving, however, his associates began to worry that once Douglass

7. *FDP*, ser. 1, vol. 2, p. 390.
8. *Life & Writings*, vol. 2, p. 210.

was abroad he might stray from the righteous Garrisonian path. He was gone for eighteen months, so he had plenty of time to wander off in his own direction.

The first signs of heresy were obscured by Douglass's provocative reassertions of the Garrisonian line. Indeed, it was Douglass's orthodoxy rather than his apostasy that raised eyebrows back home. In a farewell speech to the British people Douglass extended the argument of his *Narrative*—that slavery degraded everything it touched—by condemning the entire American nation for its complicity with slavery. Because the Constitution of the United States sanctioned slavery, because the churches of the United States defended slavery, Douglass now claimed that "the whole system, the entire network of American society, is one great falsehood, from beginning to end." Nothing was left uncorrupted. Slavery had "framed our civil and criminal code . . . , nominated our presidents, judges, and diplomatic agents . . . given to us our religion, shaped our morality."[9] With those parting words, Douglass returned to America in the spring of 1847, able to do so because his British friends had purchased his freedom.

Toward those who thought it unseemly that an American should speak so critically of his own country while in a foreign land, Douglass was unrepentant, even scornful. In his first public address upon returning to the United States he defiantly announced that "I have no love for America, as such; I have no patriotism. I have no country." Alienation so deeply felt was built into Garrison's brand of abolitionism. If all the institutions of American society were corrupted by slavery and racism, how could a former slave and a black man find any place for himself

9. *FDP*, ser. 1, vol. 2, p. 21.

in that society? How could he love a country, Douglass asked, "the Church of which, and the Government of which, and the Constitution of which are in favor of supporting and perpetuating this monstrous system of injustice and blood?"[10] The only position open to him was to advocate the overthrow of the Constitution itself.

But if this was "moral persuasion," exactly whom did Douglass think he could persuade by talking that way? No doubt his fellow Garrisonians were relieved that Douglass had returned to America spouting so much orthodoxy. But how many Americans, even northerners with antislavery sympathies, could be moved to anything but revulsion by such strident denunciations of their churches, their beloved Constitution, and their democratic politics? If Frederick Douglass retained any of his youthful interest in political activism, he would have to stop preaching only to the choir. He must have realized this, even before he came back to America.

THE ANTISLAVERY CONSTITUTION

The abolitionists Douglass met in Britain were rarely as doctrinaire as his patrons back home. Nor were his British listeners confined to abolitionists. As his audience widened, so did his argument against slavery. One early indication of this was a public letter he sent from England to Horace Greeley, the influential editor of the *New York Tribune*. To the largest readership of any American newspaper Douglass invoked "the immortal Jefferson" and used language that suggested he had been reading Jefferson's *Notes on the State of Virginia*. He claimed it was a

10. Ibid., p. 60.

crime to deprive a man of his "inalienable rights" and that slavery was "destructive to the moral sense," a clear reference to the moral philosophy that had influenced the Founders. He spoke admiringly of the English abolitionists who hung copies of the Declaration of Independence in their parlors. Never before had Douglass gone this far toward invoking the legacy of the American Revolution. He even defended his criticism of the United States as an act of patriotism. The "best friend of a nation," Douglass wrote, "is he who most faithfully rebukes her for her sins—and her worst enemy, who, under the specious and popular garb of patriotism, seeks to excuse, palliate, and defend them." This was a different Douglass, less doctrinaire and more attuned to popular opinion.[11]

By the time Douglass came back to the States he was ready to make a move. In England he had arranged for his benefactors to finance his purchase of a printing press. When Garrison balked at the idea, Douglass hesitated briefly. But after a lecture tour through the Midwest Douglass resumed his plans. He moved his family to Rochester, New York—beyond Garrison's bailiwick—and began publishing his own antislavery newspaper. Douglass claimed to be moving so as not to compete with the good work of his New England friends, but it was more than that, and the Garrisonians knew it. Their suspicions were soon confirmed when Douglass's paper, *The North Star*, revealed its editor's unmistakable interest in antislavery politics.

Douglass's dormant interest in politics was reawakened by the war with Mexico. Though the war was widely popular among citizens who saw continental expansion as America's manifest destiny, there were doubters, especially among critics

11. *Life & Writings*, vol. 1, pp. 144–49.

of slavery. That many of the Texans who had pressed for the war were slaveholders, that President James K. Polk, an aggressive expansionist, was himself a slaveholder, made the conflict seem like a southern land grab. Rather than fulfill America's destiny, critics complained, the Mexican War would increase the number of slave states and hence the political influence of the South. That was certainly the way Frederick Douglass saw it. He denounced the war as a brazen attempt to enhance the power of the southern slaveocracy.

But although he was shocked by the war itself, Douglass was at least as impressed by its political fallout. In 1846 a Pennsylvania congressman named David Wilmot introduced into the House of Representatives a "proviso" that would exclude slavery from any of the lands annexed to the United States as a result of the war. This intrigued Douglass because Congressman Wilmot was a member of the vehemently proslavery Democratic Party and anything but an abolitionist. Wilmot denied being motivated by any "morbid sympathy" for the slave. He had introduced his proviso as a northerner who resented the growing influence of the slave states in national politics. Carving more slave states out of the Mexican cession would only make matters worse. Enough northerners agreed with Wilmot to organize the Free Soil Party. Antislavery but not abolitionist, the new party was a coalition of those who shared Wilmot's resentment of southern power and those who disliked slavery itself. The Free Soil platform was summed up in its name: It was dedicated to restricting the expansion of slavery into the western territories.[12]

12. Jonathan Earle, *Jacksonian Antislavery and the Politics of Free Soil, 1824–1848* (Chapel Hill, N.C., 2004).

Douglass was fascinated by the possibility of building a larger antislavery coalition than the strictly abolitionist Liberty Party ever could. So in 1848 he urged those who intended to vote to cast their ballots for the more popular Free Soil Party. Here was the heresy the Garrisonians had long suspected. Douglass had a lot of explaining to do. He swore that he himself would abide by the nonvoting policy. His endorsement of the Free Soilers was aimed only at those who already intended to vote. He hoped only to sway such voters away from either of the two major parties, the Whigs and the Democrats, both of which Douglass blasted for toadying up to the slaveholders.

But why endorse the Free Soilers rather than the Liberty Party? It was clear from his answer that Douglass had thought a great deal about how to use politics in the war against slavery. The Free Soil Party, he explained, was the next step in the development of an antislavery majority. It brought together antislavery militants, Whigs frustrated by their party's subservience to the South, and voters who had never thought much about the threat of slavery. As a result, the Free Soilers attracted an unprecedented number of antislavery voters. Once they had accepted the need to organize a political opposition to slavery's expansion, those same voters would be receptive to a more aggressive assault on slavery itself. Douglass squirmed to make this position consistent with Garrison's, but nobody was fooled.[13]

Douglass was clearly ready to reject the nonvoting position, but his Garrisonian belief in a proslavery Constitution held him back. Before he could embrace antislavery politics, he would have to embrace the Constitution upon which the political sys-

13. *The North Star*, Sept. 1, 1848.

tem was based. Here Gerrit Smith stepped in to replace William Lloyd Garrison as Douglass's most significant mentor. Smith was a wealthy benefactor of various reform movements; his cash contributions kept Douglass's newspaper afloat in the critical early years. He lived in nearby Petersboro, New York, and within a few years of Douglass's move to Rochester the two men and their families had developed a close friendship.[14]

As a leading proponent of the idea that the Constitution was actually an *antislavery* document, Smith worked patiently to convert Douglass. In a remarkable series of editorials, private letters, and public debates in 1849 and 1850 Douglass thought through the problem. As late as March 1849 he rejected Smith's appeals and wrote off the Constitution as "a most cunningly-devised and wicked compact, demanding the most constant and earnest efforts of the friends of righteous freedom for its complete overthrow." To this Smith had two answers. First he said that the overriding purpose of the Constitution, stated clearly in its Preamble, was to "secure the blessings of liberty" to all Americans. Because slavery denied those blessings to the slaves, it was flatly incompatible with the expressed purpose of the Constitution. By this reasoning it was the duty of the government, acting under the Constitution, to abolish slavery. Second, Smith claimed that the intentions of the framers were irrelevant; the actual written text of the Constitution—and only that text—should be the basis for understanding its meaning. Because the word "slavery" was nowhere to be found in the text of the Constitution, Smith reasoned, it was illegitimate to

14. John R. McKivigan, "The Frederick Douglass–Gerrit Smith Friendship and Political Abolitionism in the 1850s," in *Frederick Douglass: New Literary and Historical Essays*, ed. Eric Sundquist (New York, 1990), pp. 205–32.

impose a proslavery meaning on clauses that did not explicitly mention slavery.[15]

Douglass could not imagine how to read the Constitution without reference to the intentions of its framers, intentions he believed were unambiguously proslavery. The framers had aimed to protect the liberty of whites, not blacks, Douglass argued. Nevertheless, he agreed with Smith that the actual text of the Constitution, "construed *only* in the light of its letter," without reference to the intentions of its authors or the context in which it was written—that Constitution, Douglass conceded, "is not a pro-slavery instrument." He also admitted that if Smith was right about the Constitution, "we should not be slow in using the ballot-box against the system of slavery, or urging others to do so." Douglass was struggling to find a way to justify his growing interest in antislavery politics. But at that point, March 1849, he could not yet see the Constitution in Smith's terms.[16]

Events in Washington soon led Douglass to reconsider the matter. Congress had become paralyzed by intense sectional disagreement over the expansion of slavery into the western territories. National politics was riveted as never before on the slavery question. Leading politicians scrambled to find another great compromise—comparable to the Missouri Compromise of 1820—that would settle the slavery issue once and for all. Whigs and Democrats agreed that agitation of the slavery question was too disruptive and should be suppressed. But Douglass took heart from all the agitation. His mind swirled with new possibilities for antislavery politics. Abolitionists had been waiting a long time for the problem of slavery to come "before the entire nation,"

15. *The North Star*, March 16, 1849.
16. Ibid. See also, *FDP*, ser. 1, vol. 2, pp. 193–97, 217–35.

Douglass wrote. "That time has now arrived." And rather than lament this development, as the leaders of the two major parties did, Douglass thought it "should be a time of rejoicing."[17]

The Compromise of 1850 was widely hailed as the final settlement of the slavery question; responsible parties swore to the heavens that they would never mention the subject again. But Douglass had other ideas about the future of antislavery politics, and he soon began hinting that he had changed his mind about the Constitution. In January 1851 he wrote to Gerrit Smith announcing that although he could "not yet see" the Constitution as an antislavery instrument, he was no longer willing to assert that it was a proslavery document, a view he now saw as "the slaveholders' side of this question." Douglass still wondered if it was proper for Smith to invoke "legal rules" that could override the intentions of the Constitution's framers, but he admitted that he knew of no legal doctrine with which to refute Smith.[18]

A few months later Douglass published an editorial announcing his "change of opinion." He recited Gerrit Smith's doctrine to the letter: The Constitution must be read in light of its Preamble, promising universal freedom, especially since there was no overt reference to slavery anywhere in the document. Viewed from this angle, the Constitution was an antislavery instrument, a weapon to "be wielded in behalf of emancipation." Antislavery politics were not merely possible but morally obligatory. The "first duty of every American citizen," Douglass now argued, was "to use his *political* as well as his *moral* power" to overthrow slavery.[19] There could be no more

17. *The North Star*, Feb. 8, 1850.
18. *Life & Writings*, vol. 2, p. 149.
19. Ibid., pp. 155–56.

pretense. Frederick Douglass had formally seceded from the Garrisonian wing of the abolitionist movement.

ANTISLAVERY POLITICS

Having embraced political activism, Douglass faced a question familiar to all radical reformers. How could he build a coalition of voters broad enough to win elections without compromising his deepest antislavery principles? Douglass felt most at home in the Liberty Party, but it could never attract enough votes to win control of the federal government. Moreover, Douglass wanted a party that would advocate the abolition of slavery in the South as well as the eradication of racial discrimination in the North. But no such party could ever win significant popular support. Douglass understood that compromise was essential to democracy itself, but there was always a risk. Too much compromise would dilute the basic principles of the antislavery cause, but too much emphasis on ideological purity would make any antislavery coalition impossible.

Douglass had trouble finding the right balance, so much so that his contemporaries charged him with being erratic and unreliable in his political allegiances. To this day historians and biographers echo the complaint. In Douglass's defense it could be said that everybody's politics were unstable in the 1850s. Major parties rose and fell; third parties flared and burned out. It was almost impossible, especially in the North, for a voter or a politician to maintain any consistent party allegiances. There were strong personal considerations as well. Douglass's embrace of antislavery politics coincided with his growing friendship with Gerrit Smith. Smith was a founding member of the Liberty Party; he did more than anyone else to persuade Douglass to accept the Constitution as an antislavery instrument and with it the political struggle for abolition. But throughout the 1850s Smith remained faithful to strictly radical abolitionist parties even as a major party took up antislavery as its leading cause. Smith's repeated runs for the presidency thus put Douglass in something of a bind. He felt a strong sense of loyalty to Smith and his principled opposition to slavery, but at the same time he was drawn to the increasingly powerful Republican Party.

Even so, Douglass's waffling reflected something more than the tug between personal and political allegiances. He had trouble reconciling his role as a radical reformer with his desire for an effective political coalition. History was of no help to him. By the mid-1850s he could look back and see a steadily expanding antislavery constituency, from the Liberty Party to the Free Soil Party to the Republican Party. But at each step along the way Douglass detected the watering down of basic antislavery principles that he so feared. His lingering Garrisonian dogmatism led Douglass to make repeated demands for ideological purity, but his instinctive pragmatism attracted him to broader political coalitions.

Douglass's zigzagging became so well known that he once joked about having to live up to his own reputation for unreliability. He more than lived up to it during presidential elections. He started each campaign season by affirming his commitment to the highest abolitionist principles, exhorting his listeners and readers not to vote for any presidential candidate who came up ideologically short. He invariably declared his undying support for the radical abolitionists, who often nominated his friend and benefactor Gerrit Smith. But as the campaign wore on Douglass would begin to buckle. He would realize all over again how terrible the proslavery Democrats really were. He would be struck anew by the exciting possibility of participating in a broader coalition. Then, usually around August, he announced a change of heart. His friends were predictably horrified; his enemies were just as predictably gleeful.

In 1852 Douglass had every reason to be openly contemptuous of the two major parties. Whigs and Democrats outdid each other in their calls for silence on the slavery question. But the Free Soilers, now calling themselves the Free Democrats, were a different story. In August both Douglass and Smith attended the national convention of the Free Democrats in Pittsburgh. Although Douglass went as a friendly representative of the Liberty Party, freely admitting that he was committed to the Liberty Party's candidate, the Free Democrats nonetheless elected him a convention secretary. In a rousing speech he urged the delegates to maintain their ideological zeal. "It has been said that we ought to take the position to gain the greatest number of voters," he declared, but that was wrong. "Numbers should not be looked at so much as right," he told the Free Democrats. "The man who is right is a majority."[20] It was a classic call for ideological integrity. More than satisfied with events in Pittsburgh, Douglass went back to Rochester, where he promptly plastered the masthead of *Frederick Douglass' Paper* with the names of John Hale and George Julian, the candidates of the Free Democrat Party.

But if ideological purity was the standard, why not stick with the Liberty Party? The Free Democrats were an antislavery party, but they advocated free soil in the territories rather than the abolition of slavery in the South. Douglass had gone to Pittsburgh as an avowed representative of the Liberty Party. Yet on September 10 he felt compelled to publish a lengthy mea culpa. It was a remarkable performance. The main issue "beyond all comparison" was slavery, Douglass began. Because the Free Democrats had passed a

20. *FDP*, ser. 1, vol. 2, p. 393.

series of strong antislavery planks, all their other positions—
however much one might disagree with them—were of no consequence. It was politically foolish to refuse a coalition with a
potentially large antislavery constituency on the grounds that
there were other points of disagreement. That "would make party
action, or combined effort impossible, by requiring complete
identity of opinion." Indeed, with its antislavery credentials well
established the Free Democrat Party was in many ways superior
to the Liberty Party. "It has the power to unite a very influential
minority on a sound principle of universal application. It can give
to the good cause the energy derived from complete organization."
And of course, it can give antislavery "the might of a multitude
instead of a few."[21] Under certain conditions, Douglass admitted,
numbers counted after all. He endorsed the Free Democrats with a
classic call for coalition building.

A few weeks later, in late September, Douglass showed up at
the national convention of the Liberty Party, where he served as
vice president. The convention nominated William Goodell for
President and Gerrit Smith for Congress. Douglass threw himself into the campaign to elect Smith, who, to everyone's surprise, won a seat in the House of Representatives from his home
district in upstate New York. Presumably, then, Douglass had
gone back to the Liberty Party. But in the middle of October
Douglass attended another Free Democrat convention, this one
in Ithaca. There he gave a long and impassioned speech denouncing the two major parties, Whig and Democrat, but allowed not
so much as a hint of whom he himself supported for President.
To this day nobody is sure.

21. *Frederick Douglass' Paper*, Sept. 10, 1852.

The record is clearer for 1856, but Douglass's position was no more stable. By then the Whig Party had collapsed and in its place a new Republican Party had emerged with broad appeal in the North. The Republicans were free soilers; they wanted to restrict the expansion of slavery into the western territories while pledging not to interfere with slavery in the states where it already existed. But the Republicans also endorsed the older Whig program of federal government support for economic development. Free soil and economic development were fused within a larger defense of the superiority of the free labor system of the North over the slave labor system of the South. Many Republicans opposed slavery not because it was cruel and not because the slaveholders were hypocrites but because it was an affront to progress. Slavery retarded the South's development by rewarding laziness rather than diligence and by stifling economic opportunities for those who worked hard. Slavery, Republicans charged, destroyed the American dream. Their policy was to sow the seeds of a prosperous free labor system throughout the western territories, and that meant prohibiting slavery's expansion. Where the Jacksonians crusaded against the Money Power, the Republicans transferred the popular fear of concentrated wealth and power to an increasingly virulent Slave Power.

At first Douglass objected vehemently to the Republican Party. Far from being abolitionists, the Republicans openly embraced the "slaveholder's view" that the Constitution protected slavery in the southern states. Their only substantive proposal—to limit the expansion of slavery into new territories—was like declaring rape and murder immoral in one state and not in another. Republicans, Douglass complained, would restrain the power of the slaveholders in the national government while leaving it completely unchecked within the South. And rather than attack slavery on "moral" grounds the Republicans offered a paltry critique of slavery's economic inefficiency. As he had four years earlier, Douglass demanded strict ideological purity. To compromise with the Republicans, he said, would bring the antislavery movement to ruin.

Douglass launched this volley beginning in late 1855, and he repeated it on several occasions, not least in late May 1856 at the presidential nominating convention of the Radical Abolitionist Party (successor to the Liberty Party), where he endorsed Gerrit Smith's candidacy for President. Why abandon basic principles to support the Republicans, he asked, when authentic antislavery voters could cast their ballots for a genuine radical abolitionist?[22]

Two months later Douglass once again stunned his readers by transferring his allegiance from Gerrit Smith to John C. Frémont, the Republican presidential candidate. Once again he offered a lengthy justification for his breathtaking turnabout. He would not abandon a single one of his antislavery convictions, Douglass protested. At stake was "a difference of Policy, not Principle." The great struggle between slavery and freedom had entered the presidential election in the form of a specific issue, "the extension or the limitation of Slavery." Douglass would have preferred to engage the battle on other terms, but like it or not, slavery expansion was where the war had commenced. "The point attacked, is the point to be defended." The Slave Power had taken its stand on the right to extend slavery's reach, and the

22. Ibid., July 27, 1855; Nov. 16, 1855; Dec. 7, 1855; April 15, 1856; April 25, 1856; Life & Writings, vol. 5, pp. 385–90; FDP, ser. 1, vol. 3, pp. 134–42.

Republican Party was in the best position to crush the Slave Power on precisely that point. The enemy of my enemy is my friend, Douglass argued. At this moment in the history of the antislavery struggle Republican candidates were "the admitted and recognized antagonists of the Slave Power." In more than a dozen years of agitation, he said, the antislavery interpretation of the Constitution "has been made appreciable but to a few minds." Except for a tiny handful of radicals, everybody in the country agreed with the Republicans that the Constitution protected slavery where it already existed. Under the circumstances the only thing the Republicans *could* propose was to keep slavery out of Kansas. And so what? Douglass asked. Should slavery be allowed to spread into Kansas simply because it could not be uprooted elsewhere at the same time? Who was to say that we could not do one good thing because we could not do every good thing? In fact, Douglass concluded, a Republican victory would mean much more than the exclusion of slavery from Kansas. It would overthrow the rule of the Slave Power, restore the freedoms of speech and the press, signal "the ascendancy of Northern civilization," reassert the national condemnation of slavery, "and inaugurate a higher and purer standard of Politics and Government." For all these reasons Douglass intended to cast his presidential vote for John C. Fremont, the nominee of the Republican Party.[23]

It was a good argument, at least as good as his argument against voting for Republicans. And therein lay Douglass's dilemma. There's a case to be made for holding to your principles; that's what reformers are supposed to do. But there's an

23. *Frederick Douglass' Paper*, Aug. 15, 1856.

equally strong case to be made for the importance of compromise, without which democratic politics would be impossible. Most people eventually figure out how to balance the two and find a stable position for their politics. Douglass could not. It was almost 1857. Leading politicians were beginning to talk about an "irreconcilable conflict" between the North and the South. And still Frederick Douglass had no stable political allegiances.

Yet there was more to Douglass's politics than endorsing candidates. As he ricocheted back and forth among political parties, Douglass settled into a new way of talking about slavery, about America, and about himself.

Liberty versus Slavery

When Douglass came back from Britain in 1848, he had gone out of his way to shock Americans by announcing that he had no love for his country. No patriotic sentiments stirred in his breast, he said. How could they, Douglass asked, when all of America's basic institutions were thoroughly corrupted by slavery? But it turned out that not all of them were corrupt. The Constitution was actually an antislavery document, and American politics was finding more and more room for antislavery activists like Frederick Douglass. Nor were all American Christians mired in slavery's corruption. From his pulpit at Plymouth Church in Brooklyn Heights Henry Ward Beecher preached a defiant antislavery gospel. He was not the only one. The churches were not entirely degraded; the Constitution was sound; politics beckoned. This was an America in which a man like Frederick Douglass might feel at home after all.

He began to recast himself. Radical alienation from America

and ringing contempt for its institutions no longer suited Douglass. It certainly had very little political appeal. But patriotic bluster was not possible either; he was still too radical for that. More than an abolitionist, he had become a "universal reformer" who counted women's suffrage, temperance, and the rights of labor among his cherished causes. Together these commitments made Douglass a fierce critic of American society. Yet his embrace of the Constitution, the churches, and party politics rendered obsolete his old stance of complete alienation. Douglass had to define himself in a way that appealed to a broad spectrum of popular opinion while sustaining his critical edge as a radical reformer. This would not be easy. Often it seemed that Douglass had as much trouble reshaping his image as he had stabilizing his politics. But as the years passed, his antislavery message became simpler, clearer, yet all the more powerful for it.

Sometimes Douglass cast himself as the excluded victim, the outsider, defiantly demanding admission as an equal member of American society. When he assumed this stance, he produced some of his most stirring speeches, the most provocative of which addressed the question, "What, to the American slave, is your 4th of July?" It was delivered at Corinthian Hall in Rochester, New York, on July 5, 1852, to an audience made up mostly of white women. Beautifully written and no doubt powerfully delivered—Douglass was by then an outstanding orator—the speech made effective use of a rhetorical device that was rapidly becoming one of his trademarks. He spoke repeatedly of *your* Fourth of July, of *your* celebration, of *your* holiday, speaking in the second person to distance himself from the event he was there to memorialize. But if all the speech had done was announce Douglass's continued alienation, it would have amounted to little more than a tiresome polemic. It was much more than that. In a career studded with great speeches, the Fourth of July address was one of Douglass's very best.[24]

He opened with several pages narrating the Founders' struggle for independence. It could easily have collapsed into platitudes, like most of the patriotic Fourth of July speeches of his day. But this was different. Douglass's rendition of historical events was suffused with his profound identification with the Founders, what they had been up against and what they had accomplished. They had refused to submit to an oppressive regime, and for that they had been condemned in their day as "agitators and rebels, dangerous men." The abusive response of their rulers in England had only strengthened their resolve. Having exhausted every means of redress, they had declared America's independence, "to the dismay of the lovers of ease, and the worshippers of property." No one listening could have mistaken the implicit analogy Douglass was drawing between those who had struggled for independence and those who were struggling against slavery. It was a masterful setup for the turnabout that was about to come.

Everything Douglass said up to that point suggested that African Americans had every reason to embrace the Fourth of July. But they could not. The continued enslavement of millions, he declared, made the annual celebration of freedom obscene and hypocritical to American blacks. How could it be *their* holiday? Thanks to the courage and principles of the Founding Fathers, Douglass told his listeners, "to-day *you* reap the fruits of their success; and *you* therefore, may properly celebrate this anniversary. The 4th of July is the first great fact in *your* nation's

24. *FDP,* ser. 1, vol. 2, pp. 359–88.

history—the very ringbolt in the chain of *your* yet undeveloped destiny." But what could this mean to the American slave? Thus the entire speech was constructed around an exquisite tension between Douglass's deep sympathy with the Revolution and his inability to celebrate it.[25] This was something more than mere alienation, and the effect was as poignant as it was polemical.

The rhetorical power of Douglass's newly ambiguous position was evident in the ease with which he could reverse the rhetorical spin of the Fourth of July speech by insisting that the revolutionaries were *his* fathers, that America was *his* country. He did this most often when speaking not of slavery but of race. He was incensed by the claim coming from various quarters, two in particular, that African Americans did not belong in the United States. Those two were the colonizationists and the emigrationists. Colonization was a movement of whites who endorsed emancipation, provided the freed slaves left the United States. Emigrationism was something else, a movement among blacks who had come to the conclusion that the United States would never accept them as equals and that they would do better by moving to some other country. Douglass hated both these movements. They shared the same flaw, he thought. Colonizationists and emigrationists held that blacks and whites could never live together as equals in America; both claimed that there was no place for blacks in the United States.

In response Douglass insisted—forcefully, eloquently, and repeatedly—that America was his country, his birthplace, the land where his ancestors had lived and died. And what was true

---

25. As Eric Sundquist puts it, "Douglass placed himself *outside* the American dream but *within* the circle of the post-Revolutionary generation's principal rhetoric." Sundquist, "Introduction," in *Frederick Douglass,* loc. cit., p. 14.

for Douglass was true for all African Americans. Blacks had fought in the Revolution, tilled the nation's soil, built its civilization. The United States—its revolutionary heritage, its opportunities, its freedoms—was the birthright of every living African American. "Notwithstanding the impositions and deprivations which have fettered us," Douglass and several black leaders declared in 1853, "we declare that we are, and of right we ought to be *American citizens*."[26] Whenever Douglass said such things, he invariably switched from the second to the first person. This is *my* country, he would say. The heroes of the Revolution are *our* Founding Fathers. This was a particularly potent argument to wield against the Supreme Court when it issued its notorious *Dred Scott* decision in 1857.

Dred Scott was a slave in Missouri who sued for freedom on the ground that his master had taken him to live for some time in the state of Illinois and in Wisconsin Territory, both of which outlawed slavery. Having lived in a free state and a free territory, Scott argued, he himself was therefore free. The Supreme Court ruled against him; Scott was still a slave regardless of where his master had temporarily taken him. But Scott's fate is not what made the Court's decision so controversial. Had Chief Justice Roger Taney issued a narrow opinion upholding Scott's enslavement nobody would have noticed. But Taney was a partisan Democrat who fully shared his party's desire to silence public discussion of slavery, especially the agitation over slavery in the territories. He therefore produced a sweeping decision declaring, among other things, that Congress had no power whatsoever to regulate slavery in the territories. Furthermore, Dred Scott had no legal standing in court because blacks could not be citizens of the United States.

26. *Life & Writings*, vol. 2, p. 258. See also *Frederick Douglass' Paper*, Oct. 2, 1851.

To prove his point, the chief justice added a little history lesson, purporting to show that as far as the Founding Fathers were concerned, African Americans "had no rights which white men are bound to respect." The Declaration of Independence was never intended to apply to blacks, Taney claimed.

Ironically, a Garrisonian might have agreed with the Court's claims about the proslavery legacy of the Founders. But by 1857 Frederick Douglass would have none of it. Piece by piece he disassembled the chief justice's opinion. But it was less Douglass's logic than his stance that gave his argument its force. Douglass claimed to speak not only "as a man" but also as "an American, a citizen." Contrary to Taney's assertions, the Founders *had* recognized the citizenship of African Americans. The *Dred Scott* decision, Douglass concluded, was a "brazen misstatement of the facts of history."[27] The Fourth of July, it turned out, mattered a great deal.

Douglass went back and forth this way all the time. "Aliens are we in our native land," he would say in one speech. "We are Americans," he would say in the next, "we address you not as aliens nor as exiles."[28] Some of this was polemical opportunism, but it was something else as well. When Douglass abandoned the Garrisonians and embraced antislavery politics, the theme of his speeches and writings began to change. Instead of denouncing the degradation of an entire nation corrupted by slavery, he located himself among America's Founders, with all their flaws. From that position he could defend American freedom against increasing threats from the proslavery South. He could turn his criticism against the North for its failure to live

27. *FDP*, ser. 1, vol. 3, pp. 178–79.
28. Ibid., vol. 2, p. 425; *Life & Writings*, vol. 2, p. 255.

up to its own revolutionary heritage. Douglass used his ambiguous relationship to America to develop an important new theme in his antislavery message: Slavery was an affront to American values. It contradicted the great principles of the Declaration of Independence. It violated the sacred purpose of the Constitution. It defiled the precepts of a professedly Christian nation. It thwarted progress and stifled individual initiative. Slavery was, to be blunt, un-American.

The Garrisonian of the 1840s had claimed that the institutions of church and state in America were already corrupted by slavery. The political activist of the 1850s warned instead that the churches, the government, and even the freedoms of the American people all were *threatened* by slavery. "Step by step we have seen the slave power advancing," Douglass wrote in 1857, "growing more and more haughty, imperious, and exacting. The white man's liberty has been marked out for the same grave with the black man's." Douglass had thoroughly repositioned himself. There would be no more blanket denunciations of America and all its works. Instead Douglass stood alongside his fellow northerners warning them of the grave threat to their cherished liberties.[29]

Yet Douglass always professed his confidence that the Slave Power would be defeated, for he had absorbed the nineteenth century's optimistic faith in progress. Because progress was governed by laws, its direction could be discerned. Civilization advanced; economies developed; morality improved—all in accordance with precepts both natural and divine. Those precepts could be flouted for a time, but they could not be undone. Slavery was therefore doomed, Douglass declared in

29. *FDP,* ser. 1, vol. 3, p. 169.

1857, by "all the laws of nature, civilization, and of progress." Sometimes Douglass invested this theme with a millennial Christianity: Slavery was rebellion "against the government of God." It was "of the Devil, and will go to its place." And just as the Lord would smite the slave masters, so would He protect the slaves. "All things are possible with God," Douglass proclaimed; "let not the colored man despair." At other times he spoke of progress in secular terms. The iron laws of political economy commanded that slavery "cannot stand," he said. "It has an enemy in every bar of railroad iron, in every electric wire, in every improvement in navigation, in the growing intercourse of nations, in cheap postage, in the relaxation of tariffs, in common schools, in the progress of education, the spread of knowledge, in the steam engine. . . ." Whether by the laws of God, or of nature, or of man, slavery was condemned to an inescapable sentence of death.[30]

The antebellum North now set the standard for moral and material progress against which Douglass calculated the baneful effects of slavery. Freedom had made the North a land of virtue and prosperity, whereas slavery had reduced the South to economic stagnation and moral depravity. Douglass took every opportunity to draw this lesson in his second and best autobiography, *My Bondage and My Freedom*, published in 1855. Compared with his 1845 *Narrative*, Douglass's second book provided a fuller account of his years as a slave; it also set a different tone, more moderate and better balanced. And it was laced with arguments against slavery that had not appeared in the first. *My Bondage and My Freedom* proclaimed the superior morality of the North, invoked Patrick Henry, and repeatedly contrasted the

30. Ibid., vol. 2, pp. 438–39; vol. 2, p. 171.

glories of free society with the degradation of slave society. Edward Covey, the notorious "negro breaker," was in 1845 the epitome of slaveholding brutality and Christian hypocrisy. A decade later he was also the product of a labor system that offered the slave "no earthly inducement" to work hard except "the fear of punishment." In the *Narrative* the master's suspicion of his slaves was evidence of his personal degradation. But in *My Bondage and My Freedom* Douglass said that it made sense for his master to assume that slaves faked their illnesses. "[H]e probably thought that were *he* in the place of a slave—with no wages for his work, no praise for well doing, no motive for toil but the lash—he would try every possible scheme by which to escape labor." The degraded conditions that slavery imposed even on free workers in the South became clear to Douglass when he arrived in New Bedford and discovered a laboring population "living in better houses, more elegantly furnished—surrounded by more comfort and refinement—than a majority of the slave-holders on the Eastern Shore of Maryland." By 1855 Douglass sometimes sounded like the proud Yankee boasting the superiority of the northern way of life.[31]

Douglass had begun positioning himself as the defender of northern freedom shortly after he made his leap into antislavery politics in the early 1850s. Within a few years he had fine-tuned his message into one great organizing theme, the historic struggle between liberty and slavery. Whenever he spoke to this theme, his words took on a remarkably familiar ring. In late 1854 Douglass gave a speech in Chicago declaring that "liberty and slavery cannot

---

31. *FDP*, ser. 2, vol. 2, pp. 109, 123, 132, 143, 177, 198. See also Eric Sundquist, *To Wake the Nations: Race in the Making of American Literature* (Cambridge, Mass., 1993), pp. 83–134.

dwell in the United States in peaceful relations." Indeed, so antag-
onistic were they "that one or the other of these must go to the
wall. The South must either give up slavery, or the North must
give up liberty. The two interests are hostile, and are irreconcilable." The following year, 1855, Douglass announced that the
"safety of liberty requires the complete extinction of its opposite."
We are witnessing "The Final Struggle," he declared a few months
later. "Liberty and slavery cannot dwell together forever in the
same country." And again in the summer of 1856, as the presidential election was gearing up: Liberty and Slavery "are as opposite
as light and darkness—as Heaven and Hell. . . . Liberty must
either cut the throat of slavery, or have its own throat cut by
Slavery." By the late 1850s most of what Douglass had to say about
slavery was framed around the theme of the titanic struggle
between liberty and slavery.[32]

Douglass always credited this theme to the Founding Fathers;
they were the ones who provoked the ongoing war of slavery and
freedom. This was quite a change on Douglass's part. In 1850 he
had had to force himself to ignore the proslavery intentions of the
Founders before he could accept the Constitution as an antislavery
document. Less than a decade later he sounded a very different
theme. "The public men of the South, and of the whole country,
were against slavery in the early days of the Republic," Douglass
wrote in 1859. They considered slavery "an evil and a curse," a
"transient system" destined for extinction. The Founders had hated
slavery after all. In providing for the abolition of the slave trade, for
example, they "thought they were providing for the abolition of
slavery. . . . All regarded slavery as an expiring and doomed system,

32. *FDP*, ser 1, vol. 2, p. 544; *Life & Writings*, vol. 5, p. 389; *Frederick Douglass' Paper*,
Aug. 24, 1855.

destined to speedily disappear from the country." By "the silent
operation of free principles," the Founders believed, slavery would
be blotted out forever. Their hope, their *intention,* was to put slavery in its proper place, on the road to ultimate extinction.[33]

In the summer of 1858 Douglass pointed to events in Illinois
as evidence that slavery and freedom were engaged in a ferocious "war of extermination." Democratic Senator Stephen A.
Douglas was fighting for his political life in the face of a hostile
administration in Washington, D.C., and a tenacious foe at
home. On the surface it looked like any other campaign for a
seat in the U.S. Senate. "This, however, is only a partial view of
the matter," Douglass said. "The truth is, that Slavery and Anti-
Slavery are at the bottom of the contest."[34] And the antislavery
spokesman, whom Douglass credited with upholding the
noblest ideals of the Republican Party, was Abraham Lincoln.

33. *Life & Writings,* vol. 2, p. 473; vol. 5, p. 402; *Douglass' Monthly,* Aug. 1859.
34. *FDP,* ser. 1, vol. 3, p. 233.

2

"I HAVE ALWAYS HATED SLAVERY"

I was about eighteen years of age, and belonged, as you know, to what they call down South the "Scrubs;" people who do not own land and slaves are nobody there. . . . I was contemplating my new boat, and wondering whether I could make it stronger or improve it in any part, when two men, with trunks, came down to the shore in carriages, and looking at the different boats, singled out mine, and asked . . . "Will you," said one of them, "take us and our trunks out to the steamer . . . ?" Each of them took from his pocket a silver half-dollar and threw it on the bottom of my boat. I could scarcely believe my eyes as I picked up the money. You may think it was a very little thing, and in these days it seems to me like a trifle, but it was a most important incident in my life. I could scarcely credit that I, the poor boy, had

earned a dollar in less than a day; that by honest work I had
earned a dollar. The world seemed wider and fairer before
me; I was a more hopeful and thoughtful boy from that time.

—*Abraham Lincoln*

"*I have with me here*"—Stephen Douglas was shouting—"a
speech made by Fred. Douglass in Poughkeepsie, N.Y., a short
time since." It was September 1 8, 1 8 5 8, and the senator was in
Charleston, Illinois, responding to Abraham Lincoln during the
fourth of their seven debates. Lincoln claimed that the rights to
life, liberty, and the pursuit of happiness were promised to blacks
as well as to whites; that was what the Founders believed, he said.
They believed no such thing, Douglas insisted. Lincoln's argument
was pure abolitionism, "black republicanism," sedition masquerad-
ing as patriotism. The proof, he said, was the speech Frederick
Douglass recently gave praising Abraham Lincoln for standing his
ground against Stephen Douglas. What better evidence could
there be of Lincoln's radicalism? Here were the very words of
America's most infamous black abolitionist as he "conjures all the
friends of negro equality and negro citizenship to rally as one man
around Abraham Lincoln." You may not believe me when I call
Lincoln a radical, Senator Douglas was saying, but surely it counts
for something that Frederick Douglass himself had embraced
Lincoln as "the perfect embodiment" of his own principles.[1]

Actually, Frederick Douglass had praised Lincoln for upholding the principles of the Republican Party, not the principle of
racial equality. Lincoln was no advocate of racial equality, but he
did hate slavery. He said so three times in his first major antislavery speech, at Peoria in 1 8 5 4. First he said that he "can not but

1. *CW*, vol. 3, pp. 1 7 1–7 2.

hate" Stephen Douglas's professed indifference to slavery. "I hate it," Lincoln then explained, "because of the monstrous injustice of slavery itself." And finally, "I hate it" because it disgraced American freedom in the eyes of the world.[2] This was strong stuff coming from a man who prided himself on restraining his passion, particularly in public. Though Lincoln had never before spoken of slavery in such forceful terms, he claimed that he felt this way all his life. "I have always hated slavery," he declared in 1858, "I think as much as any Abolitionist."[3] And in 1864 he wrote that he was "naturally anti-slavery." If slavery was not wrong, he added, "nothing is wrong. I can not remember when I did not so think and feel."[4] Was this true? Did Lincoln *always* hate slavery?

In Kentucky, where Lincoln was born and spent his earliest years, his parents belonged to the Little Mount Baptist Church, whose minister, the Reverend Jesse Head, filled them with "notions about the wrong of slavery and the rights of man."[5] Running for President in 1860, Lincoln recalled that as a small boy his father had moved the family from Kentucky to Indiana "partly on account of slavery."[6] This may or may not have been true, or it may not really matter. The fact that Lincoln remembered it that way—that he could not recall a time when he did not hate slavery—may be just as important. Lincoln almost cer-

---

2. *CW*, vol. 2, p. 255.

3. Ibid., p. 492.

4. *CW*, vol. 7, p. 281.

5. Michael Burlingame, *The Inner World of Abraham Lincoln* (Urbana, 1994), pp. 21–22.

6. Lincoln was careful to say that his father had moved "partly" because of slavery "but chiefly on account of the difficulty in land titles in Ky." *CW*, vol. 4, pp. 61–62. Lincoln's admirers were not as careful, and over the years they spread the story that Lincoln's family had left Kentucky to escape from slavery. *This* version of the story was disputed by those who knew Abraham's father, Thomas Lincoln. See *HI*, pp. 36, 240.

tainly disliked slavery by the time he was a young man. Caleb
Carman first met Lincoln in 1826 and recalled, some forty years
later, that his young friend "was opposed to Slavery & said he
thought it a curse to the Land." Orlando Ficklin remembered
the same thing. Thirty years after he and Lincoln had served
together in the Illinois legislature Ficklin recalled Lincoln as a
man who "was conscientiously opposed to slavery all his life."
Samuel Parks, who knew Lincoln from about 1840, later
affirmed the truth of Lincoln's claim that he "always hated slavery as much as any abolitionist."[7] These are mere scraps; it
would be nice to have more substantial evidence. But Carman,
Ficklin, and Parks are valuable witnesses nonetheless. They are
consistent with one another and with Lincoln's own claim that
he hated slavery for as long as he could remember.

"The slavery question often bothered me as far back as
1836–40," Lincoln recalled sometime later.[8] And it was during
those years, 1837 to be precise, when he was still in his twenties,
that Lincoln for the first time appeared in the public record as an
opponent of slavery. He was representing Sangamon County during his second term in the Illinois legislature. Along with only five
other legislators—out of eighty—he voted against a set of reso-
lutions condemning abolitionism and defending the constitutionality of slavery. Rather than declare that the Constitution
protected slavery, Lincoln would only allow that it restricted
Congress's right to interfere with slavery where it already
existed. Slavery itself, the resolution declared, "is founded on
both injustice and bad policy."[9] This was hardly abolitionism—in

7. *HI*, pp. 429, 58, 239.
8. *RW*, p. 61.
9. *CW*, vol. 1, p. 75.

fact Lincoln thought abolitionism made matters worse—but it is clear enough that by 1837 Lincoln objected to slavery, and it is probably true that he always had.

But Lincoln's youthful hatred of slavery had little to do with his youthful politics. For most of his career he agreed with the reigning political consensus that the slavery issue should be banished from the political mainstream. Then, in 1854, in an abrupt reversal, slavery became the only issue that mattered to him. By 1858 Lincoln had distilled the Republican Party's message down to a brilliantly effective sound bite: *We think slavery is wrong and they don't.* It required neither deception nor exaggeration for Lincoln to express himself in this way.

THE LOYAL WHIG

Lincoln was a politician long before he was an antislavery politician. He called himself an old-line Henry Clay Whig, and he called Clay his beau-ideal of a statesman. Like Clay, Lincoln supported the Bank of the United States to ensure a stable currency and high tariffs to promote the development of American industry. Like Clay, Lincoln advocated government support for "internal improvements," the turnpikes, canals, and railroads that would extend the market's reach deep into the heartland. These policies, taken together, were supposed to promote the development of a truly national economy powerful enough to bind every region of the country together, to build one national identity at the expense of competing regional identities. Clay called this the American System, and from 1830 to 1854 it was the heart and soul of Abraham Lincoln's political life.

In its own way it was idealistic politics. Lincoln cared deeply for the Union, and he probably agreed with Clay's argument for the unifying effects of a federally directed program of economic development. But the case Lincoln made for Whig projects had less to do with political economy than with personal experience. He had grown up on a struggling farm in a backwoods area that offered little in the way of opportunity for intelligent and ambitious young men, men like himself. From an early age he dreamed of escape. And when he left home and entered public life, Lincoln committed himself to Whig policies that would pepper the American countryside with the institutional props of upward mobility: banks and railroads, canals and turnpikes, but especially schools.

In principle Whig economics fused nicely with Whig antislavery. Lincoln believed, for example, that everyone had a "right to rise" in this world, and when he spoke against slavery, he often said that all working people, black and white alike, had a right to the fruits of their own labor. Lincoln certainly believed this precept was incompatible with slavery. But for him the right to rise was a moral conviction as much as a principle of political economy. Whig morality, not Whig political economy, most shaped Lincoln's view of the matter. And once again it was Henry Clay who established the terms on which Lincoln eventually entered the slavery debate. As late as 1864 he reminded a former Whig that they both had been followers of "that great statesman, Henry Clay, and I tell you," Lincoln added, "I never had an opinion upon the subject of slavery in my life that I did not get from him."[10] To understand Lincoln's early views on slavery, then, one must peek into the mind of Henry Clay.

Clay deplored the presence of slavery and hoped for its eventual disappearance from the United States. At the same time

10. *RW*, p. 384.

he sponsored several momentous sectional compromises in a determined effort to prevent slavery from disrupting American politics. His own solution to the problem of slavery envisioned the colonization of emancipated slaves in their "ancestral" home of Africa. By removing blacks Clay hoped to remove yet another obstacle to national unity. But colonization was more of a rhetorical gesture than a practical agenda. Removing blacks from America was a dream, a fantasy really, that Henry Clay never dared impose on any slaveholder, including himself. Clay's inability to dispense with his own slaves translated easily into the conviction that slavery was a curse in part because there was no easy way to eradicate it. The principles upon which the nation was founded cried out for the abolition of slavery, Clay said, but he could think of no practical way to escape either his or the South's dependence on this moral eyesore. Clay was the most prominent Whig politician in America, and his position on slavery enhanced the party's national appeal. His antislavery sentiments resonated with many northern voters; his adamant opposition to any policy that infringed on the rights of the slaveholders appealed to many a southern planter.

Lincoln took Henry Clay's hatred of slavery seriously. Because Clay had been defeated by James K. Polk in 1844, Lincoln wrote the following year, Texas was being annexed and slavery extended. None of this "evil" would have happened, Lincoln complained, had the antislavery men in New York voted for the Whig candidate.[11] When Clay died in 1852, Lincoln published a eulogy that scarcely mentioned the American System. Instead he praised Clay almost exclusively for his position on slavery. It had the great virtue of moderation, Lincoln said. Clay had proclaimed his hatred of slav-

11. *CW*, vol. 1, pp. 347–48.

ery in unambiguous terms yet had been critical of abolitionists and proslavery zealots alike. Lincoln then quoted, for the first but by no means the last time, one of Clay's most eloquent statements on slavery. The Declaration of Independence made emancipation inevitable because it established universal freedom as the American standard, Clay argued. What, then, must slavery's supporters do to perpetuate human bondage in America? Clay's answer was compelling, and Lincoln quoted it at length. They "must blow out the moral lights around us, and extinguish that greatest torch of all which America presents to a benighted world. . . . They must penetrate the human soul, and eradicate the light of reason, and the love of liberty. Then, and not till then, when universal darkness and despair prevail, can you perpetuate slavery, and repress all sympathy, and all humane, and benevolent efforts among free men, in behalf of the unhappy portion of our race doomed to bondage."[12]

Lincoln loved that passage. He had nothing but sympathy for Clay's inability to extract himself from the hateful slave system. He assumed that Clay's views reflected the thinking of a broad class of enlightened southerners. So, unlike Frederick Douglass, Lincoln never let loose with denunciations of the slaveholders, never called them sinners or hypocrites or sadists. On the contrary, Lincoln often said that if their positions were reversed, northerners would behave exactly as southerners did. Born to a world where slavery already existed, the slaveholders could hardly be blamed for clinging to what they knew. He would scarcely know how to eliminate slavery, Lincoln said, even if he had all the power in the world. And so, like Clay, Lincoln was

12. Ibid., vol. 2, p. 131.

content to let the problem of slavery work itself out over time. To agitate the question only made matters worse.

Through four terms in the Illinois legislature Lincoln spent nearly all his political energy defending the state bank, promoting public schools, and trying to send pork barrels home to Sangamon County. By 1842 he was tired of it and decided not to run again. The great battles over banks and tariffs and internal improvements were becoming a spent force, while off in the distance a new issue, the expansion of slavery, was beginning to make headway. Campaigning for Congress in 1846, Lincoln was visited by a delegation of antislavery men eager to flush out the candidate's views on slavery. It was a familiar tactic within antislavery politics, but it is unlikely that such a delegation had ever visited Lincoln before. The visitors left thoroughly satisfied, and he easily won the election. For someone who had always hated slavery, the transition to antislavery politics should have been smooth and comfortable. Instead it made Lincoln squirm.

The Transition

By the time Congressman Lincoln reached Washington, D.C., in December 1847 the nation's capital was consumed by the slavery issue. A Democratic President, James Knox Polk, had annexed Texas in 1845 and a year later provoked a war with Mexico, hoping to add much of it to the United States. Because Polk was a slaveholder and an ardent foe of abolitionism, many northerners suspected that the Mexican War was a proslavery swindle. Out of those suspicions a new political alignment began to coalesce in opposition to slavery's *expansion* rather than to slavery itself. It was at this point, for example, that Frederick Douglass began to contemplate the possibilities of broad-based political agitation against slavery. A great many northern Whigs feared that the South was becoming militantly proslavery, and more than a few renegade northern Democrats agreed. Hence David Wilmot's famous proviso, which would have excluded slavery from all the territories acquired during the Mexican War. The congressional struggle over the Wilmot Proviso reached its crescendo while Abraham Lincoln was in Washington.

At first Lincoln dismissed all the agitation over slavery as a "distracting question." Among friends at his Washington boardinghouse he often used humor to deflect any political discussions that veered toward the expansion of slavery. But the discomfort did not indicate any retreat from Lincoln's antislavery convictions. He later remembered voting for the Wilmot Proviso at least forty times, although four times was closer to the truth. He also voted for a bill to end the slave trade in Washington, D.C. And he drafted his own bill to allow district residents to abolish slavery entirely in the nation's capital. But he still shared the hopes of men like Henry Clay that a compromise, a "final settlement" of the dispute over western lands that would once and for all remove slavery from the national political agenda, could be reached. By some accounts Lincoln became rather fatalistic about slavery. After the annexation of Texas, he said in early 1854, he came to believe that "God will settle" the slavery question "and settle it right, and that he will, in some inscrutable way, restrict the spread of so great an evil." But "for the present," he concluded, "it is our duty to wait."[13] Not everyone was willing to wait.

As he campaigned for Whig candidates during the 1848 elec-

13. *RW*, p. 61.

tions Lincoln discovered, to his frustration, that many of his fellow Whigs were planning to vote instead for the newly formed Free Soil Party. Lincoln shared the commitment to halting the expansion of slavery into new territories, but he wondered why anyone would throw away his vote on a Free Soil candidate who could not possibly win when the Whig Party took the exact same position. Congress had no right to interfere with slavery where it already existed, he said, but it had every right to restrict the expansion of slavery into new territories. That position was not the problem, according to the Massachusetts Free Soilers. The problem was Lincoln's misplaced faith in the Whig Party's commitment to that position. The problem was Lincoln's failure to realize the growing strength of the proslavery forces in Washington. The problem, in short, was Lincoln's naive assumption that everybody "agreed that slavery was an evil." Nonsense, the Free Soilers told him. The Whigs were not to be trusted, and anyway, Lincoln's opening premise was wrong: Not everyone agreed that slavery was wrong.

The 1848 elections may have shaken Lincoln, and not simply because of the Free Soil challenge. While campaigning in Boston, Lincoln attended an antislavery speech by William Seward, the New York governor who later became Lincoln's secretary of state. "I have been thinking about what you said in your speech," Lincoln reportedly told Seward after listening to the speech. "I reckon you are right. We have got to deal with this slavery question, and got to give much more attention to it hereafter than we have been doing."[14] Politicians across the North were beginning to demand a more assertive antislavery stance, and Lincoln seemed to be listening. Two years later Lincoln's

14. *HI*, p. 691.

former law partner John Stuart predicted that at some point the only political options remaining would be abolitionists or Democrats. "When that time comes, my mind is made up," Lincoln said. "The slavery question can't be compromised."[15] Still, he hesitated.

Antislavery politics was the logical place for Lincoln to go. Instead he went home. Illinois Whigs had agreed to rotate his congressional seat, so he had no chance of being reelected to Congress. Illinois was a Democratic state, so there was no prospect of higher office back home. Nor were there any issues with which Lincoln could win an election. For the next few years he turned his attention to his increasingly prosperous law practice. He later claimed that he was "losing interest" in politics. Maybe so. But even in his semiretirement from public life Lincoln could not help noticing that the slavery issue was threatening to rip the nation apart. For the time being the Union was saved by the Compromise of 1850, a series of measures devised by Lincoln's old hero, Henry Clay, and pushed through Congress by Lincoln's longtime rival, Stephen Douglas. Whigs and Democrats alike swore unbending allegiance to the compromise as the "final settlement" of the slavery problem. Politicians North and South vowed never to breathe a whisper about slavery. It didn't work.

The northern reaction against the compromise erupted almost immediately, provoked in large part by the details of one of its measures, the Fugitive Slave Act. The Constitution protected the right of slaveholders to secure the return of their runaway slaves, but it was up to Congress to enforce the Constitution by specifying the procedures for the capture of

15. *RW*, p. 431.

fugitives. Many northern states had long tried to ensure that some measure of due process be preserved so as to prevent the kidnapping of free blacks. But the Fugitive Slave Act took runaway cases out of the northern courts, stripping away the due process rights of the accused. It also set up a payment schedule that seemed to bias the new system in favor of slave catchers. All this provoked an unanticipated furor in the North, not to mention a terrifying crisis among northern blacks. Rightly or not, voters held the Whigs responsible.

By 1852 the Whig Party was fighting for its life. Never was the strain between Lincoln's professed hatred of slavery and his continued commitment to the Whig Party more in evidence. His published eulogy for Henry Clay read like a nostalgic cry for a return to the days when everyone agreed that slavery was wrong. Lincoln had always criticized abolitionists for their sanctimonious denunciations of the South, but he never doubted that in their hatred of slavery they were fundamentally right. What shocked Lincoln now was the emergence of a new extreme in American politics, proslavery partisans who openly rejected the promise of equal rights contained in the Declaration of Independence. But he was still unable to formulate a political position that reflected his concerns over slavery. Politically Lincoln was lost. His 1852 campaign speeches picked at the sickly remains of banks, internal improvements, and protective tariffs. Nobody cared. When the returns came in, it was clear that the Whig Party was dead. So was Lincoln's undistinguished political career, unless he could establish a new political identity.

It took some time for that to happen. As the Whig Party died, a new political coalition—the American Party, commonly referred to as the Know-Nothings—attracted voters disturbed by the massive immigration of Irish and German Catholics.

Lincoln had no taste for such things. "I am not a Know-Nothing. That is certain," he explained. "How could I be? How can any one who abhors the oppression of negroes, be in favor of degrading classes of white people." So what was he? "That is a disputed point," Lincoln said. "I think I am a whig; but others say there are no whigs, and that I am an abolitionist."[16] True, he opposed the extension of slavery, but he had done that as a Whig congressman, and back then nobody had thought that made him an abolitionist. Unwilling to take up anti-immigrant politics, Lincoln turned instead to antislavery.

ANTISLAVERY POLITICS

For many northerners it was the Mexican War; for others it was the Fugitive Slave Act. But Abraham Lincoln's conversion to antislavery politics was prompted by, of all things, the Kansas-Nebraska Act, passed by Congress on May 30, 1854. It allowed the people living in the Nebraska Territory to decide for themselves whether to exclude slavery, instead of having Congress decide for them. The bill's sponsor was none other than Illinois Democratic Senator Stephen A. Douglas. The Kansas-Nebraska Act, Douglas said, did nothing more than uphold the great principle of popular sovereignty. Just as the Constitution left the regulation of slavery to the individual states, Douglas reasoned, so Congress should leave each territory free to decide for itself about admitting or excluding slavery. Who could object to so basic a principle of American democracy? Douglas asked. In fact he knew that a lot of people would object. What he did not

16. *CW*, vol. 2, pp. 322–23.

know was that the most important of those who objected would turn out to be his longtime Springfield neighbor and rival Abraham Lincoln.

But why did the Kansas-Nebraska Act provoke Lincoln to break a lifelong habit of near silence on the slavery issue? The problem was that until Douglas rammed his bill through Congress, slavery had been outlawed in the Nebraska Territory by the Missouri Compromise of 1820. To bypass this inconvenient fact—and to satisfy proslavery southerners—Douglas added to the final bill a provision explicitly repealing the Missouri Compromise. It was this, the repeal of the Missouri Compromise, that provoked a huge backlash in the North.

The Nebraska bill "took us by surprise—astounded us," Lincoln said. "We were thunderstruck and stunned."[17] Throughout the summer of 1854, as the controversy escalated, Lincoln squirreled himself away in the state library in Springfield, researching the history of slavery in the United States. Armed with his findings, he took to the stump in late August, dramatically reentering public life as one of the nation's most articulate antislavery politicians. Douglas was touring the state in a desperate attempt to contain the damage, but Lincoln hounded the senator wherever he went. In half a dozen speeches Lincoln denounced "the great wrong and injustice of the repeal of the Missouri Compromise, and the extension of slavery into free territory." Lincoln was goading Senator Douglas into public debate, and eventually Douglas had no choice but to meet Lincoln's challenge. Several debates followed, and each time Lincoln rehearsed his argument until, on October 16, in Peoria,

17. Ibid., p. 282.

he summed up his position and printed it in the *Illinois Journal*. The Peoria speech was the first major statement, in Lincoln's own words, of his antislavery politics.

Having publicly committed himself, Lincoln set about to help build an antislavery coalition with the broadest possible appeal. The coalition became known as the Republican Party. Coming to terms with antislavery politics was never as difficult for Abraham Lincoln as it was for Frederick Douglass, but even for Lincoln, it took some getting used to, and it took a lot of work. In the first years after 1854 Lincoln worked to keep the party's antislavery message clear and simple: Slavery was wrong; its expansion should therefore be restricted. He was willing to "fuse" with anybody, even the Know-Nothings, but only if they were willing to stand on the same ground: moral opposition to slavery extension, and nothing more. He knew that this ground would be attractive to many abolitionists, but he wanted his fellow Republicans to steer clear of anything that smacked of radicalism. Republicans, Lincoln insisted, had no intention of interfering with slavery in the states where it already existed and every intention of enforcing the Fugitive Slave Act. He warned Lyman Trumbull in 1856 that a radical Republican candidate or platform would surely scare off the old conservative Whigs. He warned Salmon P. Chase that if Ohio Republicans supported repeal of the Fugitive Slave Act, the party in Illinois would be doomed.

But in Lincoln's mind the biggest obstacle was the lingering party allegiances that made it hard for many Whigs and Democrats to join together as Republicans. Had the antislavery forces been united in 1856, he believed, they would have defeated the Democrat James Buchanan in the presidential election. "Can we not come together, for the future," Lincoln asked former Whigs and Democrats, "let bygones be bygones?"

Lincoln was an exemplary practitioner of the art of putting aside old differences. He hoped his new antislavery message would carry him into the U.S. Senate, but when the first opportunity arose, he was outmaneuvered. To save the seat for the new party, Lincoln threw his support to Lyman Trumbull, an old antislavery Democrat now turned Republican. His magnanimous gesture was repaid in 1858, when the Republicans nominated him to run for the other Illinois Senate seat, the one occupied by Stephen Douglas.

Lincoln was the obvious person to take Douglas on. But to Lincoln's amazement influential eastern Republicans, notably Horace Greeley, seriously considered endorsing Douglas. Greeley, the powerful editor of the *New York Tribune*, had been impressed by Douglas's recent war of words with the Buchanan administration over the admission of Kansas. Lincoln was stunned by the news of a possible eastern defection. "Have they concluded that the republican cause, generally, can be best promoted by sacrificing us here in Illinois? If so," Lincoln wrote to Trumbull, "we would like to know it soon; it will save us a great deal of labor to surrender at once."[18] That influential Republicans could think that there was any basis for allying with Stephen Douglas suggested only one thing: The Republican Party was still not unified around its core principle.

Lincoln quickly switched gears. After struggling for several years to keep the party from straying into radicalism, he spent the next two years making sure that Republicans did not abandon their core antislavery message. Douglas tussled with the administration over whether the state constitution that Kansas had submitted to Congress was valid. But as Lincoln was quick

18. Ibid., p. 430.

to point out, no Republican ever disagreed with Douglas on that
point. Mesmerized by Douglas's fight with Buchanan, Greeley
and company had blinded themselves to Douglas's fundamental
differences with the Republicans. There remained, Lincoln
wrote in May 1858, "all the difference there ever was between
Judge Douglas & the Republicans." Republicans believed Congress
should keep slavery out of the territories, he said; Stephen
Douglas did not.[19]

Slavery in the territories was merely the immediate issue,
Lincoln argued. Beneath it lay the fundamental conflict over the
right and wrong of slavery itself. This was what Greeley and the
other eastern Republicans threatened to lose sight of in their ill-
considered dalliance with Stephen Douglas. And so, from 1858
to 1860, Lincoln sharpened his message and urged his fellow
Republicans not to become distracted by secondary issues but to
stand by the "great principle" that united the party: "[S]lavery is a
moral, political and social wrong, and ought to be treated as a
wrong."[20] The "real issue" dividing Douglas and him, Lincoln
said, "is the eternal struggle between these two principles—
right and wrong—throughout the world.

> They are the two principles that have stood face to face
> from the beginning of time; and will ever continue to
> struggle. The one is the common right of humanity and
> the other the divine right of kings. It is the same princi-
> ple in whatever shape it develops itself. It is the same
> spirit that says, 'You work and toil and earn bread, and
> I'll eat it.' No matter in what shape it comes, whether

19. Ibid., p. 446.
20. Ibid., vol. 3, p. 366.

from the mouth of a king who seeks to bestride the people of his own nation and live by the fruit of their labor,
or from one race of men as an apology for enslaving
another race, it is the same tyrannical principle.[21]

Lincoln's lifelong hatred of slavery had finally fused with his
new antislavery politics. From his first reentry into politics in
1854 he repeatedly denounced slavery as an evil. At various
times he called slavery a "cancer," a "poison," or "a great national
crime." As a matter of public policy, he said, slavery should be
"resisted as a wrong" and treated "as a wrong." The sum of
Lincoln's antislavery politics could not have been clearer.

Why Was Slavery Wrong?

Some people thought it was a sin for one human being to enslave
another. Some focused on slavery's physical brutality; others on
the way it undermined the slave family or the way it dehuman-
ized its victims. Intellectuals and politicians often said that slavery was an irrational and inefficient way to organize labor. The
expansion of slavery bothered some whites because they wanted
to keep blacks out of the western territories. Still others complained of a "Slave Power" that controlled the federal government. Lincoln accepted some of these arguments, but none was
central to his own antislavery politics. He scoffed at the idea of a
proslavery Bible, but not until the very end of his life did he suggest that slavery was a sin, and even then the sin was the nation's
rather than any one master's. He never publicly condemned
slaveholders as sinners, nor did he label Christian masters hyp-

---

21. Ibid., p. 315.

ocrites. He believed that slavery was brutal, but he almost never mentioned whipping, sexual abuse, or the breakup of slave families. He assumed that the westward pattern of migration would ensure that most territorial settlers would be white, but he never so much as hinted that he opposed slavery's expansion in order to keep blacks out of the territories. Nor did he believe that black settlers should be excluded from the territories. On the contrary, when Missourians declared that they opposed slavery out of concern for white men, Lincoln objected on the ground that "I must take into account the rights of the poor Negro."[22] While campaigning for the Senate in 1858, he accused Stephen Douglas of participating in a conspiracy to make slavery national and perpetual, but he dropped that charge once the election was over, and he never made the more common claim that there was a vague Slave Power conspiracy operating in America. Instead he spoke of a "tendency" toward making slavery national and perpetual, but it was a tendency that anyone could discern without resort to conspiracy theories.

Lincoln was much more inclined to denounce slavery for denying men and women the hard-earned fruits of their own labor. He was clearly familiar with the classical economic argument against slavery, but he mentioned it only briefly. In 1845, for example, he said that allowing slavery to expand would "prevent that slavery from dying a natural death."[23] But this was a passing reference made in a private letter; it was never central to his critique of slavery. Lincoln also argued that it was much easier to prevent slavery from entering a new territory than to expel it once it was already established. Even in a democracy wealth translated into social influ-

22. *RW*, p. 432.
23. *CW*, vol. 1, p. 348.

ence and political power, he argued, and since the slaveholders were bound to be the wealthiest members of their communities, they would be hard to dislodge even where they constituted only a small minority. They would buy up the largest tracts of the best lands, limiting the opportunities for free farmers attempting to make new starts for their families. Slavery thus undermined the opportunity for upward mobility even for free men, the very thing that made the territories so attractive.

Upward mobility got closer to the heart of Lincoln's case against slavery. By asserting that wage labor was a temporary condition in the North, he disputed the proslavery theorists who claimed that the slaves were better off than northern wage earners. "The man who labored for another last year, this year labors for himself, and next year he will hire others to labor for him." Like Frederick Douglass, Lincoln occasionally offered his own rise from poverty to prosperity as a living example of what was possible in America and impossible under slavery. But this was a glib one-liner. Before 1859 Lincoln did not even attempt to formulate a coherent defense of the superiority of free labor that went much further. Even then Lincoln was practically tongue-tied in his attempt to answer proslavery theorists with his own theory of labor. He usually resorted to the increasingly dubious claim that only a small percentage of northern laborers worked for wages and that most of those who did would eventually become self-employed.[24]

After he became President, Lincoln found the eloquence he had been groping for since 1859. On July 4, 1861, in a message to a special session of Congress, he declared that the war between the North and the South was "essentially a People's con-

---

24. Ibid., vol. 2, p. 364; vol. 3, pp. 459, 462. Don Fehrenbacher, ed., *Abraham Lincoln: Speeches and Writings, 1859–1865* (New York: Library of America, 1989), pp. 83–85.

test. On the side of the Union, it is a struggle for maintaining in the world, that form, and substance of government, whose leading object is, to elevate the condition of men—to lift artificial weights from all shoulders—to clear the paths of laudable pursuit for all—to afford all, an unfettered start, and a fair chance, in the race of life."[25] By December, in his first annual message to Congress, Lincoln had finally managed to clarify his ideas about the relationship between capital and labor. Because capital was merely the fruit of labor, he said, labor was "the superior of capital, and deserves much the higher consideration." There would always be a few men with capital who did not need to work, men who paid wages to others to work for them. Nevertheless, in the free states there was simply no such thing "as the free hired laborer being fixed to that condition of life." But Lincoln stretched his reasoning beyond the upward mobility of individual workers to the larger decency of the northern way of life. Free labor, Lincoln said, "is the just, and generous, and prosperous system, which opens the way to all—gives hope to all, and consequent energy, and progress, and improvement to condition to all." It was a powerful argument, powerfully made, and it was the last time he ever made it. His excursion into political economy turned out to be rather brief, commencing in late 1859 and coming to a close two years later.[26] Thereafter he returned to the theme that had preoccupied him throughout the 1850s.

When Lincoln talked about free labor, he usually preferred to emphasize the moral premise of his defense: that all men and women were equally entitled to the fruits of their labor and with it a fair chance to raise their prospects in life. In this argu-

25. *CW*, vol. 4, p. 438.
26. Ibid., vol. 5, pp. 51–53.

ment economics and morality were inseparable. Most of the time Lincoln avoided strictly economic arguments. His major antislavery speeches in the 1850s—Peoria in 1854, the "House Divided" speech of 1858, the Cooper Union address of 1860—mentioned upward mobility only fleetingly, sometimes never. But if he was reticent about political economy, it was not because he disagreed with the economic critique of slavery. More likely, he did not feel intellectually at home in the realm of political economy. His law partner William Herndon once commented that if there was "a question of political economy," Lincoln was susceptible to the influence of friends. But on questions of justice, right, and liberty, "no man can move him—no set of men can."[27] For Lincoln upward mobility fell into the latter category; it was more a question of right than of economics. He believed that every human being was born with arms to work and a mouth to eat and that it was immoral for some people to eat while others did all the work. But he drew this conviction less from Adam Smith than from Thomas Jefferson.

"THAT ALL MEN ARE CREATED EQUAL"

This is what Lincoln preferred to say about slavery: that it was wrong because it violated the moral principle of fundamental human equality; that in proclaiming universal freedom in their Declaration of Independence, the Founders had tilted the new nation on an antislavery bias; that to defend slavery was to deny that all men are created equal; that to reject the principle of human equality was to strip the United States of its historic mission as a beacon of universal liberty in the world. Until 1854,

27. *HI*, p. 561.

Lincoln believed, only a handful of proslavery extremists made that denial. But with the repeal of the Missouri Compromise the Founders' bias against slavery was tossed aside, and the entire trajectory of American history was altered. Much more than popular sovereignty was at stake in western territories. If the Kansas-Nebraska Act were allowed to stand, national policy would no longer be based on the premise that slavery was wrong. As Lincoln saw it, the guiding principle of the American nation was under assault. To prove it, he developed his own interpretation of American history.

He began with the Declaration of Independence. It established the nation's great ideal, the right of every human being to life, liberty, and the pursuit of happiness. By this the Founders meant to say a great deal, but they did not mean to say everything. They "did not intend to declare all men equal *in all respects*," Lincoln was careful to note. "They did not mean to say all were equal in color, size, intellect, moral developments, or social capacity." Nor did they "mean to assert the obvious untruth" that all men were at present actually enjoying an equality of rights or that such an equality could be achieved immediately. But with those caveats out of the way, Lincoln went on to state precisely what the Founders did mean to do when they declared that all men were created equal. It was really quite simple: They had established the ideal that would guide the nation through its history. The Declaration of Independence, Lincoln said, "set up a standard maxim for free society, which should be familiar to all, and revered by all; constantly looked to, constantly labored for, and even though never perfectly attained, constantly approximated, and thereby constantly spreading and deepening its influence, and augmenting the happiness and value of life to all people of all colors. . . ." The Declaration "contemplated the progressive improvement in the condition of all men everywhere."[28] More to the point, it contemplated a world without slavery.

But the Founders lived in the real world with a slave system they found difficult to eradicate. They faced this reality in the Constitution, a document as crucial to Lincoln's argument as it was to Frederick Douglass's. Yet unlike Douglass or William Lloyd Garrison, Lincoln saw the Constitution as neither a clarion call to abolition nor a proslavery scandal. It was a compromise. It recognized slavery, but only out of necessity and only three times. First was the provision that prohibited Congress from interfering with the Atlantic slave trade until 1808. In the long run this was an antislavery clause, for it eventually empowered the federal government to interfere with slavery, as Congress did at the earliest possible date. The two remaining references—the three-fifths clause and the fugitive slave clause—actually protected slavery. Unlike the Garrisonians, Lincoln accepted those clauses as the necessary concessions that made the creation of the Union possible. Unlike Frederick Douglass, Lincoln did not claim those concessions had not been made. He accepted them, but that didn't mean he liked them.

In fact Lincoln detested the fugitive slave clause, the provision giving masters the right to recapture their runaway slaves in the northern states. The whole idea of it was "distasteful to me," he said. If he were called upon by a federal marshal "to assist in catching a fugitive slave, I should suggest to him that others could run a great deal faster than I could." He did not like the Fugitive Slave Act of 1850 either. "It is ungodly; it is ungodly; no doubt it is ungodly!" Lincoln said in 1860. "But it is the law of

28. *CW*, vol. 2, pp. 405–7.

the land, and we must obey it as we find it."²⁹ He would have preferred legislation that guaranteed suspected runaways the same legal protections afforded to suspects by the criminal laws of the North. But if the Fugitive Slave Law went further than it needed to go, it did not go beyond the Constitution. "We are under legal obligations to catch and return their runaway slaves for them," Lincoln admitted, despite the fact that it was "a sort of dirty, disagreeable job." He was even more blunt in a private letter to his friend Joshua Speed, a slaveholder in Kentucky. "I confess I hate to see the poor creatures hunted down, and caught, and carried back to their stripes, and unrewarded toils," Lincoln wrote in 1855, "but I bite my lip and keep quiet." So did most northerners. "You ought rather to appreciate," Lincoln told Speed, "how much the great body of the Northern people do crucify their feelings, in order to maintain their loyalty to the constitution and the Union."³⁰ Because he acknowledged that the Fugitive Slave Law was constitutional, the abolitionists gave Lincoln no end of grief. They were not in the habit of biting their lips and crucifying their feelings.

Lincoln took a similar view of the three-fifths clause. He didn't like it, but there it was in the Constitution, so he and his fellow northerners accepted it. The clause counted three-fifths of the slave population for purposes of representation in the House. Lincoln, along with many northerners, complained that the three-fifths clause increased the number of slave state representatives in Congress and thus the number of presidential electors as well. This was "manifestly unfair." But because it was part of the Constitution, Lincoln would stand by it, "fairly, fully, and

29. Ibid., vol. 3, p. 131; vol. 2, pp. 233; *RW*, p.188.
30. *CW*, vol. 2, pp. 268, 320.

firmly." However, neither he nor any other northerner was required to admit new states to the Union "on the same degrading terms." To those who insisted that slavery was none of the North's business, Lincoln pointed out that the three-fifths clause made the expansion of slavery an issue of considerable interest to the North. Every new slave state admitted to the Union extended the unfair advantage enjoyed by the slave over the free states. Under the circumstances, the northerners had a direct interest in thwarting slavery's expansion.[31]

As disturbing as the three-fifths and fugitive slave clauses were, Lincoln believed they were put into the Constitution out of *necessity*, whereas in *principle* most of the Founders were opposed to slavery. This was clear, he said, from the way the Constitution was written. Because its authors assumed that the document would outlast slavery, they would not so much as allow the word "slavery" to appear anywhere in it. Instead they resorted to euphemism. "Thus, the thing is hid away, in the constitution, just as an afflicted man hides away a wen or a cancer, which he dares not cut out at once, lest he bleed to death."[32] The Founders put slavery into the Constitution only because they had to, not because they wanted to. Because it could not be eradicated at the time without putting the creation of the new nation at risk. Because no one could imagine a way to free more than a million slaves right then and there.

But didn't this fatally taint the Constitution, exactly as the Garrisonians said? No, Lincoln argued, because the ideals of the Declaration were embodied in the Constitution. To repudiate it in the name of antislavery was to reject the very thing that kept

31. Ibid., p. 269.
32. Ibid., p. 274. See also vol. 3, pp. 307, 496.

the promise of universal freedom alive in the United States. For this reason Lincoln clung to the Constitution and to the Union it created. "Much as I hate slavery," Lincoln said, "I would consent to the extension of it rather than see the Union dissolved."[33] By this Lincoln did not mean merely that he valued the Union *more* than he hated slavery. Loyal Whig that he was, Lincoln accepted Daniel Webster's dictum: "Liberty and Union, now and forever, one and inseparable." Only within the Union, only under the Constitution, could the dream of universal liberty be realized. The "best means to advance that liberty," Lincoln believed, was to remain "true to the Union and the Constitution." They were inseparable, "*Liberty*, the *Union*, and the Constitution." If the Union died, if the Constitution failed, so would the principle of liberty "for *all* men."[34]

Lincoln's history lesson did not end with 1789. Although compelled to protect slavery where it already existed, the Founders put nothing in the Constitution to prevent Congress from restricting slavery's expansion. Indeed, they themselves repeatedly interfered with slavery and prevented its spread in the territories. Even before the Constitutional Convention the Continental Congress meeting under the Articles of Confederation enacted the Ordinance of 1787. Also known as the Northwest Ordinance, it excluded the importation of slaves into the Northwest territory, from which the future states of Ohio, Indiana, Michigan, Illinois, and Wisconsin were formed. Once the new Constitution was ratified, the very first Congress, filled with the very same Founders, quickly reenacted the ordinance.

33. Ibid., vol. 2, p. 270.
34. Ibid., p. 475.

Congress did recognize slavery in those territories where it already existed, Mississippi and Alabama, but not before prohibiting even those territories from importing slaves from the Atlantic slave trade. Thus well before the Constitution allowed the federal government to ban the Atlantic slave trade entirely, Congress signaled its determination to thwart it. In short, the First Congress interfered with slavery in the territories where it already existed. Needless to say, at the earliest possible moment, on January 1, 1808, Congress closed down America's participation in the Atlantic slave trade altogether. Finally, as part of the Missouri Compromise of 1820 Congress drew a line from east to west across the Louisiana Territory and prohibited slavery's expansion north of it.

Lincoln studied the Founders and concluded that their legacy was not as simple as the abolitionists made it out to be. The Constitution recognized and protected slavery where it had been unavoidably necessary, but it was written by men who hated slavery, hemmed it in where they could, and hoped it would eventually die. For Lincoln this divided legacy led to a crucial legal distinction between slavery in the states and slavery in the territories. Under the Constitution, the federal government could not interfere with slavery in those states where it already existed. The fugitive slave and the three-fifths clauses not only recognized the legality of slavery in the southern states but also required the federal government to defend the slaveholders' right to recover their fugitives. No elected official could swear to uphold the Constitution and subsequently refuse to enforce its slavery provisions. On the other hand, the federal government had every right to regulate slavery in the territories even to the point of forbidding its expansion. Lincoln said this many times, never more clearly than at Peoria in 1854: "I wish to MAKE and to KEEP the distinction between the EXISTING institution, and the EXTENSION of it."[35] Indeed, Congress had a moral obligation to prevent the extension of slavery, because slavery was wrong and had to be treated as such.

Such was the legacy of the founding generation. It had proclaimed universal freedom as the guiding principle of the new nation. It had abolished slavery in every northern state. It had provided for the eventual withdrawal of the United States from the Atlantic slave trade. Out of necessity, the Constitution had recognized slavery in those places where it already existed, but even as it did so, it was carefully cleansed of the word "slavery." The same men who wrote the Constitution also restricted the expansion of slavery into the territories of the Old Northwest, interfered with it in the territories of the Old Southwest, and excluded it from most of the territory acquired in the Louisiana Purchase, including Kansas and Nebraska. The Founders did all this, Lincoln said, because they recognized that slavery was incompatible with the principle of fundamental human equality. If they did not go further in abolishing slavery where it already existed, it was because they could not have established the new nation had they tried to do so. More important, having restricted slavery's expansion and cut it off from any new source of African slaves, they believed that they had put slavery on the course of ultimate extinction.

Most Americans believed it as well, or so Lincoln said. From 1776 to 1820, while "the whole Union was acquiescing in it,"

35. Ibid., p. 248.

the Founders had followed a policy restricting slavery's expansion. The "whole country looked forward to the ultimate extinction of the institution."[36] This was the antislavery consensus, and it played a critical role in Lincoln's argument against slavery.

The Collapse of the Antislavery Consensus

When Lincoln said he hated slavery as much as did any abolitionist, he added that he "always believed that everybody was against it, and that it was in the course of ultimate extinction."[37] It is possible that Lincoln did grow up believing this. He was raised in a family in which the evil of slavery was taken for granted. His parents attended an antislavery church. As a young man he was attracted to the Whig Party, which he assumed to be antislavery. "[A]ll agreed that slavery was an evil," he had claimed in 1848, provoking the scorn of Massachusetts Free Soilers. It is possible that in Lincoln's own mind there really was a time when everybody hated slavery. He even hinted that it was almost unnatural to defend slavery. The "great mass of mankind," he said, "consider slavery a great moral wrong, and their feelings against it, is [*sic*] not evanescent, but eternal. It lies at the very foundation of their sense of justice; and it cannot be trifled with. It is a great and durable element of popular action, and, I think, no statesman can safely disregard it."[38]

Up until 1854, then, "the whole public mind" rested secure that slavery's fate had been sealed by its geographical restriction.

36. Ibid., vol. 3, p. 407.
37. Ibid., vol. 2, p. 492.
38. Ibid., pp. 281–82.

"I might have been mistaken," Lincoln added, but that was what "I had believed, and now believe."[39] From the American Revolution through the Compromise of 1850 most Americans looked forward to the ultimate extinction of slavery.

There is something almost willfully naive in this vision of American history. Prior to the American Revolution slavery in the colonies pretty much hugged the Atlantic coast, held in place by imperial restrictions or ecological limits. The largest slave-produced crops in the colonies—tobacco, rice, indigo—were relatively minor players in an Atlantic slave economy dominated by the great sugar plantations of Brazil and the Caribbean. Only after the Revolution, with the invention of the cotton gin and the opening of western lands, did the southern slave economy spill across the Appalachian barrier and with dizzying speed fill half a continent with cotton plantations whose combined wealth dwarfed every other enterprise in the country. By 1850 the United States boasted one of the largest slave economies in history. Yet as this was happening before the entire world's eyes, Lincoln insisted, "the whole public mind" hated slavery and believed that its growth had been restricted and that it was on the course of ultimate extinction. So Lincoln said, and so, apparently, he believed.

The Kansas-Nebraska Act of 1854 changed everything, Lincoln said, precisely because it was designed to overthrow the antislavery consensus bequeathed by the Founders. Of course, Stephen Douglas claimed that the true founding principle of American liberty was popular sovereignty. Not only was this a nonsensical version of American history, Lincoln argued, but the very name of the principle was a fraud. A genuinely popular sov-

39. Ibid., p. 514.

ereignty would leave every individual free "to do as he pleases with himself and the fruit of his labor, so far as it in no wise interferes with any other man's rights." Nothing could be further from Douglas's bogus definition of popular sovereignty, which amounted to nothing more than "the liberty of making slaves of other people." This, Lincoln said, was a form of liberty that "Jefferson never thought of." Nor had the previous generation. Nor had anyone as recently as a year ago.[40]

Stephen Douglas also insisted that he was perfectly neutral toward slavery, that he had no strong feelings about it one way or the other. He would not say that it was right or that it was wrong, and he professed not to care whether the people of a territory voted slavery up or down. Lincoln thought this was absurd. He joked that everyone on earth had an opinion about slavery *except* Stephen Douglas. But the joke exposed an improbable moral evasion, Lincoln argued. If you won't say slavery is wrong, you must think slavery is perfectly all right, since you cannot logically say that you "care not" whether people vote in favor of something that is morally wrong. At the very least you must believe that "slavery is as good as freedom." Douglas thought of slavery "as something having no moral question in it," and that, Lincoln insisted, was not what the Founders thought.[41]

Here was the point at which history and politics fused to form Lincoln's central argument against slavery. Armed with his interpretation of the nation's origins, Lincoln pronounced Stephen Douglas's politics to be something radically new, something the Founders would never have sanctioned, something downright immoral. "I particularly object to the NEW position which the

40. Ibid., pp. 493, 250.
41. Ibid., pp. 449, 494.

avowed principle of this Nebraska law gives to slavery in the body politic," Lincoln said. "I object to it because it assumes that there CAN be MORAL RIGHT in the enslaving of one man by another." There can be no such right in a free republic, Lincoln insisted. "[N]o man is good enough to govern another man, *without that other's consent*," he declared. This, he said, "is the leading principle—the sheet anchor of American republicanism."[42]

Douglas likewise claimed that there was a natural, even a divine basis for the distinction between slave and free states. Just as small farms flourished in the Midwest, just as fishing flourished along the New England coast, so did cotton and slavery flourish in the southern states. Why worry about a hypothetical expansion of slavery into northern territories where it could not flourish? Lincoln flatly rejected this. The supposed natural barrier to slavery expansion was a "*lullaby*." If slavery could flourish on the southern bank of the Ohio River, he said, it could just as easily flourish on the northern bank. There was a moral objection as well. Slavery could not be right in one place and wrong in another. "Once admit the position that a man rightfully holds another man as property on one side of the line, and you must, when it suits his convenience to come to the other side, admit that he has the same right to hold his property there."[43] Once you take away the moral presumption of slavery's evil, Lincoln insisted, you have no reason left for resisting its expansion.

And it *would* expand, Lincoln warned. Slavery encroached "by slow degrees."[44] Once allowed in, slavery was nearly impossible to get out. Ask the people of a territory where there were

42. Ibid., pp. 274, 266.
43. Ibid., p. 262; vol. 3, p. 369.
44. Ibid., vol. 2, p. 238.

no slaves if they wanted slavery to come in and the answer would be no. But let slaveholders establish themselves in a territory, and no matter how small their numbers, slavery would become hard to remove. Those with slaves would be the wealthiest of the settlers and thus influential beyond their numbers. With slavery already in place, the settlers face a different question: Will you emancipate your neighbors' slaves? This they would find hard to do, and by this means slavery would make its way into Nebraska.

But it would not stop there, Lincoln warned, and in 1857 the Supreme Court proved his point by handing down the *Dred Scott* decision. Whereas Stephen Douglas had merely sponsored the legislative repeal of the Missouri Compromise, Chief Justice Roger Taney gratuitously pronounced it unconstitutional. Whereas Douglas had said it was best for Congress to let the territories themselves regulate slavery, Taney went further and declared that not even the territories could prohibit slavery. Why not? Because, Taney said, the Constitution expressly affirmed a right of property in slaves. Every master who chose to do so had the right to bring his slaves into the territories along with his cattle and furniture. By contrast, blacks—free and slave alike—had no rights that white men were bound to respect.

Consider the implications of Taney's decision, Lincoln warned. The judges said that the people of the territories had a constitutional right to their slaves if they wanted them. "Then I say that the people of Georgia have the right to buy slaves in Africa, if they want them, and I defy any man on earth to show any distinction between the two things." Moreover, if a constitutional right to slaves did exist, and if that right prevented the territories from restricting slavery, how could the northern states thwart the same constitutional right by abolishing slavery? The reasoning the Court had used to pry open the territories for slavery applied just as well to the states. All it would take, Lincoln warned, was one more Supreme Court decision to complete the process of making slavery national and perpetual. "We shall *lie down* pleasantly dreaming that the people of *Missouri* are on the verge of making their State *free*; and we shall *awake* to the *reality*, instead, that the *Supreme* Court has made *Illinois* a *slave* State."[45]

It would be hard to name anything in Lincoln's political life that made him angrier than *Dred Scott*. It was a "burlesque upon judicial decisions," a "slander and profanation" upon the Founders. "Dred Scottism," he said, was of a piece with "Nebraskaism." Both covered over slavery—"the sum of all villanies"—with the "deceitful cloak" of self-government in an effort to conceal the "hateful carcass" beneath. Both had to be "repulsed and rolled back." *Dred Scott* itself "must be overruled, and expunged from the books of authority."[46] Lincoln had vowed not to interfere with the Fugitive Slave Act and had bitten his lip and put up with the three-fifths clause, for these were clearly grounded in the Constitution. But nowhere did the Constitution "expressly" affirm the right of property in slaves, no matter what the chief justice said. "If I were in Congress, and a vote should come up on a question whether slavery should be prohibited in a new territory," Lincoln announced, "in spite of that Dred Scott decision, I would vote that it should," adding, "Somebody has to reverse that decision, and we mean to reverse it."[47] When Stephen Douglas denounced him for resisting a decision of the United

45. Ibid., vol. 3, p. 421; vol. 2, p. 467.
46. Ibid., vol. 2, p. 454.
47. Ibid., p. 495.

States Supreme Court, Lincoln replied with a technicality: Neither he nor anyone else would resist the Court's specific decision to deny Dred Scot his petition for freedom.

But Lincoln left no doubt that he didn't much like the specific decision either, and he took the occasion to turn the argument back against Senator Douglas. "Racial Amalgamation" was one of Douglas's bugaboos, and Lincoln had taken to pointing out that most "mulattoes" were born in the South. If Douglas was so worried about race mixing, Lincoln would say, he should advocate restricting slavery's expansion since most race mixing occurred under slavery. A few months after the Supreme Court announced its ruling, Lincoln used Dred Scott as a hypothetical example of what he meant. He pointed out that Scott's wife and two daughters were also involved in the suit. Had Lincoln had his way, the Court would have recognized their citizenship and thereby diminished "the chances of these black girls, ever mixing their blood with that of white people." By contrast Stephen Douglas was "delighted" that the Court had decided they were slaves "and thus left subject to the forced concubinage of their masters, and liable to become the mothers of mulattoes in spite of themselves."[48] This was extraordinary. Unlike Frederick Douglass, who laced his writings with innuendo about the sexual abuse of slaves, Lincoln said almost nothing about it. That he raised the issue on this occasion, in such a provocative and personal way, testifies to the depth of his anger over the *Dred Scott* decision. It was no wonder Lincoln was upset. In 1854 Congress had altered the course of American history; three years later the Supreme Court reversed it entirely.

48. Ibid., pp. 408–9.

The "Debauchment" of
Public Sentiment

Lincoln blamed the Court's decision on politicians and editors who had spent several years educating the public to accept the idea that there was nothing wrong with slavery. The republican form of government rested on public opinion, Lincoln explained. "With public sentiment nothing can fail; without it nothing can succeed. Consequently, he who moulds public sentiment, goes deeper than he who enacts statutes or pronounces decisions. He makes statutes and decisions possible or impossible to be executed." The "central idea" of the American Republic, from its founding until recently, had been "the equality of men," and with it the idea that slavery was wrong. But since 1854, since the repeal of the Missouri Compromise, politicians and editors had been cutting that central idea down to size, narrowing its meaning, limiting its scope. Some were now saying that the only equality that mattered was the equality of states rather than of men. The Supreme Court now said that the Declaration of Independence meant only that all *white* men are created equal. Proslavery writers went so far as to claim that slavery, rather than being an abstract evil, was a positive good. In the old days "our Declaration of Independence was held sacred by all, and thought to include all," Lincoln said, "but now, to aid in making the bondage of the negro universal and eternal, it is assailed, and sneered at, and construed, and hawked at, and torn, till, if its framers could rise from their graves, they could not at all recognize it."[49]

As far as Lincoln was concerned, the person most responsible for this terrible reversal of public sentiment was Stephen

49. Ibid., vol. 3, p. 27; vol. 2, pp. 385, 404.

Douglas. "Judge Douglas is a man of large influence," Lincoln said. "His bare opinion goes far to fix the opinion of others." The "susceptible young hear lessons from him, such as their fathers never heared [sic] when they were young." What would happen, Lincoln warned, if Douglas succeeded "in moulding public sentiment to a perfect accordance with his own?" What if he persuaded Americans that court decisions should be endorsed "without caring to know whether they are right or wrong?" What if he convinced most people "that there is no moral question about slavery?" What if Douglas got enough people to believe "that liberty and slavery are perfectly consistent" or that "for a strong man to declare himself the *superior* of a weak one, and thereupon enslave the weak one, is the very *essence* of liberty—the most sacred right of self government"? If Douglas succeeded in bringing public sentiment "to all this," Lincoln cried, "in the name of heaven, what barrier will be left against making slavery lawful every where?"[50]

The key to Douglas's strategy, Lincoln concluded, was his effort to persuade large numbers of whites "that negroes are not men." Unlike John C. Calhoun and other proslavery extremists, Stephen Douglas did not reject the principle of fundamental human equality; on the contrary, he defiantly asserted his devotion to the Declaration of Independence. But he and a growing legion of followers were now arguing that the principle did not apply to blacks because blacks were somehow less than human. Douglas "has no very vivid impression that the negro is a human," Lincoln said in 1854, "and consequently he has no idea that there can be any moral question in legislating about him." The only way to make Douglas's beloved principle of popular sovereignty consistent with slavery, Lincoln said, was to assume that "the negro is not a man" but a piece of property.[51] This deplorable assumption was, under Douglas's dangerous influence, becoming ever more popular among Americans. We are approaching the point at which "when men are spoken of, the negro is not meant; that when negroes are spoken of, brutes alone are contemplated."[52] The consequences were already apparent.

Thanks to Douglas's stategy, Lincoln argued, the position of free blacks in America was rapidly worsening. When Chief Justice Taney tried to justify his decision by claiming that blacks were viewed more harshly during the revolutionary era, Lincoln blew a loud whistle. "In some trifling particulars," Lincoln said, "the condition of that race has been ameliorated; but, as a whole, in this country, the change between then and now is decidedly the other way." The "ultimate destiny" of blacks in America, he said, "has never appeared so hopeless." The voting rights of blacks had been taken away in several northern states. In the South the master's right to free his slaves had been curtailed. Emancipation was once the province of the state legislatures, but some southern states had recently adopted constitutions that prohibited their legislatures from abolishing slavery. More and more Americans were sneering at the idea, once universally accepted, that the Declaration of Independence embraced blacks and whites alike. And in one of the most searing images he ever conjured up Lincoln depicted the worsening condition of the African American as a nightmarish prison. "All the powers of the earth seem rapidly combining against him," he warned. "Mammon is after him. . . .

51. Ibid., pp. 281, 239. See also vol. 3, p. 265.
52. Ibid., vol. 3, p. 445.

They have him in his prison house; they have searched his
person, and left no prying instrument with him. One
after another they have closed the heavy iron doors upon
him, and now they have him, as it were, bolted in with a
lock of a hundred keys, which can never be unlocked
without the concurrence of every key; the keys in the
hands of a hundred different men, and they scattered to a
hundred different and distant places; and they stand mus-
ing as to what invention, in all the dominions of mind
and matter, can be produced to make the impossibility of
his escape more complete than it is.

Taney's claim that "the public estimate of the negro is more
favorable now than it was at the origin of the government" was a
grotesque inversion of the truth.[53] With each passing year, Lincoln
declared, things were getting worse and worse and worse.

This "tendency to dehumanize the negro" was not merely
wrong. It was degenerate. Our "progress in degeneracy appears
to me to be pretty rapid," he told Joshua Speed in 1855. "We
began by declaring that *'all men are created equal.'* We now practically read it as 'all men are created equal, *except for negroes.'*"[54]
For Lincoln human equality was a moral principle; to attack that
principle was to tear at the moral core of the nation. No wonder
he was increasingly attracted to Henry Clay's claim that those
who denied the evil of slavery were "blowing out the moral

53. Ibid., vol. 2, pp. 403–4.
54. Ibid., vol. 3, p. 304; vol. 2, p. 323. Lincoln's letter to Speed continues: "When the
Know-Nothings get control, it will read 'all men are created equal, except negroes, *and
foreigners, and catholics.'* When it comes to this I should prefer emigrating to some country where they make no pretence of loving liberty—to Russia, for instance, where despotism can be taken pure, and without the base alloy of hypocrisy."

lights around us." By the late 1850s Lincoln had taken to asking
audiences if they had ever heard any politician, as recently as five
years back, declare that the Declaration of Independence did not
embrace blacks. A process that began with "this insidious
Popular Sovereignty" would shortly bring the United States to a
revival of the African slave trade, a federal slave code imposed
on all the territories, and a second *Dred Scott* decision carrying
slavery into the free states. All this was bound to follow from the
"gradual and steady debauching of public opinion."[55]

In a roundabout way, this brought Lincoln's antislavery politics
close to one of abolitionism's central themes, the dehumanization
of slaves. But where Frederick Douglass exposed the ways in which
slaves themselves were brutalized and degraded, Lincoln exposed
Stephen Douglas's brutalizing rhetoric. It was not that Lincoln
failed to appreciate the dehumanizing nature of slavery itself. He
once recalled that in the slave markets of the nation's capital, blacks
were driven off to the South "precisely like droves of horses."
But Frederick Douglass's archenemy was southern slavery itself,
whereas Lincoln's political opponents were northern Democrats.
They were the ones who "require me to deny the humanity of the
negro" by accepting that slaves could be carried into Kansas like any
other form of property.[56] Lincoln therefore revised the abolitionist
argument so that the critique of dehumanization worked as a political argument against the extension of slavery.

Nor was that the only echo of abolitionism in Lincoln's antislavery politics. The importance he attached to public opinion
was not all that different from the abolitionist goal of persuading Americans that slavery was wrong. Lincoln hated the way

55. Ibid., vol. 3, p. 423.
56. Ibid., vol. 2, pp. 253, 264.

politicians like Stephen Douglas were "debauching" the public sentiment of the nation, and his own antislavery politics were, in large measure, an attempt to counter what Douglas and the Democrats were doing. After 1854 Lincoln used politics to persuade as many Americans as possible that slavery was wrong. And like that of many an abolitionist, Lincoln's goal was not so much to end slavery immediately as to restore immediately the consensus that slavery should be ended. "[W]e have taught a great many thousands of people to hate" slavery, he said in 1859, people "who had never given it a thought before."[57] That was the point of antislavery politics: to teach people who had never given it much thought that slavery was wrong and ought to be treated as such.

But if large numbers of Americans had to be taught to hate slavery, how could it be that up until 1854 everyone already agreed that slavery was hateful? Either the Republicans wanted to convert people to antislavery for the first time, or they wanted to restore the antislavery consensus that favored the Missouri Compromise, but they could not logically want both. In any case, by the late 1850s Lincoln was beginning to doubt that such a restoration was possible. He was beginning to suspect that slavery was doomed, not because of northern hostility but because of southern intransigence.

"Slavery Is Doomed"

Lincoln once wrote, privately, that he did not expect to see slavery ended in his lifetime but that if its expansion was halted, the end "will come in due time." At one point in his debates

57. *RW*, p. 303.

with Stephen Douglas Lincoln said that a peaceful extinction of slavery would take "a hundred years at least," but he did not elaborate on that either.[58] Still, he was increasingly certain that the end was near. He had been moving toward this conclusion at least since 1854. Slavery and freedom, he said after the Kansas-Nebraska Act had been passed, "are like two wild beasts in sight of each other, but chained and held apart." Someday, he predicted, "these deadly antagonists will one or the other break their bonds, and then the question will be settled." Up to now—this was still 1854—only "the most artful means" had kept these "two great ideas" apart.[59] But ever since then slavery and freedom had been in open warfare, and by 1859, Lincoln concluded, the South's increasingly aggressive demands had sealed slavery's fate. There was no way to avoid it. At some point the American house, divided against itself over slavery, would cease to be so. William Seward was right to claim that the conflict between slavery and freedom was irreconcilable. The only way slavery could triumph in the great struggle with freedom was for the South to silence all further public discussion of the subject. It must squash slavery as a political issue, thoroughly and permanently. Only then would slavery be safe from the natural animosity of free people everywhere. If, however, the South pressed ahead on its reckless course, slavery was doomed. The North need only stand its ground. The Republicans need only reaffirm their intention to uphold the constitutional guarantees of slavery. The South itself would do the rest, and slavery would die.

Lincoln believed that once a certain tendency was set in

58. *CW*, vol. 3, p. 181.
59. *CW*, p. 245.

motion it was almost impossible to alter its course. Nothing any human being could do would divert the tendency from lurching toward its prescribed destiny. This was how Lincoln viewed the agitation over slavery, his friend Leonard Swett wrote. "He believed from the first, I think, that the agitation of Slavery would produce its overthrow."[60] On this Lincoln was more forthright in private than in public. "Slavery is doomed," he said in September 1859, "and that within a few years." What sealed slavery's fate was the now unstoppable public discussion of it. "[A]n evil can't stand discussion," Lincoln said. "What kills the skunk is the publicity it gives itself."[61] By their own aggressive and irresponsible demands the slaveholders had provoked the agitation over slavery, setting in motion the course of events that could end only in the extermination of slavery itself.

Republicans had no need to make any provocative gestures toward the South. They must say that they meant only to limit slavery's expansion and nothing more, Lincoln told his listeners at Cooper Union in February 1860. They must affirm their determination to uphold the Constitution. They must promise to enforce the Fugitive Slave Act. They must swear that they had no intention of interfering with slavery in the states where it already existed. They could say all these things, Lincoln told his New York audience, and should. But it wouldn't make any difference. The South could no longer be satisfied. Republicans could cede all the territories to slavery, and still, that would not be enough for the South. They could thwart all future slave rebellions, and the South would still want more. What would satisfy them? Lincoln asked. What would convince them? "This, and

60. *HI*, pp. 162–63.
61. *RW*, p. 303.

only this: cease to call slavery *wrong*, and join them in calling it *right*." And that, Lincoln said, Republicans could never do. That would be "reversing the divine rule, and calling, not the sinners, but the righteous to repentance." When it came down to the right and wrong of slavery, there was no room for compromise; there was no middle way. The North needed only stand its ground, do its duty, and "HAVE FAITH THAT RIGHT MAKES MIGHT."[62] The South would take care of the rest.

Cooper Union was the most important speech of Lincoln's political life up to that point. It was 1860, a presidential election year, and prominent eastern Republicans stocked the audience to have a look at this potential candidate. Russell Cornwell remembered sitting in the impressive new hall watching as Lincoln started out, nervously losing his place two or three times. But Lincoln, already a great public speaker, recovered quickly, and once he gained his footing, Cornwell and the rest of the audience were quickly enraptured by "the wonderful beauty and lofty inspiration of that magnificent address." Then came the climactic moment, etched in Cornwell's memory, when Abraham Lincoln quoted none other than Frederick Douglass: "It is written in the sky of America that the slaves shall some day be free." With that, Cornwell recalled, "the applause was so great that the building trembled and I felt the windows shake behind me." The most exhilarating moment of the most important speech of Lincoln's life came when he quoted the most famous runaway slave in America.[63] There was just one prob-

---

62. *CW*, vol. 3, pp. 547, 550.

63. My account of Russell Cornwell, as well as the circumstances of the Cooper Union address here and elsewhere in the chapter, draws on Harold Holzer, *Lincoln at Cooper Union: The Speech That Made Abraham Lincoln President* (New York, 2004), pp. 114–15.

lem. Lincoln never quoted Frederick Douglass, at Cooper Union or anywhere else. It was there in Russell Cornwell's memory, but it was not there in the text of the speech.

Cornwell's lapse is easily forgiven, for if Frederick Douglass's words were absent, his sentiments were almost certainly present. Lincoln may not have said that upon the American sky it was written "that the slaves shall some day be free," but he almost certainly believed it. There was no more room for compromise. A mighty struggle between slavery and freedom could no longer be avoided. "No man has the right to keep his fellow man in bondage, be he black or white," Lincoln said on the eve of the 1860 election, "and the time will come, and must come, when there will not be a single slave within the borders of this country."[64] It wasn't Frederick Douglass, but it could have been.

64. *RW*, p. 280

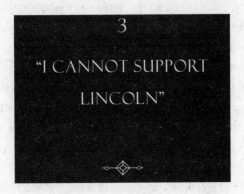

3

"I CANNOT SUPPORT LINCOLN"

As the presidential election of 1860 got under way, Frederick Douglass found himself in an uncomfortably familiar position. He did not know what to do. Should he reserve his vote for those with the highest abolitionist principles? Or should he endorse a political coalition that compromised his abolitionism but was much more likely to win voters to the antislavery cause? There was no easy answer. As he confronted the question, Douglass expressed his ambivalence in two competing interpretations of American history. The optimistic one, which he recited up until late 1859, emphasized what he called the progress of antislavery. It began with the waning of antislavery fervor after the American Revolution, followed by the revival of abolitionism in the 1830s. Antislavery sentiment grew steadily thereafter. In the 1840s a new antislavery politics emerged, and by the late 1850s antislavery activists had achieved genuine respectability. When he first escaped from bondage, antislavery speakers were mobbed and beaten in the streets, Douglass recalled, whereas now audiences listened in respectful silence. Fifteen years earlier only two members of Congress had openly identified themselves as antislavery men. Now there were more than a hundred. In 1844 the antislavery candidate for President mustered only sixty thousand votes; by 1856 the Republican candidate had received more than two million. The turning point in this narrative was the Fugitive Slave Act of 1850. It awakened thousands of northern voters to the threat of an aggressive slaveocracy, and their concerns steadily escalated over the course of the 1850s. By the fall of 1859 Douglass foresaw something that would have been inconceivable ten years earlier, the likely election of an antislavery President under the banner of the Republican Party.

But as the winter of 1859–60 descended, Douglass's mood darkened, and he retreated to a gloomier version of American history. In this interpretation the slaveholders of the South had grown ever more arrogant in their demands, ever more potent in their ability to bend northern politicians and national politics to their will. The Fugitive Slave Act was still the turning point, but now it was evidence of the slaveholders' tightening grip on American politics. Thereafter the slaveholders leaped effortlessly from victory to victory. They repealed the Missouri Compromise in 1854. They transformed Kansas from a free territory into a bloody battleground for slavery. In 1857 they secured slavery's future with the shocking *Dred Scott* decision. By 1859 the slave South held the entire federal bureaucracy hostage to a series of demands that would have made slavery both national and perpetual. Yet in the face of this rising proslavery threat the abolitionists had been neutralized, their principles progressively diluted by a series of political compromises aimed at garnering more and more votes. In 1860 the Republican Party did indeed stand on the precipice of victory, but it stood there shorn of all principle and beholden to nothing more than the naked pursuit of electoral victory.

Of course it wasn't that simple, and Frederick Douglass knew it. By 1860 Lincoln had been struggling for several years to ensure that his fellow Republicans held fast to their core belief that slavery was wrong and should be treated as such. Douglass agreed with Lincoln that nearly all the antislavery sentiment in America was now bundled into the Republican Party. And he shared Lincoln's view that the northern and southern wings of the Democratic Party were the tweedledum and tweedledee of proslavery politics. He even believed that a Republican victory would unleash hammerblows against the proslavery forces in American politics. He could not just turn away from that prospect.

How would Douglass resolve his dilemma? By taking a stance that baffled his contemporaries and has perplexed historians ever since. In July 1860 Douglass made a startling announcement. He would "sincerely hope" for a Republican victory "over all the odds and ends of slavery combined against it." But he would cast his own vote for the Radical Abolitionist candidate, knowing that the party was now a shrunken remnant of its former self. He hoped the Republicans would win, but as he wrote to his longtime friend Gerrit Smith, "I cannot support Lincoln."[1]

1. *FDP,* ser. 1, vol. 3, pp. 381–82; *Life & Writings,* vol. 2, pp. 489–90.

Reason and Passion:
The Temperamental Divide

Lincoln and Douglass were very different men. True, there were parallels. Both had grown up in poverty; they were largely self-taught; in a generation of great orators they were two of the greatest; in the century of the self-made man both came to see their own lives as exemplary. Still, they were very different men, and not merely because one was born free and white and the other black and enslaved. Their minds worked differently. Though both hated slavery, they hated it in different ways and not always for the same reasons. Their personalities were different as well. Douglass had the blustery, oversize persona of a nineteenth-century Romantic. When he spoke, he roared, his booming baritone complemented by waving arms and devastating mimicry. Abraham Lincoln was the cautious grandchild of the eighteenth-century Enlightenment. He stood still when he spoke, hands behind his back, his voice high-pitched but clear enough to be heard over large audiences. Douglass roused his listeners with his passion, shocked them with gruesome details, amazed them with his verbal pyrotechnics, and impressed them with his strong build and good looks. Lincoln disarmed his listeners with his homely appearance, folksy stories, and self-deprecating humor, leaving audiences all the more impressed by his piercing combination of lawyerly precision and simple idealism. Both men were masterful logicians, leveling their opponents' arguments with a withering lucidity. But where Douglass used logic to make people feel— viscerally—the bloody horrors of slavery, Lincoln used his oratorical skills to channel the voters' patriotic ideals into the cause of universal freedom.

For both Lincoln and Douglass the American Revolution was a touchstone, but in subtly different ways. Lincoln believed that human history had turned a corner during the eighteenth century, when a remarkable group of Founding Fathers came together to declare America's independence. Those men had affirmed the principles and established the political institutions best suited to the creation of a humane and reasonable republic. They declared that all men were created equal, they denounced slavery as a great evil, and in so doing, they set in motion a historic struggle between slavery and freedom. But because they were men of the Enlightenment, men of reason rather than passion, their highest hopes were held in check by the dictates of prudence and moderation.

Frederick Douglass came to admire the Founders as well, though less because they had articulated an important set of human freedoms than for having bowed in deference to the desire for freedom that stirred in the soul of every man and woman. For Douglass it was this innate passion for freedom that drove human history forward. Of course slavery was incompatible with the rights of man, but mostly because it was unnatural. To these familiar precepts of American Romanticism Douglass fused an increasingly messianic Christianity. The deep hunger for freedom was planted in our souls at the moment God created the first of us. Every man or woman had a *right* to liberty, Douglass argued, but only because each human being had an inextinguishable instinct to be free, an instinct that made the relation of master and slave innately vicious. "The God who made him had planted deep in his soul a love of liberty, ever driving him to resist the claims, demands, and authority of his master, and this must needs be met on the master's part with cruelty and outrage." Slavery, Douglass shouted, "must necessarily be cruel."[2] In their cruelty the slaveholders committed a grave sin against divine law, and those sinners deserved the full, furious, and bloody force of God's holy wrath. Douglass hated slavery, but he hated the slaveholders as well.

Many of the differences between Lincoln and Douglass shade into matters of personality. Douglass was impulsive and voluble, quick to react to current events, quick to take offense, quick to impugn the motives of those who disagreed with him. It made sense that Douglass published his own newspaper, he had so much to say. But it accustomed him to saying too much, to spilling forth in print rapidly with little time for reflection. Not for nothing is Douglass's biography noted for a series of sharp reversals. He was the staunchest of Garrisonians who became the target of Garrison's vengeful anger. He was a pacifist before he converted to revolutionary violence. He hated the Constitution until the moment he decided to worship it. He respected the Republican Party almost as much as he held it in contempt. It was inevitable that Douglass would blow hot and cold about Abraham Lincoln. He blew hot and cold about a lot of things.

Lincoln shied away from emotional arguments. His speeches wed reason to fact. He was a skeptic in an age of religious enthusiasm. He soared to eloquence by restating great principles rather than expressing great passion. Passionate men lost control of themselves; they took the law into their own hands; they shed blood. One of the reasons Lincoln hated slavery was that the master's authority was so lacking in restraint. Lincoln was nothing if not restrained. He shrank, as if by involuntary reflex, from all forms of social upheaval. The antislavery mobs of the 1830s

2. *FDP*, ser. 2, vol. 3, p. 280.

prompted his first memorable speech, a ringing defense of the rule of law. The anarchy in Kansas in the 1850s shocked him. He was devastated by the Civil War.

Lincoln could be gregarious in private, but as a public figure he was a man of Promethean reserve. He struggled successfully to suppress his passion and maintain his self-control. Yet he observed the flaws in other men and women with ironic detachment rather than impassioned fury or haughty indignation. He thought of white southerners as ordinary people—neither sinners nor saints—corrupted by slavery, perhaps, but no more so than any Yankee trapped by the logic of similar circumstances. A cautious and deliberate politician, Lincoln took his time making decisions. Having made a decision, he said no more than needed to be said. He had a small *d* democrat's sense of humility before the authority of the people, but he had an ear so finely tuned to the movement of public opinion that he was able to calibrate his own moves with astonishing skill. He knew just how far he could push the public mind, which arguments worked and which did not. Frederick Douglass had likewise learned to adjust his arguments for broader appeal, but he never let go of the reformer's urge to provoke his listeners and readers into furious outrage. Lincoln had always recoiled from that kind of abolitionism, yet by the end of his life he had grown genuinely fond of Frederick Douglass. In his own latter days Douglass came to appreciate the virtues of Lincoln's temperamental conservatism—but not in 1860.

That an escaped black slave approached the subject of human bondage with fiery passion requires no more explanation than the skeptical reserve of an ambitious white lawyer. Lincoln and Douglass came from different worlds. Of course they looked at the world differently, their shared hatred of

slavery notwithstanding. By the late 1850s Lincoln was carefully positioning himself as the conservative defender of the
Founders' legacy in the face of growing southern radicalism.
Meanwhile Douglass was intrigued by the prospect of apoca-
lyptic violence in his war against an increasingly reactionary
South. Lincoln was not the man to satisfy Douglass's thirst for
romantic revolution, at least not immediately. But in 1859
there was someone else who did.

—◇—

At dusk on the evening of October 16, 1859, acting on direct
orders from the Lord God Himself, John Brown led a band of
eighteen men on a raid of the federal arsenal at Harpers Ferry in
western Virginia. By midnight Brown's men had cut the telegraph wires and commandeered the railroad bridges leading
into town. They had control of the arsenal, the armory, and the
rifle factory. Then they sat back and waited for slaves from the
surrounding countryside to join their rebellion. But the slaves
never came. About twenty were brought into town by Brown's
men, but they refused to join the fight, and most of them had
the good sense to run for their lives. Little more than a year
later slaves across the South began claiming their freedom by
running in substantial numbers to armed white northerners
invading the South, this time as Union soldiers. But the slaves at
Harpers Ferry stayed put; they knew the difference between an
army of liberation and a ship of fools. By morning Brown's men
had been surrounded. Within thirty-six hours it was all over. A
handful of Brown's men escaped. Several were killed, including

two of Brown's sons. Brown and two others were captured, tried, and executed.[3]

Abraham Lincoln dismissed John Brown as a madman. Frederick Douglass said he was one of the greatest men who ever walked the earth.

"THEY DESERVE TO HAVE THEIR THROATS CUT"

Of all the compliments showered on John Brown after his impressive death, none would have pleased him more than Ralph Waldo Emerson's. Emerson called him a saint. Brown fancied himself an Old Testament patriarch, the shepherd of his flock. Alas, within this vale of tears Brown exhibited the shortcomings of mere mortals. He was an incompetent farmer, a failure at business, and a criminally irresponsible parent. He fathered twenty children and left them all but destitute, cold and hungry much of the time. Sixteen of them died—from exposure, malnutrition, sickness, or gunshot wounds—before Brown himself ascended from the earthly realm. While his family suffered, Brown was often away doing God's work, punishing America for the sin of slavery. Brown was proud that at home his sons cleaned the dishes along with his daughters. But if men could do women's work, women could not do men's. He badgered his sons, never his daughters, to join him on his adventures and succeeded in getting three of them killed in the process.

3. There are two modern biographies of John Brown. The best is still Stephen B. Oates, *To Purge This Land with Blood: A Biography of John Brown* (New York, 1970). Oates is remarkably evenhanded, whereas David S. Reynolds, *John Brown: Abolitionist* (New York, 2005) effectively recapitulates Brown's perspective.

Armed rebellion, Brown believed, was just what the slaves needed to imbue them with "a sense of their manhood," for there was nothing like killing to make a man feel like a man. At Harpers Ferry one of his sons took a lethal bullet in the gut and fell to the floor bleeding profusely and squirming in such pain that he begged his father to put him out of his misery. John Brown looked down at his writhing son and told him to shut up and "die like a man." He did invite one woman to join him; Brown was so impressed by Harriet Tubman, the fearless anti-slavery activist, that he referred to her as "he." But she wasn't man enough to join him.

Brown had a romantic disdain for the rule of law. Like Emerson, Henry David Thoreau, Theodore Parker, and Thomas Wentworth Higginson, the Yankee intellectuals who subsidized and lionized him, Brown was contemptuous of mainstream poli-tics. It was all flabbiness and corruption. Although he erupted in mighty outrage whenever proslavery forces departed from strict law and order, he considered himself exempt from such stric-tures. The truth was that Brown distrusted any earthly govern-ment other than his own. In 1856 he unleashed a bloodbath in Kansas, hacking to death six innocent settlers who had raised nothing more than their voices against their antislavery neigh-bors. His victims were German immigrants and poor southern whites, none of them slaveholders, none of them "border ruffi-ans" from Missouri, all of them men who had no particular use for slavery but who hated abolitionists even more. What had aroused Brown's wrath was their link to the territorial govern-ment. The six people he killed had all participated—as bailiffs or jurors, for example—in a court set up by territorial authorities in Kansas. Three years later Brown selected a federal arsenal as his target at Harpers Ferry. But although he aimed to attack a government installation, he had no plans to seize, much less overthrow, the government itself. Brown and his acolytes liked to imagine him as a Cromwellian figure, but Cromwell led a successful revolution to take control of the English state. Brown did draw up a constitution for a new government, but it was a preposterous document, clearly designed to govern only his armed communities up in the mountains.

Douglass knew something of Brown's intentions long before the actual raid on Harpers Ferry. The two men had first met in Springfield, Massachusetts, in 1848, and they remained friendly thereafter. Over the next decade Brown stayed at the Douglass home several times, once for three weeks, and Douglass visited Brown occasionally as well. Brown joined Douglass, Gerrit Smith, and a small group of radicals who met in Syracuse in June 1855 to create the Radical Abolitionist Party, knowing full well that the new Republican Party had already become the repository for nearly all the antislavery sentiment in America. Brown's only achievement at Syracuse was to persuade the delegates to formally endorse revolutionary violence, in effect confessing to their own political irrelevance.[4] The convention delegates also coughed up sixty dollars to help Brown wage his war in Kansas, but Kansas was merely a sideshow for him. Brown had already been talking with Douglass about his more ambitious plan to invade the South and provoke a gigantic slave uprising. But Brown knew little and understood less about slavery in the South, so it was left to Douglass to point out that the slaveholders were well armed and ferocious. The master class had only to

---

4. John Stauffer, *The Black Hearts of Men: Radical Abolitionists and the Transformation of Race* (Cambridge, Mass., 2002), pp. 8ff., sees Brown's presence at Syracuse as evidence of a more substantial political engagement than I'm able to identify.

snap its fingers, and the mighty forces of state and national power would be rushed in to put down a slave rebellion. So although he admired Brown's courage and lack of racial prejudice, Douglass was never tempted to join the "desperate" rebellion itself. Nevertheless, when Brown invaded the South, he was carrying letters from Douglass, who was instantly targeted for arrest as a coconspirator. Within days of Brown's capture Douglass fled the United States for the second time in his life, going first to Canada and then to Great Britain, where he remained for several months.

Safely out of the country Douglass shifted into hyperbole, defending Brown in implausibly grandiose terms. Most people thought Brown was some kind of lunatic, but Douglass insisted that he was perfectly sane. Brown's gruesome butchery back in Kansas contributed greatly to his reputation as a madman. Douglass skirted with dishonesty by implying that Brown's victims in Kansas got what they deserved. We shuddered at their deaths, Douglass said, the way we shudder at the execution of a murderer.[5] Before Harpers Ferry Douglass warned Brown that his invasion

---

5. The following letter was sent to John Brown after his arrest: "Sir: Altho vengeance is not mine, I confess that I do feel gratified to hear that you ware stopt in your fiendish career at Harper's Ferry, with the loss of your two sons, you can now appreciate my distress, in Kansas, when you then and there entered my house at midnight and arrested my husband and two boys and took them out of the yard and in cold blood shot them dead in my hearing, you cant say you done it to free our slaves, we had none and never expected to own one, but has only made me a poor disconsolate widow with helpless children while I feel for your folly. I do hope & trust that you will meet your just reward. O how it pained my Heart to hear the dying groans of my Husband and children if this scrawl give you any consolation you are welcome to it." GLC 7590. Mahala Doyle. Autograph letter signed: to John Brown, November 20, 1859. (The Gilder Lehrman Collection, courtesy of The Gilder Lehrman Institute of American History. Not to be reproduced without written permission.)

was bound to fail and refused repeatedly to participate. After the raid Douglass published the details of what he said was Brown's plan, hoping to show that but for a minor error of execution, Brown's raid might have succeeded in destabilizing slavery in Maryland and Virginia. But the plan Douglass described bore only passing resemblance to the raid Brown actually executed. Douglass nevertheless went to his grave singing John Brown's praises.

This was not entirely out of character; Douglass had a tendency to divide humanity into heroes and villains. The archvillains were of course the slaveholders, and none was sketched in more satanic hues than Thomas Auld, the owner who had so often protected the young Douglass. But his parade of heroes was more impressive. For some years Douglass was under the spell of William Lloyd Garrison. Later he lost himself in praise of Gerrit Smith. He wrote sycophantic letters to Charles Sumner. But Douglass's fulsome praise of John Brown set a new standard. It was not enough that Brown was "a noble, heroic, and Christian martyr"; he was also one of the greatest men in the history of the universe, almost beyond human in his greatness. Brown's soul, Douglass said, was "illuminated with divine qualities in such high degree as to raise the question, was he our brother?" Or did Brown belong to a race of men everyone thought had become extinct? His deeds filled men with wonder. The greatest minds studied Brown's character the way astronomers studied "the heavenly bodies." His posthumous hold over Douglass seemed astonishing, especially during 1860 and 1861.[6] It colored much of Douglass's reaction to Lincoln's candidacy and the early years of his presidency.

Garrison had been the inspiration for Douglass's entry into

6. *FDP*, ser. 1, vol. 3, pp. 303ff., 315ff., 325, 339–40, 412–20.

the abolitionist movement. Smith had choreographed Douglass's passage into antislavery politics. Along the way Douglass began to drop remarks about the salutary effect of killing off a few slaveholders. But it was John Brown who transformed Douglass into a steadfast supporter of revolutionary violence. Douglass credited Brown with putting the slaveholders in fear for their lives. They worried about "having their *throats cut*," Douglass wrote, "because they deserve to have them *cut*."[7] Garrison's rising disdain for American churches had dampened Douglass's religious enthusiasm, but John Brown awakened in Douglass a messianic wish for divine vengeance upon the slaveholders. Lincoln had said that the conflict over slavery was part of the eternal struggle between right and wrong; for Douglass, as for John Brown, it was also a struggle between Christ and Satan.

Similarly, Brown revitalized the spark of contempt for politics and the political process that had never fully burned out in Douglass's own mind. When they first met, in 1848, Brown told Douglass that neither moral suasion nor political action would abolish slavery. But Douglass knew better. Only a month before their first meeting he had published an essay commemorating the tenth anniversary of the English Parliament's abolition of slavery in the British West Indies. In that same publication Douglass hailed the recent abolition of slavery in the French West Indies imposed by the new government in Paris. In the northern states judges and legislators, not rebellious slaves, had abolished the institution in the wake of independence. No one understood better than Douglass that most of the major emancipations in modern history were driven by various combinations of political agitation and government action. Only in Haiti did

7. *Life & Writings,* vol. 2, p. 487.

slave rebellion play a central role in emancipation, and even there state action had been crucial.[8] Douglass had given detailed speeches praising the governments of England and France for their moves against slavery. But when he spoke of John Brown and Harpers Ferry, he shelved his faith in the U.S. Constitution and replaced it with the cynical clichés of a disillusioned Romantic. "Our civilization is yet too selfish and barbarous" to appreciate John Brown, Douglass declared; "our statesmen are yet too narrow, base and mobocratic; our press is yet too venal and truckling; our religion is too commercial" to understand or appreciate the "great character" of John Brown. But Brown himself had risen above all the venality, the mobocracy, and the racial prejudices of American civilization. "Brave and glorious old man! Yours was the life of a true friend of humanity, and the triumphant death of a hero."[9]

Such was the division within Douglass's own mind that even as he engaged with antislavery politics, he simultaneously embraced the romance of revolutionary violence. Perhaps this was because his political options were narrowing. By 1860 Gerrit Smith's influence on antislavery politics was spent. When northerners voted their antislavery sentiments, they cast their ballots for Republicans. After his name surfaced as one of the Secret Six who had bankrolled Brown's raid, Smith suffered a mental breakdown, and his family had him committed to the Utica insane asylum. With Gerrit Smith out of the picture

8. First the French Revolution destabilized the slaveholders' rule in Haiti while perhaps inspiring the slaves themselves to embark on a guerrilla war for their own emancipation. Once the rebellion was under way Spain invaded Haiti and offered freedom to those who joined the struggle against France. Then, in 1793, hoping to trump the Spanish, the radical French government back in Paris abolished Haitian slavery outright.

9. *FDP*, ser. 1, vol. 3, pp. 386–87.

Douglass's romantic attraction to heroes (and villains) drew him to John Brown. As it did so, some of Brown's contempt for politics found its way into Douglass's speeches.

The irony is that Brown's raid would have meant little had it not been for the recent upsurge of antislavery politics. Had he attacked a federal arsenal in 1829 Brown would appear today as a curious footnote in the history books. Southern shouts of outrage would have died down quickly because the entire political apparatus of the nation would have conspired to suppress the slavery issue. But in October 1859 raiding Harpers Ferry was like pouring gasoline on an already raging fire. By then a full decade piled high with great political conflicts—over the war with Mexico, the Compromise of 1850, the fugitive slave crisis, the Kansas-Nebraska Act, the *Dred Scott* decision—had steadily ratcheted up the national debate over slavery. Influential books had energized the political crisis. Early in the decade *Uncle Tom's Cabin* by Harriet Beecher Stowe rose from the fury over the Fugitive Slave Act. By the late 1850s Hinton Rowan Helper's *The Impending Crisis of the South* had thrown Congress into yet another furious debate. In 1856 the Republican Party, the first major party opposed to slavery, had flexed its muscles at the polls, and by 1859 it was bidding fair to take control of the national government the following year, a prospect John Brown himself recognized. By then the House of Representatives could not even choose a Speaker without its members hurling threats of secession and war. At the moment Brown raided Harpers Ferry, Washington, D.C., was already straddling a razor's edge. Southern leaders had a point when they complained that antislavery agitation in the North had created the circumstances that gave John Brown his great significance.

As if the rise of antislavery politics were not enough, the

North's reaction to John Brown's execution sent the South into a paroxysm of fury. Brown's dignified behavior while in prison and during his trial, capped by his eloquent closing statement at the sentencing, stirred unexpected emotions. His execution was greeted in many parts of the North as a day of mourning. It was this northern response more than the raid itself to which the South reacted in horror. Republican politicians could repeat as often as they liked that John Brown was a criminal who deserved his fate. But white southerners had heard Lincoln say over and over that the core principle of the Republican Party was that slavery was an evil and had to be treated as such. If John Brown had an impact in 1859, it was because the Republicans had succeeded only too well. Years later, in a reflective mood, Douglass acknowledged the circumstances that lent John Brown's raid its significance. A growing number of northerners had come to view slavery as immoral, he noted. After 1856 "the whole land rocked with this great controversy." An "explosive force" had already weakened the Union; the public mind was agitated to its "topmost height"; the North and South had reached their "extreme points of difference." Leading politicians were proclaiming that all hope of compromise "had nearly vanished." Only then, "as if to banish even the last glimmer of hope for peace between the sections, John Brown came upon the scene."[10]

Northern politicians scrambled to denounce the madman who invaded Harpers Ferry. They called Brown a lunatic. They belittled his insurrectionary schemes. They defended his execution for treason. Lincoln joined in, dutifully distancing himself and his party from Brown's foolish escapade. He didn't have much choice; he

10. Frederick Douglass, *Life and Times of Frederick Douglass*, intro. Rayford Logan (New York, 1881; rev. ed., 1892; repr., New York, 1962), p. 305.

wanted to be President. But Douglass resented it, and his resentment, more than ideological zeal, helps explain his exaggerated defense of Brown. Douglass knew what it was like to be denounced and shunned. After his move to Rochester and his embrace of antislavery politics the Garrisonians had subjected Douglass to a malicious campaign of vilification. Douglass had been their featured attraction; his apostasy sent Garrison and his followers over the edge, into obsession. They warned other abolitionists to stay away from Douglass. They dissected his speeches and snarled at his every move. Garrison himself published mean-spirited personal gossip about Douglass's family. So when Douglass looked around in 1860 and saw northern leaders lining up to dismiss and belittle John Brown—jumping at the crack of the South's whip, Douglass thought—he lurched instinctively in the opposite direction. In the struggle to overthrow human bondage there were no apostates and no such things as zealots.

Beyond cementing his personal loyalty to Brown, Douglass's experience with the bruising factionalism among abolitionists taught him an important lesson: There were many "right" ways to oppose slavery. Politics and moral persuasion were not mutually exclusive. A preacher's pulpit, a speaker's rostrum, a political stump—all should be put to work for the cause. He had come to disagree with Garrison's pacifism, but he rarely denounced it. He had embraced political agitation, he was flirting with the Republican Party, but he would not repudiate revolutionary violence. Antislavery reformers should not busy themselves with denunciations of those who worked to abolish slavery the wrong way. The point—the only point—was to get slavery abolished. So while everybody else was piling it on, Frederick Douglass arrived in Great Britain and rushed into his impetuous defense of John Brown and revolutionary violence.

In Scotland Douglass got word from Rochester that his ten-year-old daughter Anne, the youngest of his five children, had died on March 13, 1860. She had been ill for several months, but Douglass was gone the whole time. Stricken with grief, he risked his safety to return to America to be with his desolate wife and children. He could not have known that congressional leaders had already decided not to turn Brown's raid into a political vendetta and had quietly dropped the prosecution. By the time Douglass got back to America Republican Party leaders had succeeded in shifting the country's attention from Harpers Ferry to the presidential election of 1860. The spotlight had moved from John Brown to Abraham Lincoln.

"Who Is the Conservative?"

The raid on Harpers Ferry was not a slave insurrection, Lincoln said. "It was an attempt by white men to get up a revolt among slaves, in which the slaves refused to participate." Brown was like so many other "enthusiasts" who appeared in the pages of history. He "broods over the oppression of a people till he fancies himself commissioned by Heaven to liberate them." The attempt always failed and the would-be liberator was generally executed. There's a dismissive tone in the way Lincoln spoke of John Brown, as though he were swatting at flies. The only reason he bothered mentioning Brown at all was that the Democrats were trying to link Harpers Ferry to the Republicans. They had whipped up the public into a frenzied hatred of slavery, Democrats charged. All John Brown did was jump the gun and launch the invasion of the South that the Republicans were plotting anyway. Lincoln scoffed at this. He challenged the Democrats to name a single Republican politician who endorsed

Brown's attempted insurrection. No one, Lincoln said, can reasonably object to Brown's execution by the state of Virginia.
Though Brown "agreed with us in thinking slavery is wrong,"
Lincoln explained, there was no excuse for Brown's "violence,
bloodshed, and treason." Then Lincoln craftily turned the argument back against the Democrats. The same went for the southern states, he said: If a Republican was constitutionally elected
President and the southern states reacted by trying to destroy
the Union, "it shall be our duty to deal with you as old John
Brown has been dealt with."[11] Abraham Lincoln was running for
President as the candidate of law and order.

Politics, and politics alone, would bring slavery to heel,
Lincoln said. He could readily grant that John Brown was a man
of "great courage" and "rare unselfishness." He had nothing but
sympathy for Brown's hatred of slavery. But there was a better
way to deal with it. "We have a means provided for the expression of our belief in regard to Slavery," Lincoln argued; "it is
through the ballot box."[12] Harpers Ferry was more than a
crime; it was futile. The only way to oppose slavery seriously
was to build an antislavery coalition, organize it into a mass
political party, and take control of the state. But even then there
were limits to what slavery's enemies could do; even with their
hands on the levers of state power they would still be con-
strained by the Constitution.

Frederick Douglass liked to invoke "a higher law," but for
Lincoln there was nothing higher than the rule of law, without
which there could be no real freedom. As a young Whig back in
the 1830s Lincoln condemned Andrew Jackson's assault on the

11. *CW*, vol. 3, pp. 541, 502.
12. Ibid., p. 496.

Bank of the United States as part of "that lawless and mobocratic spirit" threatening to undermine American institutions.[13] During those same years the rise of an abolitionist movement in the North prompted a wave of antiabolitionist mob violence. The most notorious instance had taken place in Lincoln's home state of Illinois where, in November 1837, a proslavery mob at Alton shot to death an abolitionist editor named Elijah Lovejoy. Lincoln folded this event into a larger condemnation of lawlessness that he developed in his first major speech, delivered to the Young Men's Lyceum in Springfield in 1838. There he made the case for the temperamental conservatism that was to remain one of his abiding traits.

It was in the nature of mob rule, Lincoln warned, that it could not readily distinguish the guilty from the innocent. John Brown proved the point, first in Kansas and then at Harpers Ferry, where the first person killed was a black man shot accidentally by one of Brown's jittery accomplices. When innocents such as these became the victims of unchecked disorder, Lincoln argued, the public's attachment to the government and its laws would break down. He worried that this was beginning to happen in the late 1830s. The founding generation had sought fame and glory in the establishment of the United States, but their work was done. Now, he warned, a "towering genius" who hoped to achieve greatness could do so only by undermining the work of the Founders. To protect the Republic from this threat, Lincoln called for a steadfast devotion to the rule of law. Such devotion, he said, should be the "political religion" of all Americans. In earlier times Americans had to cultivate their passions so they could persevere through the bloody struggle for

13. Ibid., vol. 1, p. 69.

independence. But with those days long since over, the passions of the Revolution had properly subsided. At this point in our history, Lincoln said, passion has become the enemy. "Reason, cold, calculating, unimpassioned reason, must furnish all the materials for our future support and defence." This fear of unrestrained passion, this abiding commitment to "unimpassioned reason," stayed with Lincoln forever.[14]

Long after he had made opposition to slavery the central theme of his political identity, Lincoln still claimed that his was the true conservative position. His response to John Brown reflected this, but that was an old story, he had always thought that abolitionists went overboard. What led Lincoln to insist on his own conservatism was something else, the emergence of a proslavery extremism that claimed the conservative mantle as its own. "You say you are conservative—eminently conservative," Lincoln declared. "What is conservatism? Is it not adherence to the old and tried, against the new and untried?"[15] By that standard, Lincoln insisted, it was the Republican Party that stood for the true conservatism. It was the Republicans who wanted to put slavery back where the Founders themselves had put it. Ever since 1854 Lincoln had indeed framed his antislavery argument as a plea for the restoration of a policy that had been in place since the founding days of the Republic. Lincoln's hatred of slavery was nothing more than the reassertion of everything that Washington and Jefferson and Hamilton had said generations earlier. "Consider, then, who is conservative, your party, or ours," he said to Democrats in Manchester, New Hampshire, on March 1, 1860. The following day, in Dover, he did not leave the

14. Ibid., vol. 1, pp. 108–15.
15. Ibid., vol. 3, p. 537.

consideration up to his listeners but instead told his audience straight out that it was the "republicans who remained steadfast to the principles of the fathers on the subject of slavery." It was the Republicans, therefore, who "were the conservative party."[16] If Lincoln was positioning himself for the upcoming presidential election, it was the position with which he felt most comfortable and one that left Frederick Douglass feeling uncomfortable.

By the late 1850s much of the difference between Douglass's radicalism and Lincoln's conservatism had come down to one critical question: *What did the Constitution allow the federal government to do with slavery?* Lincoln and Douglass answered it differently. For Douglass the Constitution was an antislavery document that virtually commanded politicians to take aggressive action against slavery wherever it existed. But the Founders had freely admitted that they had compromised with slavery to create the Union, and Lincoln did not want anyone to forget it. They had made those compromises, Lincoln said, knowing slavery was evil but certain it was dying. In Lincoln's mind the founding compromises limited but did not destroy the federal government's ability to act against slavery. Still, no matter how much he personally hated slavery, the Constitution recognized it in the states where it already existed.

Douglass hated Lincoln's argument. He considered it both constitutionally implausible and morally repugnant. The more strenuously Lincoln repeated it during the 1860 campaign, the more frustrated Douglass grew. But Lincoln paid no attention; he was much more concerned by what the Democrats were saying. When they charged Republicans with plotting the abolition of slavery, Republicans insisted that they supported nothing

16. Ibid., pp. 552, 553.

more than restricting slavery's expansion. Democrats accused Republicans of planning to invade the South. Republicans answered that the Constitution prohibited them from interfering with slavery in any southern state. There was nothing new in these Republican disavowals, but they alarmed Douglass so much that he shied away from Abraham Lincoln. At heart Douglass was still a radical reformer. At bottom Lincoln was a cautious politician.

There was one more Democratic charge that Lincoln was anxious to answer. The Democrats claimed he believed in racial equality. If you think that blacks and whites are equally entitled to their freedom, they argued, you must also believe that whites and blacks could vote, work, and even marry each other as equals. Lincoln responded by carefully distinguishing race from slavery. The issue, he insisted, was not the racial equality of blacks and whites but the right and wrong of slavery. Race and slavery were two separate issues. Just because he did not want to have a black woman as a slave, Lincoln liked to say, did not mean he wanted to have her as his wife. He insisted that he could oppose slavery on moral grounds and still support discrimination against blacks.

This made no sense to Frederick Douglass. Even as a young boy he wondered out loud why black people were slaves and white people were free. Dissatisfied with the explanations he got from his fellow slaves, Douglass early on concluded that racism was nothing more than an excuse for slavery. No slavery, no racism—this was one of the Garrisonian precepts that

Douglass never abandoned. For twenty years, through all his twists and turns, he had consistently argued that racial prejudice in the North was the "spirit of slavery" extending its influence through the nation as a whole. Even after the Civil War Douglass interpreted flourishing racial prejudice as one of the lingering aftereffects of slavery. Before the war the struggle against slavery and the struggle against racism were always inseparable.

All the political pressures operating on Abraham Lincoln compelled him to separate racial equality from slavery. Everything in Frederick Douglass's experience convinced him that this was impossible.

Douglass's Strategic Separatism

Long before he was a free man, Frederick Douglass was a practicing Christian, a member of the Methodist Church. After his escape he naturally chose to attend communion among the Methodists at his new home in New Bedford, Massachusetts. When he arrived at the church one Sunday morning, the whites in the congregation were clustered up front around the altar while all the black members remained in the back of the church by the door. During the service the minister dispensed the bread and wine to any of the whites inclined to take communion. After he was certain that all the whites had been served the minister looked up to the blacks at the back of the church. "Come up, colored friends, come up!" he announced, "for you know *God is no respecter of persons*." Douglass left and never went back to that church again.[17]

The segregated church was merely Douglass's introduction to

17. *Life & Writings*, vol. 1, p. 103.

the various discriminations he ran up against in the free states. He could not find a job as a skilled caulker on the docks at New Bedford because white workers did not allow blacks to compete with them. Because he was black, he was forbidden to ride omnibuses in Boston. At theaters and lecture halls across the North, as in the churches, he could enter only if he agreed to sit up in the balcony with his fellow African Americans. Museums were closed to him. On steamships he was allowed to travel only in steerage. His children could not attend public schools with white children. In New York, where all white men could vote, Douglass could vote only because he met a property qualification imposed on blacks alone. In some states blacks could not vote at all. In the world Douglass entered after escaping from slavery black men and women were free, but they were not equal. Some of this discrimination could be traced to the things white children were taught about blacks in the North, Douglass said. But the "grand cause" of racial discrimination "is slavery."[18]

Garrisonians understood this perfectly. Slavery, they believed, had transformed "the whole system, the entire network of American society" into "one great falsehood." Northerners lived under a Constitution perverted by slavery. Their churches were corrupted by slavery. Because their institutions were shaped by slavery, northerners who accepted them were implicated in the guilt of slavery. Racial prejudice fitted right into this argument: It was a product of slavery, and in turn it helped sustain slavery. "By our deadly hate and deep prejudice against the coloured man, even when he is free," Douglass argued, northerners discouraged the slaves from striking out for their freedom. Where would they

18. Ibid., p. 104.

go? "Slavery is everywhere," Douglass said. "Slavery goes every-where."[19] The argument stayed with him long after he had left Garrison behind; the problem of slavery and the problem of racism were one and the same. In the North, Douglass once said, he "was continually reminded of his slavery by the invariable bit-terness and malignant prejudice that surrounded him." The strug-gle for equality in the North was therefore inseparable from the struggle for emancipation in the South. They were linked, Douglass said, because racial prejudice reflected what he called "the spirit of slavery."[20]

But collapsing racism and slavery into a single problem made it difficult to develop a distinct strategy for combating discrimi-nation. African Americans in the North were already organizing conventions of their own, in part because the abolitionist move-ment did not adequately address the problem of racial inequality outside the South. Reasoning that racial inequality would only disappear once slavery did, the Garrisonians questioned the moves toward independent black mobilization. At first Douglass echoed these sentiments. At a tumultuous meeting of the National Negro Convention at Buffalo, New York, in 1843, Henry Highland Garnet spoke out fervently for both black sepa-ratism and slave rebellion. Douglass spoke just as forcefully against them. But as Douglass's awareness of the scope of dis-crimination in the North grew so did his commitment to the black convention movement. In 1848 he was elected president of the National Negro Convention. Here was something else to tug Douglass away from Garrison.

19. Ibid., pp. 207, 210, 241.
20. *FDP*, ser. 1, vol. 3, pp. 278, 336.

But the questions that haunted the Garrisonian Douglass did not go away. If racial discrimination was a by-product of slavery, what good was a separate strategy for struggling against inequality in the North? And if such a strategy was feasible, should blacks form their own organizations to develop the strategy? Douglass's ambivalence about separate black organizations mirrored his ambivalence about the very concept of race. Sometimes he seemed to accept the new ethnography that distinguished human beings according to racial types. At other times he went so far as to reject the very concept of "race" as scientifically incoherent as well as incompatible with the Christian doctrine of the human family. If God truly was "no respecter of persons," whites and blacks should be free to work together, form families together, and organize together for the general improvement of humanity. But in practice, Douglass eventually concluded, separate black organization was necessary even though a raceless society remained his ideal.

By the 1850s Douglass was advocating what might be called strategic separatism. He called on all blacks, especially in the United States but also throughout the world, to appreciate what they shared and to act accordingly. "We are one people," he argued, "one in general complexion, one in a common degradation, one in popular estimation." It may be too much to say that he had become a black nationalist. But as his analysis of the problems of slavery and racism developed, Douglass, like most African American activists of his day, did assume that the mutual interests and responsibilities of black men and women united them into something like a nation. Starting from this assumption, Douglass developed a new argument for fusing the struggles against southern slavery and northern racism. He called it the elevation of the race. By this reasoning free blacks were obligated to take up the struggle for elevation not only for themselves but on behalf of their enslaved "brethren" in the South. "As one rises, all must rise," he argued, "and as one falls, all must fall."[21]

This argument cut two ways. On the one hand, the fate of free blacks was tied to the fate of black slaves. Douglass warned that if white Americans implemented an emancipation scheme that required the colonization of the freed slaves outside the United States, free blacks would lose all their claims to a foothold in the United States. In any program of forced colonization, Douglass warned, free blacks would likely be the first to go. On the other hand, the fate of black slaves depended in large measure on the example that free blacks made of themselves in the eyes of the world. Douglass argued that free blacks, in the face of "withering" discrimination, were still obliged to demonstrate their self-reliance, their virtuous character, their capacity for improvement. Doing so would help undermine the insidious premise of the colonizationists, that blacks could not thrive in white America. One indispensable piece of evidence for the competency of African Americans, Douglass believed, was their active participation in the struggle against slavery. For who could respect a freedom that was given by whites rather than earned by blacks? Douglass remained committed to the joint struggle of whites and blacks against slavery, but he also endorsed the separate organization of blacks.

The argument over separate black organization was only one of a number of bruising battles among northern blacks about the best way to proceed in the fight against racial inequality. Was the condition of free blacks in the North deteriorating, so much so that the only option left was for African Americans to emigrate? Or was the

21. *The North Star*, Sept. 29, 1848.

"progress" of antislavery evidence of a steady improvement in the prospects of blacks in America? What was the best way for free blacks to demonstrate their fitness for freedom, given all the avenues of advancement that were closed to them? Should they educate their children in the classical disciplines or train them for useful vocations? There were no easy answers to any of these questions, but Douglass took strong positions on all of them. If the doors to the professions were closed, he said, take up the mechanical arts. If the cities were swamps of antiblack prejudice, move to the countryside and take up farming. But never buckle under the weight of prejudice, Douglass declared. Never concede that blacks had reached the limits of their advancement in America. Above all else, never abandon your brothers and sisters in slavery by emigrating to some other country.

Douglass was so committed to the general elevation of blacks that he could not see the points at which the logic of his argument against slavery contradicted the logic of his argument against racism. When he was attacking slavery, he tended to idealize the North so as to contrast it with the South. On the tenth anniversary of his escape from slavery he wrote a public letter to his former master comparing the idyllic conditions he and his family enjoyed in the North with the terror and misery he had suffered as a slave. By the late 1850s he was making sweeping claims for the opportunities freedom offered blacks in the North. But when he spoke out against northern racism, Douglass moved in the opposite direction. He once said that in the southern states blacks were personal slaves, slaves to individuals, whereas in the northern states "in many respects we are the slaves of the community."[22] When he stressed the contrast

22. Ibid.

between slavery and freedom, he all but denied the existence of racial discrimination of the North. But when he took up the problem of northern racism, Douglass nearly collapsed the distinction between slavery and freedom.

The fusion of antislavery and antiracism left Douglass with no explanation for what happened in the 1850s. He correctly sensed the progress of antislavery among the mass of northern whites, but he looked away from the racism that intensified at the same time. To some extent these were parallel developments that reflected the polarization of the electorate: As one group of northerners grew more hostile to slavery, another reacted with increasingly shrill racism. But at the center of northern politics there resided a broad group of whites whose opposition to slavery was balanced by support for various forms of racial discrimination against free blacks. Whatever the explanation, it was clear that as opposition to slavery increased in the 1850s, the condition of free blacks deteriorated. A huge influx of impoverished immigrants from Ireland and Germany pushed blacks out of jobs they had occupied for decades. The Democratic Party cultivated immigrant loyalty by encouraging the new voters to think of themselves as superior to African Americans. States and cities concocted new ways to discriminate against blacks. In the face of all this, black leaders grew more and more disillusioned.

But not Frederick Douglass. Almost alone among leading African Americans he insisted that things were getting better for free blacks. There were more black doctors and lawyers than ever, he said. In the space of a generation blacks had become far more vocal and self-confident. Above all, he pointed to the rise of antislavery sentiment among whites as evidence that the prospect for blacks was improving. For in Douglass's terms, rising racism and spreading antislavery were simply incompatible.

This position left Douglass more than usually anxious during the 1860 elections. Northern voters were close to electing an antislavery President and an antislavery Congress. The Republicans seemed certain to win. The aggressive slaveocracy was about to be halted. Slavery would soon be in retreat. And if slavery was in retreat, didn't that mean that racism—the spirit of slavery—was going into retreat as well? Not in New York, Douglass's home state. On the very same day that voters went to the polls to choose a new President and a new Congress, New Yorkers were invited to repeal the discriminatory provision of the state constitution that required blacks, and only blacks, to own at least $250 worth of real property before they could vote. Douglass campaigned aggressively for the repeal, as usual linking the fate of free blacks directly to slavery. The property qualification was but one of the "peculiar insults and hardships" heaped on free blacks "on account of popular prejudice skillfully kept alive by all the wealth and power of slavery, acting through all the channels of social influence."[23] The repeal was a Republican measure, but the Republicans practically disowned it once the Democrats, hoping as usual to smear Lincoln with the abomination of racial equality, launched another round of vitriolic race-baiting. Although two out of three Republicans probably supported the amendment, the party's conservatives went against it. When New Yorkers went to the polls, they voted overwhelmingly for Abraham Lincoln and against equal suffrage.

Douglass was stunned. He expected nothing but racist demagoguery from the Democrats. But the Republicans had put the principle of human equality right into their 1860 platform, and here, at the first opportunity to stand up for what they believed,

23. *Douglass' Monthly*, Oct. 1860.

✦ ✦

they abandoned their principles. If Republicans could not be trusted on equal suffrage, how could they be trusted on slavery? After all, the vote on the property qualification was "in its nature a re-affirmation of the slavery-engendered contempt for the rights of black men." Even so, it was the Democrats who defeated the measure, and for them Douglass reserved his harshest conclusion. The defeat of the equal suffrage amendment, he said, "was the vote of drunken Irishmen, and ignorant Dutchmen, controlled by sham Democrats."[24] If the Republicans couldn't stand up to Irish drunks and dumb Germans in New York, Douglass wondered, how would they fare in the forthcoming battle with the far more aggressive slaveocracy?

LINCOLN'S STRATEGIC RACISM

Nobody loved a good joke better than Abraham Lincoln, and nobody was better at using a joke to make a point. In 1856, when the Democrats in Illinois lost the governorship along with control of the state legislature, Lincoln delighted his fellow Republicans with one of his humorous tales. Unaccustomed to losing, the Democrats reminded Lincoln of "the darky who, when a bear had put its head into the hole and shut out the daylight, cried out, 'What was darkening de hole?' 'Ah,' cried the other darky, who was on the tail of the animal, 'if de tail breaks you'll find out.'" Lincoln preferred to tell his darky jokes in Negro dialect. Like many Americans, he was fond of black-faced minstrels, some of the most popular entertainers in his day. Nor were racial epithets beneath Lincoln's dignity, though he generally used them to satirize his opponents. He belittled Stephen

24. Ibid., Dec. 1860.

Douglas's charge that Republicans wanted to "set the niggers and white people to marrying together." And when the Illinois senator disputed Lincoln's claim that the South was trying to spread slavery nationwide, Lincoln acknowledged that there was "no danger that the people of Kentucky will shoulder their muskets and with a young nigger stuck on every bayonet march into Illinois and force them upon us."[25] Lincoln was walking too fine a line. Was he merely mimicking a notorious racist demagogue or indulging in some demagoguery of his own?

It's hard to tell because before 1854 Lincoln said even less about blacks than he did about slavery. Racial equality was simply never an issue for him, one way or the other, so racial demagoguery was never part of his political identity. In his own life Lincoln had almost no social contact with African Americans, not even the small community of free blacks in Springfield, Illinois. As a practicing attorney he occasionally took on black clients, but they were few in number and provide no real evidence of Lincoln's personal views. As a politician he never showed any interest in the particular concerns of African Americans, if only because there were so few of them among his constituents. The truth is, he didn't care about blacks. Without giving the matter any real thought Lincoln quietly accepted the prevailing assumption among whites that they could not and should not live with blacks as equals. As a young member of the Illinois legislature he argued that the qualifications for voting should be higher for black men than for white men. In 1852, in his eulogy for Henry Clay, he praised his hero for recognizing that one of the benefits of colonization was "that it tended to relieve slave-holders from the troublesome presence of the free

25. *CW*, vol. 2, p. 384; vol. 3, pp. 20, 27.

negroes."[26] By that he almost certainly meant that the mere presence of free blacks stirred discontent among slaves, in which case his remark had more to do with slavery than with race. What he thought about race up until 1854 is nearly impossible to discern.

With his return to public life as an antislavery politician, beginning in 1854, Lincoln began to insist that he shared the prejudices of most whites. The first major statement of Lincoln's antislavery politics, the Peoria speech, was also the first full disclosure of his racial biases. His prejudice unfolded alongside his hatred for slavery. He began by expressing his sympathy for the difficult position white southerners found themselves in. They had not brought slavery to the South, they were stuck with it, and there was no easy way of getting rid of it. Lincoln understood and appreciated their dilemma. If he had all the power in the world, he said, he himself would not know what to do about slavery where it already existed. "My first impulse would be to free all the slaves, and send them to Liberia,—to their own native land." Here was colonization, the prolonged fantasy of statesmen from Jefferson to Clay. But Lincoln at least had the presence of mind to point out how foolishly unrealistic such a project actually was. Ship all the blacks to Africa in a day, Lincoln admitted, and they would all be dead in ten days. Moreover, there were not enough ships and not enough monies to colonize America's blacks in many times ten days. "What then?" Lincoln asked. "Free them, and make them politically and socially, our equals? My own feelings will not admit of this; and if mine would, we well know that those of the great mass of white people will not. Whether this feeling accords with justice and sound

26. Ibid., vol. 2, p. 132.

judgment, is not the sole question, if indeed, it is any part of it. A universal feeling, whether well or ill-founded, can not be safely disregarded. We can not, then, make them equals." The only real possibility, Lincoln concluded, was some system of gradual emancipation, presumably tied to a system of gradual colonization.[27]

That was the basic position Lincoln upheld well into his presidency. Freed slaves should leave the country because blacks and whites could not live together as equals. Lincoln was not shy about spelling this out, but his fullest statement came at the opening of his fourth debate with Stephen Douglas, held at Charleston, Illinois, in September 1858. Someone over at the hotel had asked Lincoln if it was true that he favored "a perfect equality between the negroes and white people." He responded at length.

> I will say then that I am not, nor have ever been in favor of bringing about in any way the social and political equality of the white and black races [applause]——that I am not nor ever have been in favor of making voters or jurors of negroes, nor of qualifying them to hold office, nor to intermarry with white people; and I will say in addition to this that there is a physical difference between the white and black races which I believe will for ever forbid the two races living together on terms of social and political equality. And insasmuch as they cannot so live, while they do remain together there must be the position of superior and inferior, and I as much as any other man am in favor of having the superior position assigned to the white race.

27. Ibid., pp. 255–56.

There were, however, limits to how much superiority whites should have. Lincoln then repeated his familiar aphorism: "I do not understand that because I do not want a negro woman for a slave I must necessarily want her for a wife. [Cheers and laughter.] My understanding is that I can just let her alone."[28] For Lincoln, unlike Frederick Douglass, the evils of slavery were independent of the inequality of the races.

Toward the end of the Charleston debate Lincoln returned to the issue to extend his argument. It was not enough that whites should occupy a position superior to blacks, that it should be illegal for blacks and whites to marry, or that blacks should be prohibited from voting and holding public office. Beyond that, Lincoln said, blacks should not even be citizens. "I am not in favor of negro citizenship," he bluntly declared. He disputed the part of the *Dred Scott* decision claiming that no blacks could be citizens, but only because he thought citizenship was an issue to be decided by the states rather than the Supreme Court. If, however, "the State of Illinois had that power I should be opposed to the exercise of it."[29] It came down to this: Because they were human beings, blacks should not be slaves, but because they were so "different," free blacks could not be treated as the equals of whites.

Curiously, Lincoln believed that colonizing blacks "in their native land" was necessary precisely because they were human beings. He complained that no political party was doing anything directly to spur colonization. But at least the Republicans were trying to create the political will for colonization whereas the Democrats were making it harder. "The Republicans incul-

28. Ibid., vol. 3, pp. 145–46.
29. Ibid., p. 179.

cate, with whatever ability they can, that the negro is a man, that his bondage is cruelly wrong." By contrast, "Democrats deny his manhood; deny, or dwarf into insignificance, the wrong of his bondage; so far as possible, crush all sympathy for him, and cultivate and excite hatred and disgust against him."[30] Lincoln was still thinking in the same syllogistic terms as Thomas Jefferson and Henry Clay. To get to colonization, you had to get to emancipation first; to get to emancipation, you had to assume the humanity of blacks. Therefore, to get to colonization, you had to assume that blacks were humans.

It is easy to string such quotations together and show up Lincoln as a run-of-the-mill white supremacist. But Lincoln's defenders have an arsenal of well-rehearsed answers. They point to the ways in which Lincoln always seemed to qualify his remarks. His feelings would not admit of racial equality, he would say, *and even if they did*, the feelings of most whites would not. Unlike Jefferson, Lincoln never said that blacks were innately inferior to whites. Instead he resorted to verbal circumlocutions and suspiciously negative constructions such as "I do not believe that blacks and whites should be treated as equals in all matters." He ridiculed Stephen Douglas's logical inferences without actually committing himself. The best example of this is Lincoln's favorite turn of phrase: "Judge Douglas thinks that because I do not want a black woman as a slave I must necessarily have her as my wife." Lincoln used all these devices, his defenders tell us, because he was on the defensive, responding to the disgraceful race-baiting of his opponents. This last point is certainly true: Racial demagoguery was a spectator sport for the likes of Stephen Douglas, in a way that it never was for Abraham Lincoln.

30. Ibid., vol. 2, p. 409.

But Lincoln did not always throw in qualifiers to mitigate his remarks. He was not always careful to construct his position in ambiguous terms. Moreover, he was responding to no one when he first proclaimed his biases in the Peoria speech. He *opened* the fourth debate at Charleston by restating his commitment to white supremacy, before Stephen Douglas had even spoken. Even if one assumes that everything Lincoln said about race had been prompted by his opponents' demagoguery, it would not mean that he actually objected to the various forms of racial discrimination to which he gave his assent. If there was something calculated in the way Lincoln talked about race—and there almost certainly was—it was not merely because he was on the defensive or because his own views were more ambivalent.

Lincoln's caginess about racial equality was prompted by something else. For him the entire issue was a distraction. He wanted questions about race moved off the table, and he needed a strategy to get rid of them. The strategy he chose was to *agree* with the Democrats that blacks and whites were not equals. Having thereby dispensed with an issue over which there was no disagreement, he hoped to turn to the issue over which there was substantial disagreement, slavery. At Peoria in 1854 and at Charleston four years later, it was Lincoln who introduced the issue of racial inequality *to distinguish it* from the slavery issue. He complained about all the "quibbling" over race because he considered it irrelevant to the debate over the right and wrong of slavery. Racial equality, he said, was one of those "false issues, upon which Judge Douglas has tried to force a controversy." When Douglas claimed that Lincoln favored a "perfect equality" of whites and blacks, he was trying to pick a fight where there was none. "The real issue in this controversy—the one pressing upon every mind," Lincoln insisted, "is the sentiment on the part of one class that looks upon the institution of slavery *as a wrong*, and of another class that *does not* look upon it as a wrong."[31] Lincoln proclaimed his commitment to racial discrimination not because it mattered to him but because it did not. He was using racism strategically, raising the issue because he wanted to eliminate it.

There were other ways of deflecting an issue, and Lincoln knew how to deploy them. He detested the anti-immigrant furor that swept the country in the early 1850s, for example, but he did not fend off that issue by agreeing that Catholics were indeed a threat to the Republic. (He never suggested, the way Frederick Douglass did, that the Democrats were the party of "drunken Irishmen" and "ignorant Dutchmen.") Instead he kept his mouth shut in public, hoping the nativist moment would pass, and it did. Later in the same decade Lincoln worried that the Republican coalition of former Whigs and former Democrats would fracture if anyone in the party raised the divisive old economic issues, in particular the tariff. So he urged his fellow Republicans to hold their tongues on the tariff, responded to private inquiries with evasive answers, and in public said nothing at all. He wanted nativism and the tariff off the table for the same reason he wanted to finesse the issue of racial equality: because the only real issue in the 1850s was slavery. But the strategy Lincoln opted for with racism was different. He did not work behind the scenes to keep Republicans from endorsing racial discrimination, and he himself would endorse it whenever he thought he had to. Lincoln fended off the supporters of racial discrimination by agreeing with them.

Lincoln's strategic deference to racism makes it hard to determine how much of it he believed and, if he did believe it,

31. Ibid., vol. 3, p. 312.

how important it was to him. He probably meant it when he
denied that he favored the social and political equality of
blacks and whites, but it is not clear that he would have had
any objections to racial equality if the majority of whites had
supported it. There is no evidence, for example, that Lincoln
believed in the racial *inferiority* of blacks. He accepted racial
discrimination because that was what most whites wanted, and
in a democratic society such deeply held prejudices cannot be
easily disregarded. If this position earns a place in the catalog
of political villainies, it comes under the heading of spineless-
ness, not racism. It is true that Lincoln supported colonization
because he believed that blacks and whites could never live
together as equals. But to draw that conclusion, all he had to
do was behold the cheers and laughter that greeted Stephen
Douglas every time he spun out one of his racist fantasies. In
Lincoln's mind white prejudice was so deeply ingrained that it
precluded the possibility of racial equality. There were blacks
in America who were saying the same thing. Finally, there is
the point made by Lincoln's defenders and not easily dismissed: Many of Lincoln's most notorious defenses of racial
inequality *were* hedged in with lawyerish qualifiers. Not
always, but often enough to raise doubts.

Even more doubts arise when we compare the public with the
private Lincoln. In numerous speeches Lincoln poked fun at
Stephen Douglas's obsession with racial "amalgamation." He
treated it as if it were a joke, so often that it is hard to avoid the
impression that he simply could not take the issue seriously. He
usually replied to one of Senator Douglas's racial tirades by denying that he was in favor of whites marrying blacks. But in 1859
Lincoln said something different when someone asked him, pri-

vately, what he thought of the Illinois law prohibiting interracial marriages. "The law means nothing," Lincoln replied. "I shall never marry a Negress, but I have no objection to anyone else doing so. If a white man wants to marry a Negro woman, let him do it," Lincoln said, "if the Negro woman can stand it."[32] Lincoln was a skilled politician and a savvy wordsmith. He knew how to leave a misleading impression when it served his purposes. But it was something else to publicly endorse a ban on interracial marriage while privately dismissing the ban as nonsense. It raises a troubling question: Was it better for Lincoln to publicly endorse discriminatory laws that he did not actually believe in? Or would it be preferable that he actually did believe what he said in public?

It was unusual for Lincoln to say things in private that flatly contradicted what he was saying in public. The interesting thing about his private musings on race is that except for a few racially inflected jokes, there are no such musings. Contrast this with Lincoln on slavery. In public he could be quite eloquent about his hatred of slavery, but in private he could be downright passionate about it. His friends commented on how agitated he often became when he talked privately about slavery. But while Lincoln paid public obeisance to the practice of racial discrimination, he never did so privately. In person, Frederick Douglass eventually concluded, Lincoln was a man utterly lacking in racial prejudice.

If it is difficult to square the public with the private Lincoln on the question of race, it is even more difficult to reconcile his endorsement of racial inequality with his vehement antiracism, of which there was a great deal. He once pondered the absurdity of race as a justification for slavery in a way that made the very

32. *RW*, p. 303.

concept of race seem absurd. He made the humanity of blacks central to his antislavery argument. He insisted that the Declaration of Independence, with its promise of fundamental human equality, applied to blacks and whites alike. His frustration with the race issue went deeper than mere strategy. "Let us discard all this quibbling about this man and the other man— this race and that race and the other race being inferior, and therefore they must be placed in an inferior position," Lincoln urged in 1858. But he did not stop there. "Let us discard all these things, and unite as one people throughout this land, until we shall once more stand up declaring that all men are created equal."[33] Lincoln was the first to point out that equality was an ideal more than a description of the way things were. But it was the ideal that embraced blacks and whites alike and toward which he wanted his country to aspire.

Lincoln was disgusted by the race-baiting of the Douglas Democrats. At one point, for example, Senator Douglas joked that "in all contests between the negro and the white man, he was for the white man, but that in all questions between the negro and the crocodile he was for the negro."[34] Lincoln was so shocked by the remark that he quoted it over and over as an example of just how depraved the Democrats had become in their contemptuous denial of the humanity of blacks. Because Lincoln was trying to deflect rather than arouse the racists, he never descended to such demagoguery.

But he did, sometimes, resort to a calculated cynicism. Even if Lincoln did not personally share the widespread belief in black

33. *CW*, vol. 2, pp. 223, 501.
34. Ibid., vol. 3, p. 445.

inferiority, his willingness to cater to it tarnishes the luster of his otherwise humane arguments against slavery. Maybe there was no other way. Maybe strategic racism was necessary to get slavery, and only slavery, onto the table. By massaging the racial prejudices of northern voters Lincoln allowed them—or enough of them—to overcome their resistance to his strong antislavery message. In the end, strategic racism helped put a Republican majority in Congress and a man who hated slavery in the White House. We don't have to like what Lincoln did, but it worked, whether we like it or not.

Frederick Douglass did not like it. Curiously, however, his criticism of Lincoln was grounded in the very same premise from which Stephen Douglas operated. Both men assumed that someone who opposed slavery must also be an opponent of racial inequality. Lincoln's public position was bound to frustrate both of them. Stephen Douglas drew from Lincoln's assertions of fundamental human equality the inference that Lincoln favored a "perfect equality" of whites and blacks. Frederick Douglass leaped from Lincoln's support for racial discrimination to the conclusion that Lincoln was not a serious opponent of slavery. Lincoln and Frederick Douglass were agreed that antislavery sentiment was "the vital element" of the Republican Party. But for Frederick Douglass this entailed support not merely of emancipation but of racial equality as well. Republicans therefore betrayed the moral center of their own party when they stood "opposed to Negro equality, to Negro advancement, to Negro suffrage, to Negro citizenship." Republican support for various forms of racial discrimination in the North amounted to "treason against the slave and the black man."[35] Under the cir-

35. *Douglass' Monthly,* Aug. 1860.

cumstances, Frederick Douglass could offer only a grudging endorsement of the Republicans in 1860. Lincoln he could not support at all.

Abraham Lincoln and Frederick Douglass agreed that there was no such thing as a constitutional right to own slaves. But for Lincoln the Constitution recognized the existence of slavery as a practical necessity, whereas for Douglass the absence of a right to own slaves obliged the federal government to overthrow slavery everywhere. Both agreed that the Fugitive Slave Act was repugnant, but Lincoln "crucified" his feelings because there was a fugitive slave clause in the Constitution whereas Douglass could not sanction obedience to a patently immoral law. Both agreed that the Bible offered no support for slavery. But where Lincoln was not sure whose side God was on, Douglass espoused a messianic Christianity in which a vengeful God commanded the bloody overthrow of the slave system. Both men insisted that blacks were humans, not brutes. For Lincoln this meant that slavery was immoral, but for Douglass it also meant that all forms of racial inequality were immoral.

This is what frustrated Douglass most of all in 1860. Like Lincoln, most northern voters finally accepted abolitionist premises, but they still rejected abolitionist conclusions. To a man like Frederick Douglass, what Lincoln and the Republican Party stood for was incoherent. No one was more eloquent than Lincoln in his insistence that the Negro was a human being and should be treated as such. By Douglass's standard, Lincoln had therefore accepted the basic tenet of abolitionism. Why, then, did Lincoln resist what were for Douglass the obvious conclusions? How, Douglass wondered, could someone who hated the

Fugitive Slave Act insist on its enforcement? How could someone who hated slavery vow to protect it in every southern state? How could someone insist on the humanity of African Americans while upholding the right of white people to discriminate against blacks in a variety of ways? How could he possibly endorse Abraham Lincoln?

As late as 1860 Frederick Douglass was still a reformer at heart. His principles led him in a straight line to the proper policies. If revolutionary violence advanced his principles more clearly than political agitation, so be it. For Douglass there was never, ever an acceptable excuse for racial discrimination. But Lincoln was a politician. He had his principles, but before they could become policies, they had to be filtered through the laws of the land and the will of the people. His temperamental conservatism led him to resist any retreat from law and order as a threat to everyone's freedom. So while Lincoln truly hated slavery, he would attack it only where it was legally and constitutionally open to attack. And he didn't much care about racism. Between the reformer and the politician there remained, at some level, an irreconcilable difference.

4

"THIS THUNDERBOLT WILL KEEP"

Back in February 1860 Lincoln had made a prediction at Cooper Union that turned out to be surprisingly accurate: No matter how often or how sincerely Republicans promised not to interfere with slavery, southerners would not believe them. If they won the upcoming presidential election and the South tried to secede, Lincoln had warned, Republicans would quash the rebellion as quickly and as thoroughly as Virginia had crushed John Brown. He doubted if the South would heed such warnings, and indeed, the South did not. Refusing to accept the undisputed results of a legitimate presidential election, the cotton states began calling for secession as soon as the outcome of the November balloting became clear. South Carolina was the first to go,

announcing its departure from the Union on December 20.
Within six weeks Florida, Georgia, Alabama, Mississippi,
Louisiana, and Texas went the same way. In February 1861 delegates from the seceded states met in Montgomery, Alabama,
drew up a constitution for the Confederate States of America,
declared themselves an independent nation, and demanded that
the United States surrender all the military fortifications within the
South's boundaries. Through it all Lincoln was under intense pressure to endorse a compromise. He had not yet been inaugurated as
President, but everyone knew that there could be no sectional reconciliation without his approval. Some urged a restoration of the
Missouri Compromise line; others argued for the principle of
popular sovereignty. Various constitutional amendments were
proposed to guarantee slavery's security.

These proposals worried Frederick Douglass. Every previous crisis provoked by slavery had ended in a filthy compromise
tilted toward the South. In 1820 the slaveholders got Missouri.
In 1850 they got a despicable Fugitive Slave Law. With that
tawdry record in mind, Douglass dismissed all the bellowing
about secession and predicted in late 1860 that the South would
never leave the Union. "The present alarm and perturbation will
cease," Douglass said in December; "the Southern fire-eaters
will be appeased and will retrace their steps." Even after the
Confederacy was formed, he still suspected that the government
"was ready for anything in the way of a compromise." Months
later, with the war already begun, Douglass worried that "we
live in an atmosphere of compromise." In September 1861—
after the first battle at Bull Run, after Congress had passed the
first law authorizing the confiscation of southern slaves—
Douglass warned yet again that "we are, in the end, to be treated
to another compromise." The following spring he suspected that

"Government compromise with the slaveholders" was "now likely." The warnings slowed down, but they never stopped. As late as 1864 Douglass lent his support to a quixotic attempt to block Lincoln's renomination, claiming that until a "sound Anti-Slavery man" was elected as President, "we shall be in danger of a slaveholding compromise."[1]

Compromise was the most lethal epithet in the reformers' lexicon. It is their refusal to compromise that makes reformers so attractive and so frustrating. They are the voices of principle in a sea of mealymouths, the self-appointed saints in a world filled with sinners. Frederick Douglass spent the Civil War years warning Americans against anything that compromised their highest principles, against any settlement that fell short of the complete abolition of slavery, the enlistment of black troops, and the guarantee of equal rights. It was the tallest order in the history of American reform, and it had to be carried out immediately. Nothing else would silence him. Anything less would be compromise.

Douglass was positioning himself. Just as Lincoln felt most comfortable playing the role of the aggrieved conservative, so Douglass preferred to present himself as the embattled patriot. He constructed this image as carefully as Lincoln, and no less sincerely. He was the American who remained true to his country even as his country snubbed his services and restricted his rights. He was the loyal citizen for whom the principle of human equality shaped his daily life, for it meant the difference between working and not being allowed to work, between voting and not being allowed to vote, between joining the armed services and not being allowed to fight for his country, between waking up a

1. *Douglass' Monthly,* Dec. 1860; Aug. 1861; Sept. 1861; March 1862. *Life & Writings,* vol. 3, pp. 400–401.

slave and going to bed a free man. How could he, how could any man or woman in America, be asked to compromise on such things? As a black man, as an escaped slave, he had far more reason to secede from America than did the South, yet it was the South that now made war upon the nation. And just as the loyalty of African Americans should be rewarded with full equality, so did the South's treason deprive slavery of any further claim to protection from the federal government. Anything less, Douglass shouted, was compromise. So he spent much of the Civil War on the attack, criticizing racist generals and attacking unprincipled politicians.

Democracy doesn't work without compromise. It is their willingness to compromise that makes politicians so indispensable and so untrustworthy. They build the coalitions that bring democracy to life by trimming their principles down to popular size. The best politicians know how to compromise just enough to arouse a constituency without forsaking basic ideals. No politician did this better than Abraham Lincoln. He maintained popular support for a terrible war by insisting that the only point of the war was the restoration of the Union. But he convinced a large number of Americans that in order to restore the Union, they had to abolish slavery. He would compromise wherever he could, wherever he had to, but never on the principle that slavery was wrong and ought to be treated as such.

As far back as 1850 Lincoln admitted to John Stuart, his first law partner, that "[t]he slavery question can't be compromised." After the Kansas-Nebraska Act was passed in 1854, he told William Herndon that the "day of compromise has passed."[2] By December 1860, with the clamor for compromise ringing

2. *RW*, pp. 431, 245.

through the North, Lincoln steeled himself against it. "Have none
of it," he warned Lyman Trumbull about proposals to revive that
despised principle of popular sovereignty. "Stand firm. The tug
has come, & better now, than any time hereafter."[3] He had no
faith that the South would reciprocate, so why offer concessions
that would only drag things out? In January 1861 he told the pas-
tor of Springfield's Second Presbyterian Church that compromise "is not the remedy, not the cure." The southern leaders
"don't want it—won't have it—no good can come of it." The
"system of compromise," Lincoln said, "has no end."[4] He had said
almost the same thing at Cooper Union nearly a year earlier.

"In Your Hands, Not in Mine"

For all his fears of compromise Frederick Douglass always maintained that because the Civil War was caused by slavery, it could
only conclude in the abolition of slavery. This was fatalism more
than faith. The "logic of events," he would say, would inevitably
force emancipation on an unwilling government. Lincoln might
stand in the way. Congress might ring its hands over the legality
of this and that. Generals might scurry to thwart the slaves who
were running to Union lines. But in the end, Douglass believed,
not Lincoln, not Congress, not even the Union army could
escape the inescapable. Oddly enough, Lincoln believed something very similar. He wore his fatalism more comfortably and,
being a politician, more discreetly than Douglass. But Lincoln
did believe there was an irresistible logic to events, that a powerful historical tendency was not easily stopped. The abolition of

3. *CW*, vol. 4, pp. 149–50.
4. *RW*, p. 193.

slavery was just such a tendency. Set in motion by the reckless behavior of the slaveholders themselves, neither Lincoln nor anyone else could fully control the destruction of slavery. Sworn to uphold the Constitution, Lincoln was obliged to try as best he could to guide the course of abolition along channels that were legally sound and politically acceptable. But at a certain point not even the President could harness the swirl of events. In the end, Lincoln said, we cannot escape our history. He hoped the secession movement could be stopped, that the upper South states would not secede, and that the Union could be restored without bloodshed. But what he hoped might happen and what he suspected was going to happen may not have been the same. For no matter how much Lincoln desired a sectional reconciliation he would not compromise on the basic Republican principles that secessionists found so threatening.

Frederick Douglass grew suspicious and impatient with the calls for compromise from both Democrats and conservative Republicans. He felt "disgust and indignation at the spectacle" of northerners cowering before the threats of an arrogant slaveocracy. "All compromises now are but as new wine to old bottles, new cloth to old garments. To attempt them as a means of peace between freedom and slavery," Douglass warned, "is as to attempt to reverse irreversible law."[5] For him, as for Lincoln, the "tug" had come, and it was best to meet it now than to put it off for another day. If there was a single "ray of hope" amid the cowardly calls for peace and reconciliation, Douglass wrote, it was Abraham Lincoln's forthcoming inauguration on March 4. He was not sure if Lincoln was the compromising type, but he was certain that appeasement would violate Lincoln's constitutional

5. *Douglass' Monthly*, Feb. 1861.

obligation to uphold the integrity of the Union. Moreover, the new President could hardly renege on the election year promises he and his party had only recently made. Douglass drew some solace from the "stately silence" that Lincoln had maintained in the months since his election. It suggested to Douglass that Lincoln was impervious to the enormous pressure on him to strike a deal. It was true that Lincoln had made no "immoderate promises to the cause of freedom," that both he and his party had repeatedly vowed not to tamper with slavery where it already existed. But those promises were contingent upon the South's remaining loyal to the Union. Secession changed everything. Republican promises were no longer binding. Slavery had destroyed the Union, and only the destruction of slavery could put the Union back together again. By inauguration day Douglass had regained some of his ingrained optimism.[6]

As Lincoln rose to take his oath of office on March 4, 1861, he had two points to make. The first was familiar and, on the surface, conciliatory. He repeated once again that he had neither the intention nor the inclination to interfere with slavery in the South. He had never wavered from this promise, Lincoln said, and would not do so now. If secession was prompted by the conviction that the Republicans would swiftly begin interfering with slavery, that conviction was groundless. There might be differences with the South over how the northern states should go about returning fugitive slaves, Lincoln admitted, but as long as Republicans accepted their constitutional obligation to return them, such differences could scarcely justify secession. No one had questioned any right expressly guaranteed in the Constitution, and no one intended to. Of course Lincoln had been saying these

6. Ibid., March 1861.

things for years, and he had long since concluded that they would do nothing to satisfy the southerners. Indeed, his hint that enforcement of the Fugitive Slave Law might be returned to the states, many of which would go out of their way to obstruct it, struck southerners as a devilish threat *not* to abide by the Constitution. And as if to goad the secessionists still further, Lincoln reasserted the very thing he believed most rankled them. "One section of our country believes slavery is *right,* and ought to be extended, while the other believes it is *wrong*, and ought to be restricted. That," he said with a touch of irony, "is the only substantial dispute."[7]

Lincoln's second point was not even superficially conciliatory. Secession was not merely unjustified, he declared; it was unconstitutional. No government could make provision for its own destruction; no contract could be abrogated at the whim of only one of its signatories. The Union was perpetual, it had existed even before the Constitution itself, and neither secession conventions nor inflammatory declarations could make things otherwise. As long as he was President and so long as he had the support of the northern people, Lincoln declared, he would assume that the southern states were still in the Union and were still subject to the authority of the government of the United States.

With those two points—that he had no intention of interfering with slavery but every intention of enforcing the law—Lincoln positioned himself where he most preferred to be, on the strategic defensive. He promised no aggression on his own part; he would only respond to the aggression of the South. He would do whatever it took to defend the Union, as he was constitutionally sworn to do. If the South chose to attack, the decision for

7. *CW*, vol. 4, pp. 268–69.

war was entirely its own. "In *your* hands, my dissatisfied fellow countrymen, and not in *mine*, is the momentous issue of civil war. The government will not assail *you*. You can have no conflict, without being yourselves the aggressors. *You* have no oath registered in Heaven to destroy the government, while *I* shall have the most solemn one to 'preserve, protect and defend' it."[8]

Lincoln's words were so blunt, so unapologetic that his incoming secretary of state, William Seward, urged him to end on a more conciliatory note. Ironically, it is that final note that has come down through history as among Lincoln's most eloquent perorations. "We are not enemies, but friends. We must not be enemies," Lincoln said. "Though passion may have strained, it must not break our bonds of affection. The mystic chords of memory, stretching from every battle-field, and patriot grave, to every living heart and hearthstone, all over this broad land, will yet swell the chorus of the Union, when again touched, as surely they will be, by the better angels of our nature."[9] But the coda could not undo the content. Lincoln's speech was unstinting in its determination to suppress the slaveholders' "insurrection." It seemed to be aimed less at persuading the South to abandon secession than at persuading the North to resist it. When Lincoln reiterated that he would not touch slavery in the southern states, he was speaking, at least in part, to a northern electorate that had no taste for an abolition war. By positioning the North as the defender of the Union rather than as the invader of the South, Lincoln could not have believed he would persuade the secessionists, but he surely hoped to stiffen the North's determination to uphold the Union at whatever cost.

8. Ibid., p. 271.
9. Ibid.

Douglass was infuriated by the inaugural address, the peroration in particular. Sectional reconciliation was the last thing he hoped for. He remained convinced that the Constitution fully empowered the government to stamp out slavery wherever it existed. But Douglass seemed most annoyed by something else in the speech. Lincoln not only disclaimed any power to interfere with slavery, but also said he had no "inclination" to do so. Douglass took Lincoln's disinclination as a moral impulse rather than a legal disclaimer. He thought Lincoln was asserting his indifference to slavery when in fact the President was simply stating that he had no inclination to overstep his constitutional authority. After all, moral indifference to slavery was precisely what Lincoln had taken the northern Democrats to task for during the 1850s. Douglass had hoped that secession would finally persuade Lincoln and the North that a Union destroyed by slavery could only be restored by slavery's destruction. But on inauguration day Lincoln said no such thing. His election had not been enough to set abolition in motion. Nor, it seemed, was secession.

Lincoln the politician was positioning himself as the conservative defender of the nation's founding principles. Douglass the reformer was reminding everyone that the greatest of all the founding principles was universal freedom. Lincoln put the "momentous" question of war and peace in the South's hands. Douglass threw the question of freedom and slavery back into Lincoln's hands. What would it take, he asked, to force the North to face the issue of emancipation? The answer was simple: war.

It began in the early morning hours of April 12, 1861, when southern rebels opened fire on Fort Sumter in Charleston Harbor. Lincoln immediately began issuing orders that, lacking any congressional sanction, were based entirely on the President's authority as the commander in chief. Notwithstanding his reverence for legality and his temperamental conservatism, Lincoln had an expansive conception of his constitutional war powers. With Congress out of session Lincoln himself called up a vast army and authorized enormous military expenditures. The upper South responded quickly. Within six weeks Virginia, Tennessee, Arkansas, and North Carolina joined the Confederacy. The last embers of sectional reconciliation were extinguished.

"The Harpoon Has Struck the Whale to the Heart"

The government's assault on slavery commenced almost immediately. Little more than a month after Fort Sumter, Lincoln's secretary of war, Simon Cameron, signed off on a policy declaring runaway slaves contraband of war. On July 4 Lincoln sent Congress a recommendation, drafted by his treasury secretary, that it pass a confiscation act giving congressional sanction to the contraband policy. Congress readily complied. The Senate Judiciary Committee reported a bill on July 15, and after several amendments and revisions both houses of Congress passed the first Confiscation Act in early August 1861. Lincoln signed it four days later. While the contraband and confiscation policies were taking shape, Lincoln ordered the federal government to begin the aggressive suppression of the illegal Atlantic slave trade. By the end of the year federal prosecutors had seized half a dozen ships and brought several smugglers to trial. In the fall Lincoln began pressuring the border states to enact emancipation statutes on their own. By December, only eight months after the war had begun, Lincoln told the historian George Bancroft that "slavery has received a mortal wound . . . the

harpoon has struck the whale to the heart."[10] As Douglass
predicted, war changed everything, even before the first significant battle was fought.

On Thursday night, May 2 3, three black field hands showed up
at the Union encampment at Fortress Monroe in northern
Virginia. The slaves were owned by Colonel Charles Mallory, the
commander in charge of Confederate forces in the area. Union
commanders and soldiers had only to look across to enemy lines
and see slaves at work building Confederate fortifications. The
three slaves were about to be shipped out of the area, away from
their wives and children, "for the purpose of aiding secession
forces" farther South. Union General Benjamin Butler had only
just arrived, but already he saw that he could use the labor of such
"able bodied" men himself. On Saturday he wrote to his commanders in Washington, D.C., explaining the problem. If he
returned the slaves, the Confederates would immediately put
them back to work building their batteries. The enemy could
never have built its fortifications so quickly had it not been using
slave labor, Butler noted. "As a military question it would seem to
be a measure of necessity to deprive their masters of their services," Butler wrote to the secretary of war three days later.

"How can this be done?" he asked. It was a lawyer's question;
Butler wanted to know how it could be done *legally*. He had
already put the slaves to work on Union fortifications and sent
Colonel Mallory a receipt for his slave property. The slaves,
Butler suggested, should be designated "contraband of war" and,
like all such property, be returned to its owner once peace was
restored. Virginia commanders were already complaining. One
Major Cary showed up at Butler's headquarters demanding to

10. *RW*, p. 2 1.

know if the Union general intended to abide by his "constitutional obligations to deliver up fugitives under the fugitive slave act." Butler must have enjoyed telling him that the Fugitive Slave Act did not apply to foreign countries, "which Virginia claimed to be." Secession, it seems, had stripped the South of its constitutional right to claim fugitive slaves. This, Butler told Major Cary, was "one of the infelicities" of the position Virginia had put itself in.[11]

The secretary of war approved of Butler's decision. Two months later Congress backed the decision up with a Confiscation Act, the first of two, that effectively nullified all those Republican promises to return fugitive slaves to their rightful owners. The theory behind the new law was that runaway slaves could be confiscated or held as contraband only if they had been used in the Confederate war effort. In practice there was no way to know how most fugitive slaves had been used or would be used if they were sent back to their masters. This made it difficult to enforce the Fugitive Slave Law in any consistent way. Slaveholders from the border states were soon complaining that military commanders were holding their runaways as contraband. The "incidents of war," as Lincoln liked to call them, were rapidly turning the Fugitive Slave Act into a dead letter. So much for Republican pledges never to interfere with slavery in the southern states.

In late July Union forces suffered a humiliating defeat in the first major engagement of the war, beside a stream called Bull

---

11. U. S. Department of War, *The War of the Rebellion: A Compilation of the Official Records of the Union and Confederate Armies* (Washington, D.C., 1880–1901), ser. 1, vol. 2, pp. 649–50; Ira Berlin et al., eds., *Freedom: A Documentary History of Emancipation, 1861–1867* (Cambridge, Mass., 1985), ser. I, vol. 1, p. 71.

Run, at Manassas Junction, not far from Washington, D.C. Up to then Republican congressmen were reluctant to toss aside their constitutional misgivings about confiscating slaves. Only a week before Bull Run the Senate Judiciary Committee had sent a confiscation bill to the floor, where it was destined for some rough treatment. But military defeat transformed the bill's fate. Republicans concluded that suppressing the southern rebellion would be a more difficult undertaking than most northerners had thought. Within a few weeks of the disaster at Manassas Congress passed the first Confiscation Act. Democrats denounced the law as revolutionary and, more seriously, as unconstitutional and illegal. It was not six months since Lincoln's inauguration, and already Republicans were using the war to justify unprecedented attacks on southern slavery.

But the attacks were limited, both legally and practically. There was, to begin with, the problem of the army. The administration could accept the principle of treating runaways as contraband, and Congress could legalize the confiscation of slaves, but it was up to the Union army to physically accept fugitives, and in 1861 the Union officer corps was divided on the matter. General George McClellan, commander of the Union armies, ordered his officers to turn away the fugitives. General Henry W. Halleck went out of his way to enforce his own similar order. Both generals objected to anything that smacked of antislavery radicalism. Indeed, so strong were the proslavery sentiments of some Union officers that Lincoln believed a general mutiny would spread through the army if he openly embraced a policy of emancipation. Still, General Benjamin Butler accepted runaways gladly, and there were others. To outsiders like Frederick Douglass it looked as if the Union had no consistent policy on fugitive slaves, and in a sense he was right. A struggle between the military and civilian authorities was compounded by a struggle between proslavery and antislavery forces within the army. Until these were resolved, the government's policy appeared to be more inconsistent than it actually was. Beginning in late 1861, however, Lincoln and Congress stepped in to clarify matters in favor of runaway slaves. In December Lincoln ordered McClellan to stop Union troops from turning away slaves who had escaped to Washington, D.C., and to arrest any masters who tried to recapture fugitives in the nation's capital. A few months later Congress forbade the Union army from returning fugitives anywhere. By early 1862 the proslavery generals had lost their battle.

Even so, there were legal problems with both the contraband and confiscation policies. General Butler had invoked the law of nations to justify holding slaves as contraband; the authors of the Confiscation Act relied on the law of the seas. But neither international law nor admiralty law was relevant to the suppression of a domestic rebellion. Lincoln had qualms about the dubious legality of both policies, but he had an additional concern about the Confiscation Act. He was not sure *Congress* had the constitutional authority to enact it. The contraband policy had emerged from within the military and been approved by the secretary of war; its legitimacy therefore derived from the war powers of the President. Lincoln believed that the Constitution gave the President, as commander in chief in a time of war, powers he did not have in peacetime. But no such authority resided in the legislative branch, Lincoln thought. Indeed, he and the Republicans had been claiming for years that under the Constitution, Congress had no right to interfere with slavery in the states. Congress could confiscate slaves, but it could not emancipate them.

The reason General Butler sent Colonel Mallory a receipt for his three fugitives was that slaves confiscated by the Union were still, strictly speaking, slaves. Contraband property was supposed to be held only for the duration of the war, after which it would be returned to its rightful owner. Congress remained bound by the constitutional restriction against bills of attainder, which prohibited the permanent confiscation of property without due process. Even Republicans sympathetic to emancipation— Joshua Giddings and Orville Hickman Browning, for example— understood that there was nothing in the Constitution allowing Congress to *free* the confiscated slaves.[12] The question of congressional authority was not quickly resolved. As late as 1864, long after he had issued the Emancipation Proclamation, Lincoln refused to sign the Wade-Davis bill because it contained a clause emancipating the slaves in the rebel states. "That is the point on which I doubt the authority of Congress to act," Lincoln told Senator Zachariah Chandler of Michigan. Moreover, the President added, "I do not see how any of us now can deny and contradict all we have always said, the Congress has no constitutional power over slavery in the states."[13] He thought it was dangerous, both legally and politically, for Congress to claim a power that he and his fellow Republicans had long denied.

But the war powers of the executive were, in Lincoln's mind, sufficient to free the slaves. "I conceive that I may in an emergency do things on military grounds which cannot be done constitutionally by Congress." Once someone was freed it would be virtually

12. Louis S. Gerteis, *From Contraband to Freedman: Federal Policy toward Southern Blacks, 1861–1865* (Westport, Conn., 1973); Herman Belz, *A New Birth of Freedom: The Republican Party and Freedmen's Rights, 1861–1866* (Westport, Conn., 1976); Allen C. Guelzo, *Lincoln's Emancipation Proclamation: The End of Slavery in America* (New York, 2004).

13. *RW*, p. 228.

impossible to reenslave him, Lincoln thought, even if a presidential emancipation technically expired with the war. It is unclear how early he adopted this position. It was Congressman John Quincy Adams who, a generation earlier, had first suggested that in theory the war powers of the commander in chief could emancipate slaves. This gave the argument a respectable Whig pedigree that must have impressed Lincoln. Also, from the earliest days of the war Senator Charles Sumner, who fancied himself Adams's successor, pressed Lincoln to use his war powers in just that way. The first indication that Lincoln accepted this view of his war powers may have come in a typically backhanded way that obscured the radicalism of his move.[14]

"TO LOSE KENTUCKY IS TO LOSE THE WHOLE GAME"

In September 1861 Lincoln overruled General John C. Frémont's proclamation granting freedom to slaves in Missouri. Frémont was already well known for his expeditions in the West when Lincoln, partly in deference to Frémont's politically influential relatives, installed him as the military commander of the entire western theater. The President stationed him in St. Louis with orders to keep a lid on the volatile situation in Missouri, one of the four border states that Lincoln was desperately trying to keep in the Union. This was an assignment that required both military and political skills, neither of which Frémont possessed in any measurable degree. His heavy-handed policies and arro-

---

14. Ibid. On John Quincy Adams's influence on abolitionists, see Gilbert Hobbs Barnes, *The Anti-Slavery Impulse, 1830–1844* (New York, 1933), pp. 121–29; John Stauffer, *The Black Hearts of Men: Radical Abolitionists and the Transformation of Race* (Cambridge, Mass., 2001), pp. 27–34.

gant demeanor alienated Missouri's Unionists, while the secessionists went on a rampage throughout much of the state.
Unable to defeat the disloyal element by rallying those loyal to
the Union, Frémont resorted to high-handed declarations of
martial law. He established military tribunals and empowered
them to execute those deemed traitors, and he had very broad
notions of who counted as a traitor. On August 30 he went even
further by announcing not only that the property of all traitors
would be confiscated but that their slaves would be freed.

Frémont had created a legal and political nightmare. The
Constitution allows the government to suspend habeas corpus in
a national emergency, but this was a dangerous power to be
exercised by Congress and the President, not by rogue generals.
Nor was there anything in either the contraband policy or the
Confiscation Act that had authorized outright emancipation. In
other words, Frémont's proclamation was illegal. Lincoln acted
quickly to undo the damage. He warned the general not to execute anyone without the President's explicit approval and told
him to rewrite his proclamation to conform to the Confiscation
Act: It could apply only to those engaged in open rebellion, and
their slaves could be confiscated but not emancipated.
Astonishingly, Frémont announced that he would disregard
Lincoln's suggestions unless the President explicitly ordered
him to act. "I very cheerfully do," Lincoln wrote him back. At
issue was not only the legality of emancipation but the principle
of civil *versus* military authority. As Lincoln pointed out, Frémont
was behaving like a military dictator, as though he could do "*anything* he pleases." Yet his proclamation was "*purely political,*"
Lincoln snapped; it had no military justification at all.[15] Thus by

September 1861 Lincoln seemed to accept the distinction between a "purely political" and therefore illegitimate emancipation and a military justification, which implicitly carried more weight.

At least as worrisome as its illegality was the political fallout from Frémont's reckless behavior. If the proclamation was allowed to stand, there was a good chance that the four border slave states that had remained in the Union would flip sides and join the Confederacy. Missouri was one of them, but the biggest concern was Kentucky. As one Unionist warned in a telegram to the White House, "[t]here is not a day to lose in disavowing emancipation or Kentucky is gone over the mill dam." Lincoln knew this. To lose Kentucky would be a disaster—probably a fatal disaster—for the Union cause. "Kentucky gone," Lincoln said, "we cannot hold Missouri, nor, as I think, Maryland." If that happened, we "would as well consent to separation at once, including the surrender of this capitol."[16] With a stroke of his irresponsible pen Frémont had put the entire Union effort— and with it the fate of emancipation—at serious risk.

Lincoln had every reason to fear the loss of the border states. With Maryland out of the Union the nation's capital would have been completely encircled by Confederate states. Baltimore's crucial industrial facilities, in particular its indispensable rail yards, would have been put to work in the service of the Confederacy rather than the Union. The loss of Missouri would have opened a third front in the trans-Mississippi West; St. Louis would have given the Confederacy the armor plate works that supplied the Union navy with the "Pook's turtles" that allowed the North to dominate the inland waterways. With Kentucky

16. Guelzo, *Lincoln's Emancipation Proclamation*, p. 53; *CW*, vol. 4, p. 532.

gone the military border would have shifted hundreds of miles to the north all the way to the Ohio River, making the job of conquering the western Confederacy immeasurably harder, probably impossible. The two hundred thousand border state whites who eventually joined the Union army might well have fought instead for the Confederacy. So great a transfer of manpower would have crippled the Union's military strategy of laying siege to successive Confederate strongholds, Fort Donelson, Vicksburg, Atlanta, and Petersburg. Those sieges were among the most important Union victories of the Civil War, but they required the Union to maintain far more troops in the field than did the Confederates. So did the flanking maneuvers demanded by the invention of rifles. Faced with the loss of hundreds of thousands of soldiers, the Union could not have pursued its most consistently successful strategies for winning the war. For all these reasons, it is difficult to dispute the judgment of the scholar who has explored this issue more thoroughly than anyone else: Lincoln was right to be concerned about the border states. Without them the North would probably have lost the Civil War, and the slaves would have lost their only real chance for freedom.[17]

Far from inhibiting emancipation, Lincoln actually paved the way for it by carefully securing the loyalty of the border states. By late 1861, as it became clear that Missouri, Kentucky, and Maryland would remain loyal, Lincoln began pressuring them to emancipate their slaves on their own. Abolition by state legislatures was still the only legally certain route to emancipation. Everyone knew that as soon as the first slaveholder sued

17. William W. Freehling, *The South vs. the South: How Anti-Confederate Southerners Shaped the Course of the Civil War* (New York, 2001).

his way to the Supreme Court, the chief justice—Roger Taney, author of the *Dred Scott* decision—would instantly declare that contraband and confiscated slaves could not be freed by any power of the federal government, congressional or executive. The same fate would have awaited Frémont's attempt to free slaves by martial law had Lincoln himself not blocked it first. The most legally secure way to free the slaves, Lincoln understood, was for state legislatures to do it, just as the northern states had done after the Revolution. With most of the slave states out of the Union, the only place to try legislative emancipation was in the four border states. Delaware, with the fewest slaves, seemed the likeliest place to start. In November 1861 Lincoln drafted two versions of a voluntary emancipation statute and circulated it privately to see how much support it had within the Delaware legislature. Congress had no right to interfere with slavery in any state, but there was nothing to stop it from enticing the states with a colonization plan along with appropriations to compensate them for the slaves they chose to free on their own.

In December Lincoln urged Congress to set up such a scheme. The federal government would purchase slaves from any state that sold them voluntarily, whereupon the government, as rightful owner, would free the slaves it had purchased. This, Lincoln indicated, could leave the government with large numbers of dependent freed people on its hands. To accommodate them, Lincoln suggested that Congress appropriate funds for the purchase of colonies where freed people might go if they so chose. With these proposals Lincoln revealed his ideal version of emancipation: It would be gradual; it would be enacted voluntarily by the vote of the state legislatures; the owners of freed slaves would be compensated. Congress would meanwhile appropriate funds to encourage the voluntary colonization of the freed people "so far as individuals may desire." It was classic Lincoln, employing conservative means to radical ends.[18]

In the course of spelling out his proposal to Congress in December Lincoln let slip, as if in passing, one of the most important announcements of the war: that the slaves confiscated by the Union were "thus liberated." Liberated *how*? And by *whom*? The Confiscation Act made no provision for the liberation of slaves confiscated from rebel masters. When Lincoln ordered Frémont to revise his proclamation to conform to the Confiscation Act, he meant that Frémont could confiscate but not emancipate slaves. Hence the significance of Lincoln's surreptitious announcement in his first annual message to Congress. By early December 1861 Lincoln had already decided that confiscated slaves were effectively liberated, presumably by the war powers of the commander in chief but also by the practical, political, and moral impossibility of returning them to their rebel masters. This was no slip of Lincoln's tongue. He had deliberately bundled the confiscated slaves with those transferred by the states and subsequently freed by the federal government, suggesting to Congress that steps be taken to help colonize "both classes" of recently emancipated blacks. The following month Lincoln told Senator James H. Lane of Kansas that the government had no right to return confiscated slaves to their masters and that even if it did have such a right, "the people would not permit us to exercise it." He was still more emphatic on July 1. "No Negroes necessarily taken and escaping during the war are ever to be returned to slavery," Lincoln told Orville

18. *CW,* vol. 5, pp. 29–30, 48.

Browning. By what authority the slaves were freed Lincoln did not say, though he still insisted the Congress had "no power" over slavery in the states.[19]

There is not much doubt about Lincoln's trajectory at the end of 1861. He had begun by then to pressure the border states, where his war powers could not reach, to emancipate the slaves on their own. He steadily intensified that pressure during the first half of 1862. As for the seceded states, he had approved the contraband policy, signed the Confiscation Act, and clarified the legal status of slaves thus taken by declaring them "liberated." Nine months in office were enough to justify the greatest fear the secessionists had about Lincoln: His promises to the South meant nothing. He would not enforce the Fugitive Slave Law. He would interfere with slavery in the southern states. He would even emancipate slaves seized from southern masters. Eventually Lincoln would use the tremendous economic and political power of the federal government to promote the abolition of slavery everywhere, guided only by his avowed hatred of slavery. In fact it was more complicated than that.

If anything guided Lincoln, it was the demands of war. But his response to those demands reflected his hatred of slavery. The war precipitated the contraband policy, got the Confiscation Act through Congress, and was making the Fugitive Slave Law a dead letter. Emancipating slaves from the seceded states, for so long disavowed, was becoming a "military necessity." By the end of 1861 slavery had been dealt a mortal wound, just as Lincoln said, just as he had predicted. But Lincoln obscured every one of his moves by smothering them with legal qualms, revealing

19. Ibid., p. 48; *RW*, pp. 123, 64.

them in backhanded ways, and slipping them virtually unnoticed into his public messages. He was doing what he could to make it look as if the wound to slavery were self-inflicted.

Anyone hunting for clues to Lincoln's thinking would have found scattered through his first annual message to Congress in December still more hints about his personal inclinations on matters of race and slavery. He suggested opening diplomatic relations with Haiti and Liberia, and he actively pressed for the suppression of the illegal Atlantic slave trade. Though these were matters peripheral to emancipation, they tell us something about the President's state of mind in late 1861.

In the 1790s, after the freed people of Haiti had declared their independence from France, the administration of President John Adams had initiated the process of establishing diplomatic relations with the new Caribbean nation. But Thomas Jefferson, immediately upon taking office as President in 1801, gratuitously insulted the Haitian representatives who had already arrived in Washington. Jefferson quickly scuttled all efforts to grant their country diplomatic recognition and instead began scheming with Napoleon to reestablish slavery and French dominion on the island. Every succeeding administration had followed Jefferson's lead in denying formal diplomatic recognition to Haiti. The same thing happened to Liberia, the African nation established by expatriate American blacks. In February 1862 Frederick Douglass cited the refusal to recognize Haiti and Liberia as evidence that the U.S. government was unduly influenced by the slaveholders. But two months before Douglass spoke, Lincoln had given public notice that the sixty-year diplomatic snub was about to end. Early in his first annual message to Congress, in December 1861, the President said, in a disarmingly perplexed tone, that he was "unable to discern" any good reason for continuing the long-standing American policy of denying diplomatic recognition to the two black republics.[20] He therefore urged Congress to appropriate the funds necessary to maintain a chargé d'affaires in each nation. The following April the Senate obligingly passed an authorization bill, the House concurred two weeks later, and by mid-July Lincoln had appointed the first U.S. diplomatic representative to Haiti. He had made it clear that he would have no objections if Haiti returned the favor by sending a black diplomat to Washington, and in February 1863 Ernest Roumain arrived in the nation's capital and initiated a period of friendly relations between Haiti and the United States.

Closer to Lincoln's heart was the suppression of the illegal Atlantic slave trade. Ever since the importation of slaves had been banned in 1808 the U.S. government had, in Frederick Douglass's words, "winked at the accursed slave trade."[21] Shortly after Lincoln took office, the government stopped winking. Within weeks of his inauguration the new President ordered his secretary of the interior, Caleb Smith, to assume a centralized responsibility for the prosecution of those who smuggled African slaves into the country. Smith understood how deeply Lincoln detested slave traders, and he quickly assembled a crackerjack team of lawyers and investigators. In August Smith's men organized a seminar in New York to train federal marshals and prosecutors throughout the Northeast in the legal mechanisms for the suppression of the slave trade. Before the year was out, they had succeeded in capturing five ships, freed hundreds of slaves, sent them to their freedom in

20. *CW*, vol. 5, p. 39.
21. *Douglass' Monthly*, Feb. 1862.

Liberia, and begun prosecuting a number of smugglers. One of them, Nathaniel P. Gordon of Portland, Maine, was sentenced to death after his ship, the *Erie*, had been captured with 893 slaves off the coast of Africa. The death penalty had never been used against a slave trader, and Gordon's case drew howls of sympathy from many quarters. But Lincoln resisted the pressure and refused to commute the death sentence. Gordon was hanged on February 21, 1862.[22]

A few weeks after Gordon's execution, undeterred by the criticism, Lincoln ordered his secretary of state, William Seward, to open negotiations with the British for a treaty to jointly suppress the Atlantic slave trade. Frederick Douglass had recently complained that for twenty-five years the United States had refused "to unite in a treaty by which slave-traders could not shelter their hell-black traffic under their respective flags."[23] But Lincoln was anxious for such a treaty. The British were delighted, negotiations proceeded swiftly, and on April 10 the President sent a slave trade treaty to Congress. By a unanimous voice vote the Senate ratified the treaty two weeks later. Within minutes of the vote an ecstatic Senator Charles Sumner carried the ratification personally to Seward's office, and the secretary, nearly as thrilled, sent it quickly on to Lincoln. This time the public reaction was overwhelmingly favorable, so much so that two months later Congress had no hesitation in passing enforcement legislation recommended by Lincoln. With these new prosecutorial powers at its disposal the administration redoubled its efforts, and within eighteen months Lincoln proudly

22. Ron Soodalter, *Hanging Captain Gordon: The Life and Trial of an American Slave Trader* (New York, 2006).

23. *Douglass' Monthly*, Jan. 1862.

reported to Congress that "so far as American ports and American citizens are concerned, that inhuman and odious traffic has been brought to an end."[24]

"No Good Shall Come to the Negro from This War"

From the day the new President was inaugurated Frederick Douglass worried that Lincoln would cave in to proslavery pressure, which was far more powerful than abolitionism, even in the North, by announcing a new sectional compromise. To some degree he was misled by the care Lincoln took to position himself as a conservative, and to some degree Douglass was performing his own role as the uncompromising reformer. Overall, Douglass's criticism of Lincoln had more to do with the way they positioned themselves than with the positions they took. Whatever his reasons, Douglass went out of his way to notice Lincoln's penchant for conservative means but studiously disregarded nearly all his radical moves. Even at the end of 1861, after the mortal wound to slavery had already been struck, there was still a long way to go. To an instinctive reformer like Douglass this was no time to ease up on the criticism.

In truth most of Lincoln's moves toward emancipation were made quietly, sometimes invisibly. Lincoln had silently accepted the contraband policy. He had grumbled about the Confiscation Act before signing it. His draft emancipation statutes for Delaware circulated behind the scenes; Douglass could not have known about them. So unobtrusively had Lincoln slipped his

24. *CW*, vol. 7, p. 36.

decision to free the confiscated slaves into his first annual message to Congress that Douglass missed it along with everybody else. By contrast Douglass could not help noticing Lincoln's very public repudiation of Frémont and his equally public concern for the loyalty of the border states. By the end of the 1861 Douglass had begun to argue that Lincoln, far from being an antislavery President, was actually determined to thwart the destruction of slavery. Such, at least, was the stance he took. And it was probably just as sincere as Lincoln's continued disavowal of any intention to interfere with slavery in the states.

After the disappointment of the inaugural address Fort Sumter briefly raised Douglass's spirits. He threw himself into the propaganda war, declaring his desire to see the South beaten and humiliated before the wrath of an inflamed North. He had a clear, simple theme: The war was nothing more than the extension of slavery's violence into the free states. The depravity and arrogance that slavery bred into the southern ruling class had now spilled beyond the South and was threatening, actually threatening, to drag the free people of the North down into slavery along with southern blacks. Ironically, Douglass's militant rhetoric placed him more squarely in the mainstream than ever before. In the spring of 1861 bloodthirsty words were hemorrhaging from all quarters, above and below the Mason-Dixon line. But Douglass had an agenda that most northerners did not. His aim was the destruction of slavery, not the mere restoration of the Union. Slavery was the source of the bloodshed, he argued, and bloodshed would be necessary to bring it down. When whites warned that emancipation would unleash the "wholesale murder" of blacks, for example, Douglass didn't flinch at the prospect. Such a slaughter would be a terrible but necessary precursor to the freedom of the slave.

Douglass had a favorite metaphor. Slavery, he said several times in 1861, was "the stomach of this rebellion." Slave labor fed the rebel armies, clothed the rebel troops, funded the rebel war. "Strike here," Douglass insisted, "cut off the connection between the fighting master and the working slave, and you at once put an end to this rebellion."[25] This was abolition as a military necessity, and eventually northerners accepted it. But not right away. In the spring of 1861 most people agreed that slavery had caused the war, but few could see how abolishing slavery would end it. Most Yankees reasoned that a cause and a cure were two different things. You might as well tell a smoker that his lung cancer would go away if he just stopped using cigarettes. Once again Douglass was baffled that northerners accepted his premises but not his conclusions.

By June 1861 Douglass's impatience was already showing. Even many radical Republicans agreed that the constitutional ban on bills of attainder restricted Congress's power to emancipate slaves. But Douglass airily dismissed the "supposed constitutional objections" to abolition. There were those who worried "that the Constitution does not allow the exercise of such power," Douglass said. "As if this were a time to talk of constitutional power!" It was perfectly all right to suppress the South for trampling the Constitution, but if the Constitution stood in the way of abolition, then the Constitution be damned. Douglass felt the same way about public opinion; he invoked or rejected it as it suited his immediate purposes. At first he warned that public opinion would turn violently against Lincoln and the Republicans if they abandoned their principles for the sake of yet another sectional compromise. But when Republicans warned of a political backlash if they moved too swiftly against slavery, Douglass denounced them for their pusillanimous subservience to public opinion. Politicians had an obligation to lead, he said, and in the case of slavery they had nothing to worry about. "The people will follow in any just and necessary path," Douglass insisted, "and do so joyfully."[26] But the politicians knew better.

By the summer of 1862 Lincoln would be proclaiming his constitutional power to emancipate slaves and struggling to bring public opinion along with him. But Douglass was there a year earlier, and he was impatient with every move that fell short of complete abolition. He gave a passing nod to General Butler's policy of holding fugitive slaves as contraband of war. It was only "a temporary arrangement," Douglass grumbled, "carefully left open to the most sudden reversal." It freed no one. What about the first Confiscation Act? A "tame and worthless statute," in Douglass's view.[27] He did not notice Lincoln's year-end announcement that slaves seized under the Confiscation Act were "thus liberated." Nor was he impressed by Lincoln's proposal that Congress compensate the states if they abolished slavery on their own. By the ordinary standards of American politics, Lincoln's moves had been radical and astonishing, but to Douglass they were slow at best and suspect at worst.

As for Lincoln's delicate maneuvering to keep the border states in the Union, Douglass thought it was a criminal waste of time. Slaveholders were slaveholders, Douglass insisted; whether in Kentucky or in Mississippi, they were not to be reasoned with. There was some truth in this; Lincoln did overestimate the anti-slavery sentiments of border state Unionists. Even so, this was

26. Ibid., July, Aug., and Sept., 1861.
27. Ibid., Aug. and Oct., 1861.

Douglass at his most myopic. He reasoned that because Kentuckians defended slavery, they had no moral claim to the solicitude of the government. He thereby confused the moral worth of the border states' position with the strategic soundness of Lincoln's. The President himself was reasoning the other way around: Because the government could not survive the loss of the border states, he had no choice but to step warily around Kentucky's concern for slavery. There is no doubt that Lincoln nourished a naive faith in the willingness of the border states to accept what was coming and, with a little financial nudge from Congress, abolish slavery on their own. In fact Lincoln had too much faith in southern Unionists in general. But Douglass had a naive streak of his own. He professed to believe that slavery would come tumbling down in the border states if Lincoln merely proclaimed its destruction, that the end of slavery in Kentucky would topple dominoes across the rest of the South, leading to the complete collapse of the Confederacy. In a way Lincoln and Douglass shared flip sides of the same delusion. Lincoln hoped that if the border states abolished slavery on their own, the Confederacy would throw up its hands in defeat. Douglass hoped the same thing would happen if the federal government declared slavery abolished in the border states.

Its hard to tell whether Douglass believed this or not. In different circumstances he knew perfectly well that the slaves could not simply walk off their plantations and bring slavery to an end on their own. He had spent ten years warning John Brown that it would never happen. He told Lincoln the same thing in the summer of 1864: The slaveholders had plenty of ways to keep slaves from hearing about the Emancipation Proclamation and still more ways of preventing them from attempting to claim their freedom. Nevertheless, inspired by his vision of a spontaneous emancipation rolling forth from Kentucky, Douglass hurled some of his sourest invective at the Lincoln administration's successful attempt to keep the border states from leaving the Union.

The government, Douglass declared in late August, "has resolved that no good shall come to the Negro from this war." By late summer he was complaining about the meager accomplishments of the administration. Republicans, he argued, were paralyzed by long years of northern subservience to the Slave Power and to the racist tradition that denied African Americans any rights beyond those of a beast of burden. In Douglass's mind, Frémont was the hero of the hour. He discounted as frivolous pretexts the stated reasons for Frémont's subsequent dismissal. He did not indicate the slightest misgiving about generals making important public policy decisions on their own. Frémont's proclamation "strikes the rebellion at its source," Douglass declared.[28] The general had fused the cause of the war to its remedy, slavery to emancipation. Nothing else mattered. He was unimpressed by the growing numbers of Union troops who, disregarding their orders, continued accepting fugitive slaves into their camps while thwarting their masters' attempts to recover them. Instead Douglass took scornful notice of every military commander who turned away fugitive slaves, as the army had always done. "We are catching slaves instead of arming them," he said.[29]

By December Douglass had announced that the loyal people of the North were "disgusted with the tenderness with which the Administration treats the cause of the war." He urged Congress to wrest control of the war from the President, some-

28. Ibid., Oct. 1861; *Life & Writings*, vol. 3, p. 158.
29. *FDP*, ser. I, vol. 3, p. 466.

thing it was not prepared to do. That left Douglass at the start of 1862 more dejected than ever. The "friends of freedom, the Union, and the Constitution, have been most basely betrayed, deceived and swindled." Elected on the basis of its hostility to slavery, the government had in fact shown itself to be "destitute of any anti-slavery principle or feeling. . . ." But the tide of history was against the Republicans, Douglass believed. Sooner or later emancipation would be forced upon them, just as it would be forced upon the slaveholders. With a peculiarly Lincolnian turn of phrase Douglass expressed his continued belief "that slavery is to receive its death wound from the present rebellion."[30] On this, at least, Lincoln and Douglass were agreed.

The closer Lincoln drew to the radical conclusion that emancipation was essential to the suppression of the southern rebellion, the more frustrated Douglass seemed to become. At times he seemed to disagree with Lincoln on matters over which they were in complete agreement. Both men had concluded by late 1861 that the destruction of slavery was inevitable, but rather than embrace Lincoln's reasoning Douglass assailed it. Their positions were not identical, but they were clearly too close for comfort.

DOUGLASS'S LOGIC, LINCOLN'S NECESSITY

In early February 1862 two of Lincoln's sons, Willie and Tad, became very sick. They had probably contracted typhoid fever from the White House's polluted water supply. Tad was ill for

---

30. *Douglass' Monthly*, Dec. 1861 and Feb. 1862. See also *FDP*, ser. I, vol. 3, pp. 473–521, for three speeches from the first three months of 1862, when Douglass was at his most critical of Lincoln.

several weeks but eventually recovered. Willie, Lincoln's favorite, did not. As the boy's condition worsened, Lincoln was thrown into despair. He sat by Willie's bedside night after night until, on February 20, the ten-year-old boy died. Elizabeth Keckley had just laid Willie's body out on his bed when Lincoln came into the room. "I never saw a man so bowed down with grief," she remembered. Lifting the sheet that covered the body, Lincoln looked into his son's face. "My poor boy," he said, "he was too good for this earth." Then he buried his own face in his hands as his body convulsed from sobbing. Lincoln was distraught; for months he periodically shut himself alone in his office and broke down. He began having long talks with Phineas D. Gurley, a Presbyterian clergyman, and Mary Todd Lincoln believed that her husband's grief over Willie's death turned Lincoln toward religion for the first time in his adult life. Nevertheless, Willie's death reinforced Lincoln's powerful streak of fatalism. "There's a divinity that shapes our ends," he quoted from Shakespeare, "Rough-hew them how we will."[31]

Frederick Douglass had a fatalistic streak of his own. He believed that slavery's destruction was inevitable no matter how cleverly mere mortals sought to prevent it. "I wait and work," he concluded somewhat dejectedly, "relying more upon the stern logic of events than upon any disposition of the Federal army toward slavery." Timid politicians and racist generals notwithstanding, he observed, "one thing is certain—slavery is a doomed institution." It was not the Republicans but the slaveholders who, "in their madness," have "invited armed abolition

31. Paul Angle, ed., *The Lincoln Reader* (New Brunswick, N.J., 1947), p. 429.

to march to the deliverance of the slave." It was not loyal northerners but southern traitors who had "accelerated" slavery's
decline "and precipitated its disastrous doom."[32]

Douglass called it the "inexorable logic of events"; for
Lincoln it was the logic of necessity. But it meant nearly the
same thing: Slavery was doomed by the slaveholders themselves,
the conclusion unavoidable. Yet Douglass was frustrated by this
element of Lincoln's thought. "Nothing short of dire necessity,"
he complained, would force the government "to act wisely."[33]
Precisely. Lincoln would strike directly at slavery as soon as its
military necessity was clear to himself and to the American people. He had revoked Frémont's order because it was "not within
the range of *military* law, or necessity."[34] In his more reflective
moments Douglass accepted this. "Governments act from necessity," he admitted toward the end of 1861. "They move only as
they are moved upon.——Our government is no exception to this
rule. It cannot determine what shall be the character of
events."[35] For Douglass necessity would ultimately force Lincoln
to adopt an emancipation policy. For Lincoln "military necessity"
would make emancipation legitimate to northerners who would
accept it under no other circumstances.

If Lincoln came early to the conclusion that emancipation
was inevitable, he was willing to wait until public opinion caught
up with him. He said so as early as September 1861. Douglass
and the Radical Republicans, led by Senator Charles Sumner of

32. *Life & Writings*, vol. 3, pp. 158–59; *Douglass' Monthly*, May 1861.
33. *Life & Writings*, vol. 3, p. 159.
34. *CW*, vol. 4, p. 531.
35. *Douglass' Monthly*, Nov. 1861.

Massachusetts, were fuming about Lincoln's rebuke to Frémont. "It would do no good to go ahead any faster than the country would follow," Lincoln said in response. "I think Sumner and the rest of you would upset our applecart altogether if you had your way. We'll fetch 'em," Lincoln promised, "just give us a little time.

> We didn't go into the war to put down slavery, but to put the flag back, and to act differently at this moment, would, I have no doubt, not only weaken our cause but smack of bad faith; for I never should have had votes enough to send me here if the people had supposed I should try to use my power to upset slavery. Why, the first thing you'd see, would be a mutiny in the army. No, we must wait until every other means have been exhausted. This thunderbolt will keep.[36]

Lincoln made it clear that he questioned neither the wisdom nor the desirability of emancipation, only its timing. "The only difference between you and me" on the matter of emancipation, Lincoln told Sumner in late 1861, was "a month or six weeks in time."[37]

In the same month that Lincoln stressed the issue of timing to Charles Sumner, Frederick Douglass came as close as he ever did to appreciating its importance in the government's move toward emancipation. As he often did, Douglass invoked the impersonal logic of events that was driving both the North and the South "to extremities not dreamed of at the beginning of the war." Once again he insisted that the abolition of slavery was "the natural consequence of the war, whether our Government or

36. *RW*, p. 295.
37. Ibid., p. 433.

✧ ✧

Generals would have it so or not." Nevertheless, he conceded that the government's reluctance to "strike the blow at present may be necessary to make it all the more powerful, effectual and successful when it is struck."[38] That pretty much summed up Lincoln's position.

Douglass had embraced antislavery politics, but he still lived in the world of reform, still moved in the circle of reformers. As much as he admired Senator Charles Sumner, the dean of congressional radicals, Douglass did not even associate with the Radical Republicans. He was still a reformer at heart. He was impatient with restraints—political restraints but legal and constitutional ones as well. His impulse was to nudge, to provoke, to condemn all halfway measures. Douglass could savor victories only briefly before his instinctive sense of mission returned, for there was always more to be done. He was relentless. He was inconsistent. But he had a reformer's gifts as well: polemical brilliance and a ferocious critical bite. When Douglass moved into antislavery politics, he brought the sensibilities of a reformer with him. He expected nothing from slaveholders and Democrats. Republicans he held to a higher standard, but it was a reformer's standard that almost no politician could meet. For nearly two years after the Civil War began there was nothing Abraham Lincoln could do to satisfy Frederick Douglass.

Lincoln was a politician, not a reformer, an elected official rather than a freestanding critic. And he was the President of the United States, not a senator from Massachusetts. Lincoln and Douglass could have agreed down to the last jot and tittle—on racial equality, on the Constitution, on colonization—and still,

38. *Douglass' Monthly*, Nov. 1861.

Lincoln would have been restrained by his oath of office and the will of the people in ways that Douglass was not. "We reason as though Mr. Lincoln wielded a dictatorial, unrestricted power at the White House," Eugène Pelletan told his fellow radicals. "But Mr. Lincoln simply presides over a republic where popular opinion rules, and he is surrounded by divers opinions on the question of slavery."[39] It is important to democracy that reformers like Frederick Douglass could say what needed to be said, but it is indispensable to democracy that politicians like Abraham Lincoln could do only what the law and the people allowed them to do.

By early 1862 there was no disagreement between Lincoln and Douglass over whether slavery should be abolished. The issue was how. For all his talk of violent slave insurrection—and he talked a lot about it after Harpers Ferry—Douglass actually endorsed all paths to emancipation. He was a flexible dogmatist. The goal mattered much more than the means of achieving it. Twenty years earlier, when his own freedom was at stake, Douglass had backed a proposal by his English friends to purchase his liberty from the man who still technically owned him, thus making it possible for Douglass to return safely to America. Righteous abolitionists cried foul, but Douglass cared more about securing freedom than securing freedom in the purest way. In this sense he was somewhat more pragmatic than the President. Lincoln believed that some ways of abolishing slavery were better than others, that some were downright unlawful, and still others—remorseless insurrection in particular—were terrible and should be avoided. For Douglass the crime of slavery was so great that any means of overthrowing it were justi-

39. Quoted in Guelzo, *Lincoln's Emancipation Proclamation*, p. 30.

fied. By contrast, Lincoln was "conservative as to *means*," his friend Joseph Gillespie explained, but "radical he was so far as *ends* were concerned."[40]

To some extent it suited Lincoln's purposes to have radicals like Douglass attacking him. It made the President appear more conservative than he actually was, but it also exposed his genuine preference for conservative approaches to emancipation. He pressed for emancipation, but he recoiled at some of the ways radicals wanted to get there. Even as he invoked his war powers to free confiscated slaves, he remained "anxious and careful" not to let the Civil War "degenerate into a violent and remorseless revolutionary struggle."[41] In time Lincoln would launch an aggressive war on slavery, but not until he and the northern people accepted emancipation as a military necessity. Even then Lincoln had no desire to cast himself as a revolutionary hero. When he made his move, he was careful to insist that it was the unavoidable consequence of the slaveholders' own recklessness. "The powder in this bombshell will keep dry," Lincoln said of abolition in September 1861, "and when the fuse is lit, I intend to have them touch it off themselves."[42] Regardless of who lit the fuse, the bomb went off in 1862.

40. *HI*, p. 507.
41. *CW,* vol. 5, p. 49.
42. *RW*, p. 295.

5

"WE MUST FREE
THE SLAVES OR BE
OURSELVES SUBDUED"

JANUARY 1, 1863

Lincoln had not slept at all. Early the
next morning, New Year's Day, he went
to his office and wrote out the final
Emancipation Proclamation. From
there he sent it to the State Department
to have an engrossed copy prepared for
his signature. But when Secretary of
State Seward hand-delivered the official
proclamation later in the morning, it
contained an error. It went back to the
State Department to be corrected. The
signing was delayed until after the annual
New Year's celebration hosted by the
President and First Lady.

For the next three hours Lincoln
stood shaking hands as guests streamed

❖ ❖

through the White House. Finally, at two o'clock in the afternoon, the festivities ended, and Lincoln went back upstairs,
where the corrected copies awaited his signature. By then he
was exhausted. Sitting at his desk, Lincoln picked up his pen, but
his hand shook so badly he had to put it back down. He tried
once more, but again the trembling forced him to stop. As
Seward stood by watching, Lincoln explained that the tremor
was caused by the hours he had spent shaking hands, not from
any misgivings about signing the proclamation. Finally, holding
the pen as tightly as possible and in a somewhat shaky script, he
affixed his full signature, Abraham Lincoln, to the document. In
cities and towns across the North men and women had gathered
in wait to celebrate the news. By late afternoon the telegraph
wires were buzzing with word that the President had at last
signed the Emancipation Proclamation.

Henry Wadsworth Longfellow had organized a Jubilee
Concert at Boston's Music Hall. The leading lights of New England
civic and literary culture were in attendance. Decorating the walls
were the coats of arms of the United States of America and the
Commonwealth of Massachusetts. The Boston Philharmonic
opened the program, playing just long enough to bring the hall to
silence. Josiah Quincy, Jr., took the podium to introduce a
speech by Ralph Waldo Emerson. When Emerson finished, the
orchestra played Beethoven's Egmont Overture, followed by
Mendelssohn's Hymn of Praise—"most appropriate for the occasion," the *Boston Morning Journal* reported, "illustrative of the
darkness of the past, the dawning of the glorious future." With
the distinguished historian Francis Parkman looking on, Oliver
Wendell Holmes rose to recite his "Army Hymn," with two new
stanzas he had written for the occasion.

We lift the starry flag on high,
That fills with light our stormy sky.

No more its flaming emblems wave
To bar from hope the trembling slave;
No more its radiant glories shine
To blast with woe a child of Thine.

The celebration concluded with more music: Beethoven's Fifth Symphony, the Hallelujah Chorus from Handel's *Messiah*, and Rossini's rousing William Tell Overture. An announcer interrupted the closing concert to let the audience know that the Emancipation Proclamation had indeed been issued by the President and would appear on the telegraph wires later that evening. The Music Hall erupted in "tumultuous applause" as the ladies and gentlemen gave nine cheers for Abraham Lincoln. "It is not often that a more brilliant assembly is seen," the *Morning Journal* declared, "not often so great an occasion—never one more important—the celebration of a day which will hold a place in history forever."[1]

Meanwhile, at the Tremont Temple nearby, the Union Progressive Association had organized a daylong celebration of its own. Some of the greatest names in American abolitionism were scheduled to speak before the largely black audience. William Lloyd Garrison was expected to appear, though he never showed up. But Wendell Phillips did. So did William Wells Brown, and so did Frederick Douglass. The morning session began with a speech by William C. Nell thanking the President for the proclamation and "alluding in a feeling manner to the

1. *Boston Morning Journal*, January 2, 1863.

attachment of the colored race to their home and native land."
Some speakers attributed emancipation to divine will; others
promised that "when we get through with the enemies of the
black man in Dixie," they would carry the struggle against racial
prejudice into the North. William Wells Brown read the text of
the preliminary proclamation and later, in a speech of his own,
defended the ability of the freed slaves "to take care of themselves." The morning session closed with "three cheers for civil
and religious liberty, three for the President of the United
States, and three for the Army and Navy." The afternoon session
convened at two-thirty for another round of speeches, one of
which was interrupted when a messenger entered the hall "with
the intelligence that the President's Proclamation was coming
over the wires." The announcement caused "considerable com-
motion" and shouts of "Glory to God! &c." The evening session,
the best attended of the three, was devoted to still more speakers professing their faith in the freed slaves, their willingness to
work hard and their burning desire for education.[2] Just before
adjournment news of the final proclamation arrived. "The
joyous enthusiasm manifested was beyond description.

> Cheers were proposed for the President and for the
> proclamation, the whole audience rising to their feet and
> shouting at the tops of their voices, throwing up their
> hats and indicating their gratification in every conceiv-
> able manner. When the cheers had somewhat abated, the
> whole audience stood up and joined in singing the
> jubilee song 'Blow ye the trumpet blow,' and then fol-

2. Ibid., January 7, 1863.

lowed a beautiful prayer of thanksgiving by the Rev. Mr. Waterston, which moved many to tears, and was frequently interrupted by shouts of 'Amen,' 'Glory to God in the highest!' 'Hallelujah,' &c.

After the meeting at the Tremont Temple, the *Boston Evening Transcript* reported, a large number "wended their way to the Twelfth Baptist Church, where they joined in prayer and singing, and partook of a repast which had been prepared."[3]

They were in the same city, on the same day, celebrating the same event. Yet it was as if the Tremont Temple and the Music Hall occupied parallel universes, a mile away but a world apart. It wasn't just the contrasting skin colors of the respective audiences. At the Music Hall they talked about history; at the Tremont Temple they talked about God's will. One audience sat listening to a great orchestra, spectators to an important event. The other rose to its feet, shouting and singing glorious hymns, deeply engaged by the event being celebrated. Both groups gave thanks to the United States and cheered the President, but at the Tremont Temple the jubilation was leavened by lingering concerns: for an emancipation that, though begun, was far from complete; for the future prospects of the freed people; for the racial discrimination that persisted in the North even as slavery collapsed in the South. At the Music Hall Abraham Lincoln got nine cheers. The folks at the Tremont Temple gave him three, reserving three for civil and religious liberty and three more for the Union military. Frederick Douglass was at the Tremont Temple.

3. Ibid., January 2, 1863.

Toward Emancipation

Lincoln's pace was set by military affairs, but it accelerated in 1862. Beginning in the winter of 1861–62, a succession of Union victories in the West secured the loyalty of both Kentucky and Missouri, enabling the President to go public with his campaign to pressure the border states into adopting emancipation on their own. The Republican-controlled Congress came back into session and quickly sent him a raft of antislavery bills, all of which he signed into law. By late spring military affairs had intruded again, but this time it was Union failure in the East that spurred Lincoln. After one last effort to prod the border states into action he decided by mid-July to issue an emancipation proclamation. The proclamation itself was one of several orders which together shifted the Union military toward a policy of "hard war" against the Confederacy. As if to emphasize its military rationale, Lincoln withheld publication of the proclamation until a Union victory made emancipation look like a demonstration of northern strength rather than an act of northern desperation. This was something Frederick Douglass understood early on; the fate of emancipation hinged on the fortunes of the Union army.

Douglass kept up his criticism after the New Year, denouncing the "imbecility" of Lincoln's letter to Frémont and wondering why the President seemed "ashamed to tell the world what he is fighting against."[4] But he began to understand that most of the pressure on Lincoln was coming from proslavery Democrats who had, by early 1862, regained their momentum and were roundly condemning the increasingly radical drift of the war. From then on

4. *FDP*, ser. I, vol. 3, pp. 483, 477.

Douglass fell into a pattern of tempering his own misgivings about Lincoln whenever he realized that the Democrats, not the abolitionists, were the real alternative to the Republicans.

As the likelihood of emancipation grew, Democrats began to demand an answer to the question, "What shall be done with the slaves?" But Douglass shrewdly observed that the increasing prominence of the question "implies at least the presence of danger to the slave system."[5] Then, too, Douglass was buoyed by a very real shift of public opinion in favor of abolition. "Tongues that used to bless Slavery now curse it," he declared in February 1862; those who once praised the patriotism of slaveholders "are but now having the scales torn from their eyes by slaveholding treason and rebellion."[6] It would be impossible, he predicted, for the President, his cabinet, or the army to withstand for long "the mighty current of events, or the surging billows of the popular will."[7]

But Douglass feared military defeat more than he feared the Democrats. In the first half of 1862 Douglass's writings suddenly exploded with detailed commentary on the movement of troops, and his volatile mood now rose and fell with the fortunes of war. As he and other Americans beheld the spectacle of a seemingly paralyzed Union army, Douglass's anger gave way to a sober concern for the fate of his country. In these months he wrote more movingly than ever of his deep attachment to "our *great* Republic—for such it truly is." He spoke with pride of the fact that African Americans were the most reliably loyal group in the country, that "there are no black rebels" anywhere in the United States. "I am an American citizen," Douglass told a

5. *Douglass' Monthly*, Jan. 1862.
6. *FDP*, ser. I, vol. 3, pp. 495–96.
7. *Douglass' Monthly*, Feb. 1862.

Boston audience one February evening. "In birth, in sentiment, in ideas, in hopes, in aspirations, and responsibilities, I am an American citizen." Moreover, "I am such by choice" as well as by lineage. Years earlier Douglass had been offered citizenship in England but instead returned to his "mission" in the United States. "I have never regretted that decision," he continued, "and tonight, I allow no man to exceed me in the desire for the safety and welfare of this country." In truth Douglass wanted to remain in England, but his family called him home. Nevertheless, nothing he was now saying was different from what he had said in the past. But his tone had changed. He was more somber, almost frightened. "God forbid," Douglass said, "that when the smoke and thunder of this slaveholding war shall have rolled from the troubled face of our country it shall be said that the harvest is past, the summer is ended and we are not saved."[8]

"We Must Free the Slaves or Be Ourselves Subdued"

As Douglass worried for his country, Lincoln was losing patience—with his generals and with the border states. Early in 1862 the Delaware legislature rejected his proposal for voluntary, compensated emancipation. In March Lincoln turned up the pressure by sending Congress a proposed resolution for federal compensation to the owners of slaves in any state whose legislature enacted an emancipation statute. He justified this as a military measure designed to deprive the Confederacy of any hopes of enticing more slave states to leave the Union. Yet he stepped up the pressure on the border states only after the mili-

8. *FDP,* ser. I, vol. 3, pp. 474–75, 493–94.

tary pressure on those states had eased considerably. Union general George Thomas had kicked invading Confederate troops out
of Kentucky. Ulysses Grant had taken control of Forts Henry
and Donelson in Tennessee, foreshadowing the North's military
domination of the West. The Confederates had been swept from
much of Missouri and defeated at Pea Ridge, Arkansas. And
naval commander David Farragut had launched a spectacular
flotilla up the Mississippi River from the South to give the
Union control of New Orleans.

Military necessity was Lincoln's rationale for pressuring the
border states, but his motives were more complicated than his
rationale. He hoped that if he dangled the carrot of compensation in public, the border states would feel more pressure to
accept his proposal. But just in case they needed more goosing,
Lincoln added a not so veiled threat to his March message to
Congress. He reminded the border states of his pledge to use
"all indispensable means" to end the war and that as long as the
war continued, "it is impossible to foresee all of the incidents,
which may attend and all the ruin which may follow it."[9] The
message was clear enough. If the border states did not accept
this offer of compensated emancipation, the "incidents" of war
could leave them without slaves and without compensation
either. Only a dunce could miss Lincoln's point.

But miss it, or at least disregard it, the border states did. When
his proposal elicited no comment from border state congressmen,
Lincoln called them to the White House. He told them honestly
that he had always hated slavery and wished to see it abolished,
but he justified his proposal on military grounds. By abolishing
slavery on their own, the border states would dash one of the

Confederacy's fondest hopes and thereby speed the collapse of the rebellion. To the President's face the legislators were as respectful as they could bring themselves to be, but when they got back to Capitol Hill their tongues loosened up as one after another they denounced Lincoln's proposal as an unwarranted and unconstitutional interference with slavery in the states. Lincoln was startled by the border state reaction, but he should have known better. His proposal did, after all, have the aroma of radicalism about it. "[F]or the first time in two generations," a Republican newspaper explained, "we have the recommendation from the presidential chair of the *abolition of slavery* and of measures by Congress to invite and assist it."[10] Over the vociferous objections of the border state representatives both houses of Congress passed the President's resolution and Lincoln signed it a week later.

By the spring of 1862 public opinion had shifted far enough for the Republicans in Congress to make several dramatic moves of their own. They passed a law prohibiting Union officers from turning back slaves who ran away to Union lines. In brazen defiance of the Supreme Court's *Dred Scott* decision, Congress expressly prohibited the expansion of slavery into federal territories. The lawmakers also ratified Lincoln's treaty with Britain for the suppression of the Atlantic slave trade and then followed it up by passing vigorous enforcement legislation. Most dramatically, Congress abolished slavery in the District of Columbia. The bill had almost everything that Lincoln preferred: Emancipation was not gradual, but the masters were to be compensated. It did not allow the people of Washington or their representatives to vote on it themselves, as he would have liked. Nevertheless, he

10. Quoted in Allen Guelzo, *Lincoln's Emancipation Proclamation: The End of Slavery in America* (New York, 2004), p. 107.

signed the bill and sent it back to Congress with a message stating that "I have ever desired to see the national capital freed from the institution in some satisfactory way."[11] For the first time in American history the federal government used its power to abolish slavery. Frederick Douglass could scarcely believe what was happening. "I trust I am not dreaming," he wrote.[12]

But Lincoln, careful and deliberate where Douglass was quick and impulsive, was not yet prepared to make emancipation an explicit aim of the war. Douglass's suspicions were aroused when Lincoln rebuked yet another Union general who had overstepped his authority by declaring the emancipation of the slaves on the coastal islands of Georgia, South Carolina, and Florida. The general, David Hunter, issued his edict on May 9; Lincoln repudiated it ten days later in a very public proclamation. Nobody in the government had had advance knowledge that Hunter would issue such a proclamation, Lincoln said, and so Hunter could have had no authorization to issue it. Indeed, military commanders had no business making such decisions. Then Lincoln slipped in another one of his backhanded revelations. "I reserve to myself," he said, any decision "to declare the Slaves of any state or states, free." Back in December Lincoln had taken it upon himself to declare confiscated slaves liberated. Now he was going much further by suggesting that as commander in chief he could declare *all* the slaves in the seceded states free if he deemed it "a necessity indispensable to the maintainance of the government."

As he had with General Frémont, Lincoln repudiated General Hunter because he objected not to emancipation but to generals making policy decisions that properly belonged to civilian authori-

11. *CW*, vol. 5, p. 192.
12. *Life & Writings*, vol. 3, p. 233.

ties. As if the hint of his own inclinations were not broad enough, the President used the proclamation revoking Hunter's order to take another jab at the border states. He quoted his own resolution of the previous March urging Congress to compensate any state that voluntarily emancipated its slaves. He pointed out that both houses of Congress had passed the resolution by large majorities. Emancipation was coming, Lincoln hinted. "You can not if you would, be blind to the signs of the times," he said. He invited the border states to take advantage of the opportunity presented them by taking the lead in one of the greatest deeds of human history. "May the vast future not have to lament that you have neglected it." A diligent reader finishing Lincoln's words might have found it odd that a proclamation ostensibly designed to overturn General Hunter's emancipation order had devoted the bulk of its space to calling upon the border states to join him in the march of human history by emancipating their own slaves and to declaring the President's authority to free the slaves in the rebel states whenever "military necessity" required it.[13]

Military necessity presented itself in June 1862. Following the Union's disastrous defeat at the First Battle of Bull Run the previous summer, Lincoln had installed George B. McClellan as commander of the Army of the Potomac and, for a period, commander of all Union armies. McClellan devoted the fall and winter to whipping his army into shape, and he was good at it. But as the winter months passed, his great flaw as a general became increasingly apparent: He could build a well-disciplined army, but he was unwilling to use it. Frederick Douglass captured the problem nicely. They had got up a huge army on the Potomac, he said, but it "has remained idle through the summer,

13. *CW*, vol. 5, pp. 222–23.

✧ ✧

waiting for autumn—idle through the Winter, waiting for Spring, and which will probably remain idle through the Spring, waiting for good roads."[14] By the spring of 1862 Lincoln had all but ordered McClellan to move against the Confederate armies defending Richmond, Virginia. The result was the Peninsula campaign, McClellan's cumbersome plan to capture the Confederate capital. Though his forces vastly outnumbered those of the enemy, McClellan was paralyzed by the aggressiveness of the Confederates. By the end of June the Peninsula campaign was over. McClellan withdrew his army south to the James River and then sat there and did nothing other than blame Lincoln and the politicians for his own failure.

At that point, early July 1862, the stars fell into alignment. The reluctance of the border states to emancipate their slaves converged with McClellan's reluctance to fight. With rumors swirling that McClellan was part of a military plot to march on Washington and overthrow the government, Lincoln decided to go see the general himself on July 7 at Harrison's Landing. There McClellan handed the President an astonishing letter detailing his objections to the drift toward emancipation and hinting at his own willingness to be appointed "Commander in Chief" of the Army. At last Lincoln realized that McClellan's unwillingness to fight was driven as much by politics as psychology. He also realized that if voluntary emancipation in the border states were to happen, it would have to start happening immediately. On July 12, a few days after returning from Harrison's Landing, Lincoln called the border state congressmen to a second meeting. This time the President warned them in the bluntest possible terms that if they hesitated any longer, emancipation would be forced

14. *Douglass' Monthly*, Feb. 1862.

on them by "the incidents of war." He told them that he had revoked General Hunter's proclamation not because he objected to military emancipation but because it was a decision only the President could make. He also made it clear that in revoking Frémont's and Hunter's orders, he had deeply upset many loyal citizens whose support the Union could not afford to lose. The representatives took their leave and, two days later, informed the President that they had voted more than two to one against his proposal. Lincoln must have seen their rejection coming, for he had already made a decision of his own.

Attorney General Edwin Stanton's son had died, and Lincoln was riding to the funeral with Gideon Welles, his secretary of the navy, and William Seward, the secretary of state. Lincoln was still aching from the death a few months before of his own son Willie, and the grief he now shared with Stanton drew the two men close to each other. In the carriage Lincoln told Welles and Seward that he had decided to issue a proclamation of emancipation as a military necessity. He had "about come to the conclusion," Lincoln said, "that we must free the slaves or be ourselves subdued." It was July 13, 1862, the day after his unproductive session with the border states and less than a week after his meeting with McClellan. The army had failed to strike the "vigorous blows" needed to put down secession, so it was time for his administration to "set the army an example, and strike at the heart of the rebellion." He had hoped that the border states would take the lead on the measure, but at that point any further efforts would "be useless." Then he repeated something he had been saying for over a year. "Slavery was doomed," he said, and it was the slaveholders who made it so.[15]

15. Howard K. Beale, ed., *Diary of Gideon Welles* (New York, 1960), vol. 1, pp. 70–71; *RW*, pp. 469–70.

A few days later Congress made its own move. Republican moderates, disgusted by McClellan's failure, joined with the radicals to pass the Second Confiscation Act on July 17. Unlike the first one, which was restricted to slaves employed in support of the Confederacy, the new law authorized the confiscation of slaves of any master who was actually in rebellion—but with the crippling proviso that the master's treason be proven in a court of law. Knowing that Lincoln was jealous of his war powers as commander in chief, Congress stipulated that the law could go into effect only with a presidential proclamation. But Lincoln planned more than that, not simply a confiscation proclamation but an emancipation proclamation. It was the last of a series of proclamations that he brought to his cabinet in July, all of them aimed at shifting to a policy of hard war against the Confederacy. When he revealed it to the entire cabinet on July 22, Lincoln said that although he was interested in their advice, he had no intention of reversing himself. At the suggestion of the secretary of state, Lincoln withheld the publication of the Emancipation Proclamation until the North had a decisive military victory under its belt. To release it so soon after the disaster of the Peninsula campaign would make emancipation look like an act of desperation. Lincoln agreed, and the wait began.

WAITING FOR ANTIETAM

For two months, from July 22 to September 22, Lincoln sat on the Emancipation Proclamation, waiting for a military victory. A second defeat at Bull Run only prolonged the agony. Lincoln did not know how much time he would have before the victory he was waiting for, but he used his time strategically—almost deviously—to prepare public opinion for what was coming. He began to drop hints of his decision, something he almost never did. At the same time, knowing that the proclamation would be seen as a radically new direction for the war, Lincoln tried to position it ahead of time as a conservative gesture. Frederick Douglass was thrown off the scent by Lincoln's calculated distractions, so much so that he chose that moment, August 1862, to unleash one of his most vitriolic denunciations of the President.

Douglass was already upset by Lincoln's recent order revoking General Hunter's emancipation edict in South Carolina. Once again Douglass put the goal of emancipation above the threat of a military usurpation of civilian authority. The President, he complained, had "repeatedly interfered with, and arrested the antislavery policy of some of his most earnest and reliable generals." But wasn't this part of a larger pattern? Since the day he took office every move Lincoln made, Douglass said, "has been calculated in a marked and decided way to shield and protect slavery." Had Lincoln not put aside his constitutional authority, not to mention his moral duty, to emancipate the slaves? Had he not ignored the enforcement provision of the Second Confiscation Act by refusing to issue an emancipation proclamation? When Douglass published this in August 1862, he had no idea that Lincoln was waiting for the military victory that would give added force to his impending proclamation.[16] His frustration must have been unbearable; along with every other careful observer of politics and war, Douglass sensed how close the government was to proclaiming emancipation. Why had it not done so already? What was Lincoln waiting for?

Horace Greeley felt the same way. The influential editor of the *New York Tribune* was, like Douglass, on the edge of his seat

---

16. *FDP*, ser. I, vol. 3, p. 539.

waiting for the announcement that never came, though Lincoln had tried to tip him off. Unaware of the impending proclamation, Greeley published his call for emancipation in a melodramatic "prayer of twenty millions" on August 19. Lincoln's reply of August 22 was a masterpiece of indirect revelation. His primary goal was what it had always been, the President said: "I would save the Union. I would save it the shortest way under the Constitution." If he could do this most quickly without emancipating any slaves, that was what he would do. If he needed to emancipate some slaves and not others, he would do that. But if he concluded that restoring the Union required him to free all the slaves, Lincoln wrote, he would not hesitate to free all the slaves.[17] As in his proclamation reversing General Hunter's order a few months before, Lincoln's letter to Greeley opened the possibility of a broad emancipation by cloaking it in a respectable commitment to the preservation of the Union. Lincoln was not dissembling. He wanted people to read the forthcoming proclamation as a conservative gesture, the latest move in a policy whose primary purpose remained the reestablishment of the Union. That was precisely how Frederick Douglass read it: as evidence that Lincoln cared a great deal about the restoration of the Union and very little about the abolition of slavery.

By then Douglass's suspicions about Lincoln had recently been refreshed. As the prospect of emancipation became clearer, there were renewed calls for free blacks to leave the United States, all of which aroused Douglass's furious indignation. As in the 1850s, Douglass waged his war on two different fronts. The first battle, against emigrationism, was actually a continuation of

17. *CW*, vol. 5, p. 388.

the dispute among black leaders that peaked in 1859 and 1860 and continued into the earliest months of the Civil War. The racist backlash of the 1850s had prompted a handful of black leaders to step up their campaign for emigration to someplace where African Americans would be freed from humiliating discrimination and the blighting prejudice of whites. But the war itself raised the hopes of American blacks and so dampened much of whatever enthusiasm there had been for emigration. It did not discourage James Redpath, a white Briton, who persisted in his campaign to encourage black Americans to migrate to the Caribbean. With funding from the Haitian government Redpath opened an office in Boston in late 1860 to drum up support for black emigration to the island nation. Because Redpath had been one of John Brown's most devoted followers, Frederick Douglass was less skeptical than usual about his proposal for an émigré colony in Haiti. But within months Douglass's skepticism revived. "We are Americans," he insisted, and we "shall rise or fall with Americans." As he had a decade earlier, he rejected the proposition that whites and blacks could not live together as equals. There was no such thing, Douglass wrote, "as a natural and unconquerable repugnance between the varieties of men." The barriers of "race," he noted, were "arbitrary and artificial," and as such they could be overcome by "interest and enlightenment."[18] The Haitian experiment turned into a debacle. Of the two thousand or so blacks who actually emigrated, only a few hundred remained a couple of years later. Most of the others had either died of tropical diseases and malnutrition or returned home to the United States in desperation.

18. David W. Blight, *Frederick Douglass's Civil War: Keeping Faith in Jubilee* (Baton Rouge, 1989), pp. 127–34.

One of Douglass's complaints was that the emigrationists gave aid and comfort to white racists who, as the prospect of emancipation rose, were reviving the idea of colonization. By late 1861 it was beginning to dawn on many northerners that large numbers of slaves might be freed by the war. In December Lincoln urged Congress to consider the establishment of colonies, preferably in Central America, as potential homes for emancipated slaves. Within months the lawmakers appropriated some six hundred thousand dollars to finance the voluntary colonization of those freed by the various incidents of war, including the abolition of slavery in the District of Columbia. The closer Lincoln got to proclaiming emancipation, the more aggressively he pursued his colonization scheme. By dropping hints of a forthcoming emancipation in the form of proposals for colonization, he was doing something peculiar, not to say unseemly. He was appealing to northern racism to smooth the way for emancipation.

On August 14 the Interior Department's commissioner of emigration, the Reverend James Mitchell, escorted a delegation of five African Americans, most of them local preachers, to the White House, where Lincoln treated them to a bizarre lecture on race relations in America and the benefits of colonization. He began with broad rhetorical questions. "[S]hould the people of your race be colonized, and where?" Indeed, "why should they leave this country?" He did not expect his guests to answer. Rather, he came prepared to address the questions all by himself. The "physical difference" between blacks and whites was a "great disadvantage to us both," Lincoln said, "as I think your race suffer greatly, many of them by living among us, while ours suffer from your presence. In a word," the President said, "we suffer on each side." Blacks suffered, Lincoln said, not merely by their atrocious enslavement but by the refusal of whites anywhere in America to treat even the most accomplished blacks as their equals. Whether this was right or wrong was not the issue, Lincoln said; it was enough that all parties acknowledge it as a fact.[19]

It was easy enough to see how blacks suffered from the presence of whites. But what could Lincoln have possibly meant by saying that whites suffered by the presence of blacks? The answer was the terrible war that slavery had brought to America. "[W]ithout the institution of Slavery," Lincoln explained, "*and the colored race as a basis*" there would be no war.[20] This was an outrageous thing to say. For years, in the face of Democratic race-baiting, Lincoln had insisted that slavery and race were two different matters. Now he was trying to have it both ways. On the one hand, racism was a powerful force independent of slavery, so that emancipation would not free blacks from the crippling effects of discrimination. On the other hand, Lincoln declared that "race" was the basis of slavery, and he conflated the two with a sophomoric syllogism: Whites are at each other's throats over slavery; slaves are black; therefore, whites suffer from the presence of blacks. It sounded as though Lincoln were blaming the Civil War on blacks.

The remainder of Lincoln's remarks went into the details of emigration to Central America, which he thought a more practical destination than Liberia. He ended with an almost pathetic request. There was, he knew, great resistance to colonization among free blacks. But without leadership from the best and brightest of American blacks the less educated slaves would never seek their freedom in Central America. Therefore, the

19. *CW*, vol. 5, p. 371.
20. Ibid., p. 372.

✧ ✧

cause of emancipation would be greatly enhanced if a mere one hundred, even fifty, perhaps only twenty-five educated black families set the example by emigrating first. Whites in turn would see this, and their hostility to abolition would melt away. Thus colonization prompted by a small but prominent group of free blacks would do great service to the cause of humanity.

Was Lincoln serious? He had always supported colonization, and in August 1862, when he knew that emancipation was coming, his moment of truth had arrived. If he expected the freed slaves to leave the United States, he had to have someplace for them to go, and he had to make emigration seem desirable. But from the beginning there had always been something fantastically improbable about colonization, never more so than on the day Lincoln met the black delegation. By 1862 there were more than four million African Americans in the United States. No colony anywhere on earth was prepared to absorb even a fraction of that number. It would cost a fortune to set up such a colony and transport millions of American blacks. But such problems paled beside the greatest obstacle of all: Blacks did not want to go. Some colonizationists were prepared to force blacks to leave, but not Lincoln. He always insisted that emigration was to be voluntary. Lincoln was weeks, maybe days from proclaiming emancipation, and he had no place to colonize the freed slaves, they didn't want to go, and he had no intention of forcing them. What could he possibly have been thinking?

Maybe Lincoln was deluding himself. Colonization often did that to its supporters, especially if they were sincere, and there was no reason to doubt Lincoln's sincerity. Still, there was something contrived about his meeting with the black delegates, as if it had been staged for public consumption. There was virtually no dialogue between the President and his visitors; Lincoln simply lectured them with what sounded like prepared remarks. Also, there was a reporter in the room taking stenographic notes of everything the President said. Lincoln made sure that his high-handed remarks would appear verbatim in the national press the very next day. In short, it was not a meeting, it was a performance. Lincoln was using his handpicked delegates, none of them important black leaders, in an effort to make emancipation more palatable to white racists. The whole world could see that Lincoln was prepared to tell blacks right to their faces that the nation would be better off if they went somewhere else. As in the 1850s, Lincoln carefully avoided claiming that he personally believed blacks were inferior to whites; he even said that because of slavery, blacks were suffering the greatest wrong that could be inflicted on any people. But he was once again using racism strategically. It was a low point in his presidency.

Frederick Douglass was stunned when he read reports of the meeting. The President's remarks, he said, were "characteristically foggy, remarkably illogical and untimely." They exposed Lincoln's "pride of race and blood, his contempt for Negroes and his canting hypocrisy." Worse, Lincoln's published words gave license to all the "ignorant and base" racists "to commit all kinds of violence and outrage upon the colored people of the country." In words saturated with sarcasm Douglass went on to expose the fallacious reasoning behind Lincoln's utterances. Anyone with "an ounce of brain in his head" knew that in other parts of the Americas blacks and whites were perfectly capable of living together peacefully and as equals. To blame the Civil War on the presence of blacks was like the horse thief blaming the horse for his crime. Racism and slavery were indeed linked, Douglass reasoned. But Lincoln ought to know "that Negro hatred and prejudice of color are . . . merely the offshoots of that root of all crimes and evils—slavery." He dismissed the "arrogant and malignant nonsense" that posited a "natural" repugnance between blacks and whites.[21]

Because he had always equated the struggle for racial equality with the struggle against slavery, Douglass read Lincoln's deference to white prejudice as evidence of an abiding indifference to slavery. Though he had been elected as an antislavery President by antislavery voters, Douglass argued, Lincoln's actual record in office revealed that he was instead "a genuine representative of American prejudice and Negro hatred." To Douglass, therefore, Lincoln's most recent capitulation to prejudice could only reflect a lack of commitment to emancipation. "This address of his leaves us less ground to hope for anti-slavery action at his hands than any of his previous utterances." Lincoln's support for colonization proved to Douglass that Lincoln was not a true antislavery man.

Douglass's logic made perfect sense, but it was not Lincoln's logic. To Douglass colonization presupposed racism, the spirit of slavery. But to Lincoln colonization presupposed emancipation. His meeting with black leaders was prompted not by his resistance to emancipation but by the fact that he had already decided to proclaim it. The black delegation could not have known that, and neither could Douglass. Instead he saw all the evidence piling up against emancipation. Voluntary emancipation in the border states was a fool's errand, he thought. The letter to Horace Greeley was a public profession of Lincoln's indifference to slavery. By August 1862 it all added up to the conclusion, erroneous but understandable under the circumstances, that Abraham Lincoln would never issue an emancipation proclamation.

21. *Douglass' Monthly*, Sept. 1862.

THE PROCLAMATION

Lincoln was scheming, Douglass was fuming, and all the while Robert E. Lee was making plans. He would invade the North in a bold attempt to win the war in the East before the Confederacy was defeated in the West. Lee had sent McClellan's vast Union forces into retreat. Weeks later Confederate hopes were raised by a second dramatic southern victory at Bull Run. Seizing the moment, Lee turned his mighty Army of Northern Virginia toward Pennsylvania. He was hoping to unhinge Union morale by bringing the war onto Yankee soil. But his great plan was cut short on September 17, when he met the Union's Army of the Potomac at Sharpsburg, Maryland, beside Antietam Creek. It was a brutal battle. But despite several blunders that prolonged the fighting and increased the casualties, and despite the Confederate escape across the Potomac, Antietam was a strategic defeat for Lee. The South's attempt to invade the North was turned back, and the Union had a clear military victory on its hands. It was time for Lincoln to let the world know.

Five days later, on September 22, he released the preliminary Emancipation Proclamation. It gave the southern states one hundred days, until January 1, 1863, to lay down their arms. If they did not, the United States government would "thenceforward" consider every slave in the rebellious South to be free. Africans had been enslaved in North America for more than two and a half centuries. Now, a mere eighteen months after promising never to interfere with slavery in the southern states, Lincoln committed all the military and financial might of the United States to the emancipation of millions of African Americans. And it would be an emancipation of the most revolutionary kind. It would be imposed by force as the Union army

❖ ❖

marched through the South. It would be immediate rather than gradual. The freed slaves would not be required to emigrate. And the slaveholders would get nothing, not one cent, in compensation. Abolitionists thought it was about time, but in the larger span of American history Lincoln had moved with remarkable speed toward a remarkably radical conclusion.

Frederick Douglass was beside himself. "*Abraham Lincoln,*" he exclaimed, "in his own peculiar, cautious, forbearing and hesitating way, slow, but we hope sure, has, while the loyal heart was near breaking with despair, proclaimed and declared" that as of the following January 1 the slaves in the rebellious South "Shall be Thenceforward and Forever Free." Emancipation once proclaimed was irreversible, Douglass argued. "Abraham Lincoln may be slow, Abraham Lincoln may desire peace . . . , but Abraham Lincoln is not the man to reconsider, retract and contradict words and purposes solemnly proclaimed over his official signature."[22] If Douglass still chastised Lincoln for moving too slowly, this was a minor quibble now. At long last Lincoln had declared his intention to do what Douglass had for months been calling on him to do: invoke the war powers of the chief executive to emancipate the slaves on grounds of military necessity.

Emancipation as a military necessity was an idea associated chiefly with radicals and abolitionists. Nearly all northern Democrats denied the existence of any constitutional power to emancipate slaves. For a long time so did most Republicans, and those who did not dispute the President's *power* to emancipate usually disputed its *prudence*. Even within Lincoln's cabinet there were objections to the proclamation. Seward thought there was no need for it since slavery's death became inevitable on the day

22. Ibid., Oct. 1862.

Lincoln was inaugurated. It was already dying, he argued, so why issue a proclamation that would only alienate the Europeans? Chase thought it would be more effective for Union commanders to issue individual emancipation proclamations while in the field, where they could back them up with military might. Why issue a general proclamation that depended on future military success? Most of Lincoln's generals opposed emancipation as well. Fearing that large numbers of escaping slaves running to Union army lines would interfere with the war effort, the generals argued against emancipation on strictly military grounds. But Lincoln had a more capacious sense of what counted as military necessity, one that looked beyond the immediate convenience of Union command-ers. So he sided with the radicals, having long since concluded that as commander in chief the President had the power to free slaves. The big difference, but the only difference, was that unlike Charles Sumner and Frederick Douglass, Lincoln refused to use his power until it was very clearly a military necessity and until the public was prepared to accept it as such.

Even so, Lincoln fully expected the proclamation to provoke a political backlash, especially among northern Democrats. Republican setbacks in the fall elections proved him right. Democrats campaigned heavily against Lincoln's turn to the "radical fanaticism" of emancipation, as well as his recent sus-pension of habeas corpus. But Lincoln sensed that his oppo-nents could score points on emancipation chiefly because of his failure to win the war. In July and August Lincoln issued calls for six hundred thousand more troops under the new mil-itary draft policy. He began firing generals who believed in a limited war that did not disturb southern property: Don Carlos Buell went two weeks before the elections, George McClellan shortly thereafter. And when he released the final proclamation on January 1, 1863, Lincoln added a provision allowing the enlistment of blacks in the Union army for the first time in more than half a century. Lincoln had turned to emancipation hoping to accelerate a Union victory, but he also hoped that military success would make it easier for people to accept emancipation.

But not even strict military necessity could be severed from the moral conviction of slavery's evil. The eloquent message Lincoln sent to Congress in December 1862 revealed how in his mind military and the moral rationales collapsed into one another. "The fiery trial through which we pass, will light us down, in honor or dishonor, to the latest generation," the President said. "In *giving* freedom to the *slave*, we *assure* freedom to the *free*—honorable alike in what we give, and what we preserve. We shall nobly save, or meanly lose, the last best, hope of earth." To that end Lincoln proposed a series of constitutional amendments that would resolve the legal uncertainties still hovering over military emancipation. They would guarantee the freedom of those slaves emancipated by "the chances of war." They would offer federal bonds to yet again entice the border states to free their slaves, gradually and voluntarily. To reach loyal masters in those parts of seceded states already under Union control and thus excluded from the proclamation, Lincoln proposed compensation for their emancipated slaves. Finally, he proposed federal funding for a scheme of voluntary colonization. The war powers allowed Lincoln to emancipate slaves only in those parts of the Union in rebellion against the government. The amendments he now proposed were designed to secure the freedom of every slave in the United States. It was a nice plan, but it was not very practical, and Congress would not go along with it.

Treasury Secretary Chase had warned Lincoln that Republican lawmakers were in no mood to compensate any slaveholders since by then everyone knew that slavery was on its deathbed everywhere in the Union. Lincoln knew this reasoning well; he had been warning the border states about it for months. But for him the relative conservatism of compensated emancipation took some of the radical sting out of an unavoidably revolutionary process. And he knew that the Constitution gave neither the President nor the Congress the authority to free slaves in any parts of the country that were loyal to the Union. No one could really be sure that "the chances of war" would fully undermine slavery in the border states. Indeed, until the end of the war Lincoln was not sure that emancipation was secure even in those parts of the South covered by the proclamation. After all, the British had offered freedom to escaping slaves during the American Revolution, and thousands of slaves had taken them up on the offer. But the British had lost the war, and so slavery had survived. What if the South won this war? Lincoln's innately cautious disposition, especially his meticulous concern with legal technicalities, made him less certain than most of his fellow Republicans about the ultimate fate of slavery.

Lincoln was not the only skeptic. At the time and ever since critics of the proclamation dismissed it as a paper tiger. They likened it to a papal bull against the comet. It was an empty decree, they said; it freed no one because it applied only to those areas that were not under Union control. This was always an odd criticism. No one understood better than Lincoln that the proclamation's reach depended on how effectively the Union army could enforce it. Frederick Douglass was particularly lucid on this point. All proclamations, all laws, all judicial decrees emanating from the government are "paper orders," he wrote, "and

would remain such were they not backed up by force." By order-
ing the Union army to begin practicing "hard" war, by instituting
a military draft, by enlisting black troops, and by ordering his
generals to emancipate the slaves as they swept through the
South, Lincoln was doing everything possible to ensure that the
Union used its military might to enforce his proclamation.
Indeed, emancipation itself increased the Union's firepower by
making the arrival of the army more immediately destructive.
That was the whole point. To make sure it worked this way,
Lincoln assigned several military officers to enforce military
emancipation in tandem with Union invasions. Lincoln trans-
formed the Union troops into an army of liberation.

Frederick Douglass argued that once the final proclamation
was issued all that was necessary for emancipation to take effect
was for the Union to win. If anything, Douglass seemed more
confident of a Union victory than Lincoln, and for that reason
his first response to the Emancipation Proclamation was to insist
that it would ensure the ultimate abolition of slavery. Republican
setbacks in the November elections led to some speculation that
Lincoln might not release the final proclamation on January 1.
Douglass was not worried. He wished Lincoln had issued the
proclamation sooner, he did not approve of the hundred-day
delay, but he correctly judged that having made the decision,
Abraham Lincoln was not the type of man to reverse himself.
He knew in his bones that the proclamation was a death sentence for slavery, but he did not know—nobody could—
precisely how the sentence would be carried out or how long it
would take.

So it was with a mixture of exhilaration and uncertainty that
Frederick Douglass went to Boston, to the Tremont Temple, to
celebrate the release of the proclamation on New Year's Day

1863. He thanked God for letting him live to see that day, he said, "the beginning of the end of slavery." A generation earlier the descendants of the Puritans had "deemed it a duty" to break up abolitionist meetings. Only a year before, Douglass reminded his listeners, in the very same Tremont Temple, abolitionists were mobbed and beaten by crowds who still demanded silence on the matter of slavery. Now look, he said. With freedom for the slave came freedom for all; the right to speak freely and assemble peaceably was now possible, now that slavery's end was near. He echoed Jefferson. "Error cannot safely be tolerated unless truth is free to combat it," Douglass declared, "and the only antidote for error is freedom, free speech and a free press." Across the country people were finding out "that the blacks were Americans, and that the color of a man's skin does not disqualify him from being a citizen of the United States."[23] Even so, Douglass warned, this was but a "rosy dawning." A long day's work lay ahead, beginning with raising a black army. On this too Lincoln would need some prodding.

BLACK TROOPS

Almost immediately after the firing on Fort Sumter blacks across the North began offering themselves as soldiers in state militias and the Union army, only to find their enlistments blocked by law and prejudice. As northern blacks discussed the issue among themselves, they began to argue that the North was impeding its own war effort by not taking advantage of black soldiers. They watched in frustration as slaves running for freedom to Union lines, having been encouraged to do so by some Union com-

23. *Boston Morning Journal*, January 7, 1863.

manders, were turned back by others. Black troops quickly became part of Douglass's argument for emancipation as a military necessity. Don't just free the slaves, he said. Put them in uniforms and give them guns. Transform the slaves from a bulwark of secession into agents of freedom. Do that, and the slaveholders' rebellion would be crushed all the more quickly. Yet even after the North's humiliating defeat at the First Battle of Bull Run, despite calls for ever-larger numbers of volunteers, Union policy followed northern public opinion in adamant opposition to the enlistment of blacks. Douglass considered this madness. "The national edifice is on fire! Every man who can carry a bucket of water, or remove a brick, is wanted," he declared. And yet the policy makers of the Union remained "determined that the flames shall only be extinguished by Indo-Caucasian hands." But it was northern voters, as much as northern politicians, who objected to the use of black troops. As one northern soldier put it, "We don't want to fight side by side with the nigger. We think we are a too superior race for that." For Douglass this was the kind of "stupid prejudice" that ruled the hour.[24]

Many whites feared that plantation slaves, reared to servility and dependence, were simply not ready to perform as self-disciplined troops. "Negroes—plantation negroes, at least—will never make soldiers in one generation," wrote a white missionary from South Carolina.[25] To many northerners, among them Abraham Lincoln, it was hard to believe that men raised in fear and trembling could exhibit the courage and self-confidence necessary for good soldiering. However misguided this argu-

24. James M. McPherson, *The Negro's Civil War: How American Negroes Felt and Acted During the War for the Union* (New York, 1965, 1967), pp. 162–63.
25. Ibid., p. 164.

ment was, it was not the same as the racist assertion that innately inferior blacks could *never* make good soldiers. The racists held out no hope for the future. But those who feared that plantation slaves might not make good soldiers were increasingly happy to be proved wrong.

Lincoln was afraid, he said in September 1862, that if blacks were armed, "in a few weeks the arms would be in the hands of the rebels." He was also restrained by his concern to hold on to whites in the border states. To "arm the negroes," he said at one point, "would turn 50,000 bayonets from the loyal Border States against us that were for us."[26] But even as he said these things, Lincoln was beginning to change his mind. Both remarks were made in those critical months between his first drafting of the preliminary Emancipation Proclamation and his release of the final document on January 1, 1863. By then more and more northerners were warming to the idea of black soldiers. Union military reverses and war-weariness had led to a troubling decline in white enlistments. Then, too, emancipation itself changed the logic of the situation. As northern voters grew comfortable with the prospect of black freedom, it made more sense to enlist blacks in a war for their own emancipation. Congress reflected this shift in public opinion. During the summer of 1862 the lawmakers included a clause in the Second Confiscation Act authorizing Lincoln to enlist as many black soldiers as he deemed necessary to put down the southern rebellion. At the same time Congress repealed the discriminatory provision of the 1792 Militia Act that had barred blacks from serving in the army.

By the end of the year Lincoln had changed his mind as well.

26. *CW,* vol. 5, p. 357.

Shortly before he issued the final proclamation, he instructed the War Department to begin recruiting black soldiers. When he issued the final proclamation he publicly authorized the enlistment of blacks. Within months Lincoln had become a full-throated convert to the cause of black enlistment. In a March 26, 1863, letter to Governor Andrew Johnson of Tennessee Lincoln wrote that the "colored population is the great *available* and yet *unavailed* of, force for restoring the Union." The same number he had only recently used to indicate his suspicion of black troops now entered Lincoln's writing as an expression of his newfound enthusiasm. "The bare sight of fifty thousand armed, and drilled black soldiers upon the banks of the Mississippi, would end the rebellion at once," he wrote.[27]

Lincoln had good reason to change his mind. By early 1863 favorable reports of the performance of black troops began filtering back to Washington and into the northern press. The President read them with growing enthusiasm. And having converted to the cause, Lincoln became convinced that there was a psychological as well as a purely military advantage to enlisting blacks in the Union army. "It is important to the enemy that such a force shall *not* take shape, and grow, and thrive, in the South," he explained to General David Hunter, "and in precisely the same proportion, it is important to us that it *shall*."[28] Frederick Douglass had been saying the same thing since the war began.

Not surprisingly, Douglass threw himself wholeheartedly into the campaign to promote the enlistment of blacks as soon as the proclamation took effect. Throughout the first half of 1863 Douglass traveled the North, telling black audiences that it was

27. Ibid., pp. 149–50.
28. Ibid., p. 158.

their moral obligation to fight for the Union. Even the discrimination black soldiers suffered in the army—lower pay, conde-
scending white officers, little prospect of promotion to the
officer corps, relegation to menial tasks and garrison duty—did
not dissuade Douglass from urging blacks to fight. "Young men
of Philadelphia, you are without excuse," Douglass said in one
speech. "The hour has arrived, and your place is in the Union
army."[29] He acknowledged the discrimination, he protested
against it, but for Douglass this did not justify anyone's refusal to
enlist. The destruction of slavery was too great a cause.

But although northern public opinion was shifting, it was
not nearly as enthusiastic about black troops as were Douglass
and the President. This was particularly true of whites in the
army, soldiers and officers alike. Notwithstanding favorable initial reports, black troops had not yet participated in any serious
battles. Then, beginning in late spring of 1863, black soldiers
proved themselves in three widely reported engagements. At
Port Hudson in southern Louisiana, on May 27, two regiments
made up of free blacks from New Orleans and freed slaves
from nearby plantations marched heroically into the face of
Confederate artillery fire in an effort to dislodge the enemy
fortification. The attack itself failed but the behavior of the
troops impressed everyone who witnessed it. Official reports
claimed that the battle at Port Hudson should lay to rest any
lingering doubts about whether blacks could fight effectively.
Less than two weeks later there were similar reports of courageous black troops who drove back a Confederate bayonet
charge at Milliken's Bend on the Mississippi River north of
Vicksburg. The assistant secretary of war, Charles Dana, wrote

29. *FDP,* ser. I, vol. 3, p. 597.

that "the bravery of the blacks in the battle of Milliken's Bend completely revolutionized the sentiment of the army with regard to the employment of negro troops."[30] Most impressive of all was the July 18 assault on Fort Wagner, at the entrance to Charleston Harbor, by the Fifty-fourth Regiment, a unit recruited primarily from free blacks in Massachusetts. In the face of murderous Confederate fire the black soldiers advanced relentlessly on the fort. A huge proportion of the regiment fell in the battle, and when white troops failed to come to their aid, the Fifty-fourth was forced to retreat. But the extraordinary heroism of the soldiers' behavior resounded throughout the North. Lincoln's enthusiasm was vindicated.

But by then Douglass was having his doubts. The problem was not only discrimination, though Douglass strongly protested against it. More specifically, he was upset by Lincoln's failure to respond aggressively to the South's refusal to treat captured black soldiers as prisoners of war. Instead the Confederacy defined them as insurrectionists, the punishment for whom was execution or enslavement. But more worrisome than the official policy, which southern officials enforced irregularly and with some reluctance, was the violent behavior of southern troops in the field. There were reports of several brutal massacres of black soldiers by Confederate troops. Douglass wanted Lincoln to respond in kind. "For every black prisoner slain in cold blood, Mr. Jefferson Davis should be made to understand that one rebel officer shall suffer death," Douglass wrote. Although he complained vehemently about Lincoln's refusal to address the issue—"What has he said?" Douglass demanded. "Not one word"—his tone was notably less harsh than it had been a year

30. McPherson, *Negro's Civil War*, p. 187.

earlier.[31] After all, by the summer of 1863 Lincoln had already committed himself to emancipation and had become an enthusiastic supporter of black enlistment. And so, at the urging of his friend George Stearns, Douglass "was induced to go to Washington and lay the complaints of my people" directly before the President.[32] Abraham Lincoln and Frederick Douglass were about to meet for the first time.

31. *Douglass' Monthly*, Aug. 1863.

32. Frederick Douglass, *Life and Times of Frederick Douglass*, intro. Rayford Logan (New York, 1881; rev. ed., 1892; repr., New York, 1962), p. 346.

"MY FRIEND DOUGLASS"

In July 1863 the fortunes of war tipped decisively in favor of the Union. After months of searching for a general who would fight Lee's army, Lincoln was at last able to savor two great military victories. For three days at the beginning of July Union troops successfully fought off Lee's second invasion of the North, at Gettysburg, Pennsylvania, sending the Confederate army scurrying back to Virginia in disastrous defeat. Out in the West, meanwhile, Ulysses Grant's troops captured the city of Vicksburg, Mississippi, after a long siege, giving the Union uninterrupted control of the entire Mississippi River. Northern morale soared. The Confederacy never recovered from the devastating losses.

That same month, northern opposition to the war reached a dramatic climax. Ever since the beginning of the year the uproar against emancipation, against black troops, and against the draft had been swelling through the North. Antiwar rioters swept through the streets in several cities, assaulting and murdering innocent blacks. The largest and most notorious of the draft riots paralyzed New York City for three full days in late July. But the New York riots disgraced the antiwar movement; thereafter it restricted itself to legitimate political opposition. Sensing the depth of popular outrage against the rioters, Lincoln seized the moment and on July 30 issued an Order of Retaliation aimed at halting Confederate abuse of black prisoners of war. For every captured Union soldier killed by the Confederacy Lincoln ordered a rebel soldier executed. For every Union soldier enslaved or sold into slavery by the Confederates "a rebel soldier shall be placed at hard labor" and shall remain there until the Union soldier was released and treated as a proper prisoner of war.[1]

With northern morale buoyed by the Union's greatest victories, with black soldiers having proved themselves in battle even as antiwar violence peaked, Frederick Douglass made his first trip to Washington, D.C. A year earlier he would have gone into print or taken to the speaker's platform to voice his grievances. But a lot had happened since the summer of 1862, and Douglass was now satisfied enough with the Lincoln administration to choose a different course.

THE FIRST MEETING

In the early-morning hours of August 10, 1863, Douglass walked from his hotel to the office of Samuel C. Pomeroy, the senator

1. *CW*, vol. 6, p. 357.

from Kansas. Pomeroy quickly offered to serve as Douglass's escort, easing his access to the men he most wanted to see. First was Edwin Stanton, the secretary of war. Douglass found Stanton "cold and business-like"—Stanton was that way with everybody—but sympathetic to Douglass's concerns. They talked for half an hour. Douglass argued that heroes and cowards were distributed equally among blacks and whites, that the administration's policy should assume no distinction at all between black and white troops—in pay, uniforms, rations, and opportunities for promotion. Stanton told Douglass that he supported equal treatment for all soldiers, that he had sent a bill to that effect to Congress, but that the Senate had refused to pass it. Stanton also said that he believed in promotion by merit and would sign off on any commission recommended to him by superior officers. He offered Douglass himself a commission as an assistant to General Lorenzo Thomas, who "was now rigorously engaged in organizing Colored Troops on the Mississippi."[2]

2. My account of the first meeting is based on the following sources. Frederick Douglass to George L. Stearns, August 12, 1863. The letter to Stearns, two days after the White House visit, is the earliest and—I assume, therefore—the most reliable of the several descriptions Douglass left of his first meeting with Lincoln. My own account takes the Stearns letter as the baseline but adds material from Douglass's later accounts. On December 3, 1863, Douglass included a general description of the meeting and his initial impressions of Lincoln in a speech delivered at a convention of the American Anti-Slavery Society in Philadelphia. The text is in *FDP*, ser. I, vol. 3, pp. 606–8. Douglass's most detailed account, though far removed from the event and thus less reliable, was in the last of his three autobiographies, first published in 1881 and revised eleven years later. See Frederick Douglass, *Life and Times of Frederick Douglass*, intro. Rayford Logan (New York, 1881; rev. ed., 1892; repr. New York, 1962), pp. 347–49. In 1888 Douglass contributed a chapter to Allen Thorndike Rice, *Reminiscences of Abraham Lincoln* (New York, 1888), pp. 185–95. This last reminiscence is vague, collapses several different conversations into one, and adds no new information. Lincoln himself left no account of the meeting. His secretary, John Hay, made a

Stanton was not trying to flatter Douglass, but he may have been trying to get rid of him. For whatever reason, the commission he promised Douglass never came.

From the War Department Douglass and Pomeroy went directly to the White House. The senatorial escort may have smoothed the way, though Douglass was by then far more prominent than the senator from Kansas. Even so, the degree to which Lincoln made himself available to visitors is astonishing; if nothing else, it reveals how far removed his was from the imperial presidency that emerged in the twentieth century. But the President's openness also reflected his personality. Lincoln was an unpretentious man as well as a hand-clasping politician. By neither instinct nor desire did he seal himself off from the public. Douglass was but one of hundreds who got to meet with Lincoln during his four years in the White House. Still, not everyone got in. When he arrived Douglass found a large crowd of applicants lining the stairway, hoping for a moment with the chief executive. Douglass expected to wait for some time. Instead he submitted his card and within minutes one of Lincoln's assistants appeared, called out, "Mr. Douglass," and escorted him upstairs. "Yes, damn it," someone grumbled as Douglass elbowed his way past the waiting crowd, "I knew they would let the nigger through."

It was immediately evident that this was not going to be a quick, staged event in the President's office. Lincoln was at work in a simply furnished room upstairs, papers scattered every-

---

brief reference to it in his diary confirming some of the substance of Douglass's August 12 letter to Stearns. For providing me with a copy of the indispensable Stearns letter I am greatly indebted to Professor John R. McKivigan, editor of the Frederick Douglass Papers.

where. There was no hint of formality in either the man or his surroundings. Douglass found Lincoln stretched out on a sofa reading, his long legs reaching into "different parts of the room." As soon as he entered, "the President began to rise, and continued to rise until he stood over me." Lincoln reached out to shake Douglass's hand. "Mr. Douglass, I know you," he said. "I have read about you, and Mr. Seward has told me about you."

He quickly put Douglass at ease. "There was not the slightest shadow of embarrassment from the first moment." The President received me, Douglass said, "just as you have seen one gentleman receive another." For all his earlier criticism, Lincoln had always struck Douglass as a fundamentally honest man and the meeting confirmed that impression. "I have never seen a more transparent countenance," Douglass wrote.

Douglass began by thanking Lincoln for issuing the recent Order of Retaliation for the Confederate abuse of black prisoners, hinting perhaps that it was about time. But at that point, a rare one for a man so loquacious and opinionated, Douglass preferred to hear what Lincoln had to say.

Lincoln jumped at Douglass's tacit invitation, an equally rare move for a man so famously "shut-mouthed" and deliberate in his choice of words. With "an earnestness and a fluency of which I had not suspected him," Douglass recalled, the President proceeded "to vindicate his policy respecting the whole slavery question and especially that in reference to employing colored troops." Lincoln was particularly concerned to refute two charges often made by his radical critics, including Douglass. The first was that Lincoln took too long to make decisions, that he was "tardy" and "hesitating" about emancipation or about the enlistment of black troops.

But you were "somewhat slow" to issue the Order of Retaliation, Douglass chided the President.

Lincoln replied that the "country needed talking up to on that point." He had hesitated to embark on such a policy when he thought that "the country was not ready for it." Blacks were widely despised in America, Lincoln said, and if he ordered retaliation too quickly, "all the hatred which is poured on the head of the Negro race would be visited on his [Lincoln's] administration." Had he issued the order any sooner, Lincoln said, "such was the state of popular prejudice that an outcry would have been raised against the measure. It would be said—'Ah! we thought it would come to this. White men were to be killed for negroes.'" There was "preparatory work" to be done. "Remember this, Mr. Douglass," Lincoln added, Port Hudson, Milliken's Bend, and Fort Wagner "are recent events; and . . . these were necessary to prepare the way" for the policy of retaliation.

If we can credit Douglass's autobiographical account of the meeting, published almost twenty years later, Lincoln disliked the very idea of retaliation. He said that it was "a terrible remedy," that "it was very difficult to apply—that, if once begun, there was no telling where it would end—that if he could get hold of the Confederate soldiers who had been guilty of treating colored soldiers as felons he could easily retaliate, but the thought of hanging men for a crime perpetrated by others was revolting to his feelings. He thought that the rebels themselves would stop such barbarous warfare—that less evil would be done if retaliation were not resorted to."[3]

3. Douglass's 1881 account is ambiguous on this point and has created some confusion. It reads as though Douglass was still hoping for Lincoln to order retaliation, when in fact the order had been issued ten days earlier. Lincoln in turn appeared to be questioning a policy he had already adopted. Douglass did not mention this in his two earlier accounts of the meeting. The simplest explanation is that twenty years later Douglass simply misremembered the details. On the other hand, it would not have

Years later Douglass remembered having raised the issue of equal pay for black and white soldiers as well as more opportunities for black soldiers of proven ability to earn promotions. Lincoln's answer, as recorded by Douglass, is suspiciously precise for an eighteen-year-old memory. But it is perfectly plausible that Douglass would have raised the issue—he had been speaking out against such discrimination for months—and the reply he puts into Lincoln's mouth is likewise in character. It confirms how sensitive Lincoln was to the racial prejudices of white Americans, even if he himself did not share those prejudices. Stanton had told Douglass that he would sign off on promotions for any black soldiers recommended to him by their superior officers; Lincoln in turn promised that he would "sign any commission" for a black officer that Stanton recommended to him. But on the matter of equal pay, Douglass remembered that Lincoln's answer was more expansive.

> He began by saying that the employment of colored troops at all was a great gain to the colored people—that the measure could not have been successfully adopted at the beginning of the war—that the wisdom of making colored men soldiers was still doubted—that their enlistment was a serious offense to popular prejudice—that they had larger motives for being soldiers than white men—that they ought to be willing to enter the service

---

been out of character for Lincoln to decry the necessity of a retaliation policy that he thought he had to adopt but was still reluctant to enforce. If so, Douglass's autobiographical account was not so much mistaken as unclear. In any case, Douglass recalled being impressed by Lincoln's resistance to retaliation. In it Douglass "saw the tender heart of the man rather than the stern warrior . . . and, while I could not agree with him, I could but respect his humane spirit." Douglass, *Life and Times*, pp. 347–49.

upon any condition——that the fact that they were not to receive the same pay as white soldiers seemed a necessary concession to smooth the way to their employment at all as soldiers, but that ultimately they would receive the same.[4]

Lincoln had often admitted that his concern to prevent a popular backlash sometimes caused him to move slowly, in this case more slowly than Douglass would have liked. But the President was not willing to admit the validity of another line of criticism about his policies: that he vacillated. This he flatly denied.

"I think the charge cannot be sustained," Lincoln insisted. "No man can say that having once taken the position I have contradicted it or retreated from it."

For Douglass this was "the best thing" Lincoln had to say. It was the President's way of assuring Douglass "that whoever else might abandon his anti-slavery policy President Lincoln would stand firm to his." Because of Lincoln's assurance, Douglass left the meeting more certain than ever that "slavery would not survive the war and that the Country would survive both slavery and the War."

Douglass was impressed. Not because he was persuaded by all of Lincoln's answers: He could not countenance the idea that the President had to tailor his policies so as not to rankle prevailing racial prejudices, no matter how politically necessary Lincoln believed it to be. Rather, Douglass was struck by the patience with which the President listened, the sincerity and humaneness of his replies, and the decency with which he treated a longtime critic. Abraham Lincoln, Douglass concluded, although "wise, great and eloquent," will nevertheless "go down to posterity, if the country

4. Ibid., p. 348.

is saved, as Honest Abraham." Throughout the world his name will be spoken "side by side" with that of Washington.[5]

But as always with Douglass, there was still more to be done. Not even the greatest captain can rescue a beleaguered ship on his own. If Lincoln was to succeed, if the country was to be saved, it was up to the crew to pitch in. Emancipation had been declared. Black troops had been enlisted. Retaliation had been proclaimed. But these were battles in a war that had yet to be won, skirmishes in a revolution that was still incomplete. The Confederacy had to be defeated, surely, but just as surely emancipation had to be secured.

REDEFINING THE UNION

Lincoln never stopped saying that his first priority was to restore the Union. Douglass was suspicious of such talk; it sounded too much like those calls for compromise that would guarantee slavery's future. But it meant something different for Lincoln. He thought slavery was an anomaly in a Union founded on the principle of universal freedom. A Union with slavery was inherently unstable, a house so divided against itself that it could not stand that way forever. So when he called for the restoration of the Union, Lincoln did not necessarily imagine the restoration of slavery as well. For Lincoln the Union, properly understood, was incompatible with slavery, and he began to say so very early in his presidency.

This was "essentially a People's contest," Lincoln declared in his first major statement after the inauguration, a special message to Congress on July 4, 1861. The Union the North was struggling to maintain was a rare and important form of government, he

5. *FDP*, ser. 1, vol. 3, p. 608.

said, a form whose "leading object, is to elevate the condition of men—to lift artificial weights from all shoulders—to clear the paths of laudable pursuit for all—to afford all, an unfettered start, and a fair chance, in the race of life."[6] Lincoln had used similar language often during the 1850s. Slavery was evil, he said, because it deprived blacks of their equal right to the fruits of their labor. Now he was saying that the very same right was the "leading object" of the Union he was struggling to preserve. There was no place for slavery in a Union such as that.

Later that year Lincoln elaborated on the argument in his most successful outing into the thicket of political economy. In his first annual message to Congress he set about to answer the "mudsill" theory of some of slavery's defenders, the theory that defined labor as naturally and necessarily inferior to capital. Because capital is nothing more than the fruit of human labor, Lincoln answered, labor is in fact superior to capital and must necessarily be so. Under a "just and generous" system of government, such as prevailed in the North, those who begin their adult lives working for wages have every opportunity to advance to economic independence. Freedom thus "opens the way to all—gives hope to all, and consequent energy, and progress, and improvement of condition to all."[7] Once again Lincoln spoke of freedom as universal, something that applied to all and thereby gave hope to all. It was the very opposite of slavery. This made it easy for Lincoln to continue to claim, even after the Emancipation Proclamation, that his first goal was to restore the Union, for the Union of which he dreamed was the home of universal liberty. In the months and years that followed Lincoln

6. *CW*, vol. 4, p. 438.
7. Ibid., vol. 5, p. 52.

became more explicit about this: The restored nation would be a Union without slavery. But he also abandoned the emphasis on economic opportunity that had crept into his speeches between 1859 and 1861. Instead he returned to the core principle of fundamental human equality that had animated his great antislavery speeches in the 1850s. Nobody since Jefferson himself had invested such eloquence in the ideal of human equality, and Lincoln never more so than in November 1863 at Gettysburg.

The founders, Lincoln said, had set out to establish a nation "conceived in Liberty and dedicated to the proposition that all men are created equal." A nation without slavery: That, Lincoln said, is what this civil war is all about. For that the soldiers buried beneath them at Gettysburg had given their lives. It was "the cause for which they gave their last full measure of devotion." But their work was unfinished. It was left to the living—"we here"—to complete their work by resolving "that this nation shall have a new birth of freedom—and that government of the people, by the people, for the people, shall not perish from the earth." America reborn, a nation redeemed, could now stand before the world, Lincoln said only a few months later, as "the home of freedom disenthralled, regenerated, enlarged, and perpetuated."[8] The "new birth of freedom" was genuinely new; the restored Union would not be a mere duplicate of its antebellum predecessor.

CONSOLIDATING THE REVOLUTION

In choosing a battlefield, Gettysburg, to reassert the highest ideals of the Union, Lincoln could make no starker demonstration of the intermingled fates of slavery and the war. By late 1863 he firmly

8. Ibid., vol. 7, pp. 22, 53.

believed that emancipation would help end the war more quickly. Reviewing the remarkable events of the year, he recalled how tenacious the rebellion had seemed only twelve months before. The army had been bogged down, commerce had stalled, and European states were threatening to recognize the Confederacy. But the proclamation turned everything around. "The policy of emancipation, and of employing black soldiers, gave to the future a new aspect," Lincoln said. One hundred thousand former slaves were already serving in the U.S. military, and "it is difficult to say they are not as good soldiers as any." And thanks to the decisive military victories of the summer there was no longer any prospect that a major European state would intervene or recognize the Confederacy. Moreover, emancipation, once proclaimed, was quickly proving impossible to restrict to the disloyal South. By late 1863 Lincoln saw evidence of an abolition juggernaut pressing inexorably into areas well beyond the proclamation's reach. "Influential citizens" in Tennessee and Arkansas, "owners of slaves and advocates of slavery at the beginning of the rebellion, now declare openly for emancipation in their respective States." Maryland and Missouri, jealous to protect slavery only months before, "only dispute now as to the best mode of removing it within their own limits."[9] This was not quite the scenario that either Lincoln or Douglass had imagined earlier in the war. Lincoln had hoped a voluntary emancipation in the border states would propel the destruction of both slavery and the Confederacy. Douglass had thought that forcing emancipation on the border states would do the same thing. But it happened the other way around: It took military emancipation in the Confederacy to force voluntary emancipation onto the border states. No matter. By the end of 1863

9. Ibid., pp. 49–50.

Lincoln was pleased to report to Congress on the progress of both war and emancipation.

But even as he was reviewing the past, Lincoln was forced to look ahead. Southern Louisiana had come under Union control the year before and Lincoln pressed his generals, first Benjamin Butler and then Nathaniel Banks, to begin the reconstruction process. Lincoln saw this as an extension of the war and thus the President's responsibility, but Congress was itching to put its own stamp on the process. In an attempt to preempt the legislators Lincoln issued a Proclamation of General Amnesty and Reconstruction, laying out his tentative plan for bringing the defeated southern states back into the Union. Lincoln would pardon most Confederates, excluding high civil and military officials, those who had resigned civil or military positions in the Union to support the Confederacy, and anyone who had participated in the abuse of Union prisoners of war, specifically including black prisoners of war. Those who qualified for amnesty would be required to swear an oath of loyalty to the United States and to uphold that oath in practice. To such persons Lincoln promised the restoration of property, "except as to slaves." When 10 percent of the state's electorate, measured by the number of those who had legally voted in the 1860 presidential election, had sworn the loyalty oath, those persons would be permitted to organize a new state government that conformed to the requirements of the U.S. Constitution. This was the so-called 10-Percent Plan. In addition to its formal requirements, Lincoln suggested that the new state governments legally recognize the "permanent freedom" of the slaves, provide for their education, and establish, if necessary, a "temporary arrangement" for putting the freed slaves back to work. This was an oblique reference to the disreputable Banks Plan, under which freed people were forced to sign contracts and return to work for their former masters.[10]

In both his annual message to Congress and his reconstruction plan Lincoln addressed the troubling question of the legal status of men and women who had been freed as an act of war. What would happen to them when the war ended? To ensure that presidential proclamations of freedom survived the peace, Lincoln said that "there had to be a pledge for their maintenance" from the returning southern states. In addition, thousands of slaves serving in the U.S. military had run to Union lines from parts of the South not covered by the second Confiscation Act or the Emancipation Proclamation. They "have aided, and will further aid," in the restoration of the Union, Lincoln said. "To now abandon them would be not only to relinquish a lever of power, but would also be a cruel and an astounding breach of faith." It was for this reason—to ensure the freedom of emancipated blacks—that Lincoln's plan required adherence to provisions of the Emancipation Proclamation as a precondition for readmission to the Union. And what about those who remained enslaved, those not technically covered by the proclamation itself? Besides continuing to press the border states to emancipate the slaves on their own, Lincoln urged Congress to enact any measure that would facilitate the final and complete emancipation of every slave in America.[11]

Primarily because of its provision for making emancipation permanent, Lincoln's plan for reconstruction satisfied most Republicans, including the radicals. But it did not satisfy the freed people of Louisiana, who resented being sent back to the harsh

10. Ibid., pp. 54–55.
11. Ibid., p. 51.

labor regime of their former masters. Nor did it satisfy the large and vocal Free Colored community of New Orleans, whose members wanted to vote and participate in the reconstruction of the state. As a result, Lincoln's plan angered several Republican radicals and many abolitionists. They thought that requiring only 10 percent of the rebels to swear a loyalty oath was too lenient, that General Banks's labor system was too harsh, and that the absence of voting rights for blacks was an outrage. Among those who were upset, none was more so than Frederick Douglass.

Lincoln spelled out his plans in December 1863; in January Douglass resumed his criticism of the President. At Gettysburg the President had eloquently invoked "our Fathers" to reassert the founding principle of fundamental human equality. Douglass now turned that language back against Lincoln to demand racial equality along with abolition. Slavery "had received its death-blow when our fathers—I say *our* fathers—emphatically declared that all men were created equal." But the founders' hopes were foiled by a long history of compromise by those who refused to treat blacks and whites as equals. In the government's continued failure to pay black soldiers or to promote them equally with whites Douglass saw the egalitarian legacy of the American Revolution insulted once more. So hostile was Douglass to the merest recognition of racial distinction that he objected even to the word *white* in laws passed by Congress. "I dread that word," Douglass declared. "It is unlike nature, it is unlike God." Looking beyond emancipation, Douglass demanded "the complete, absolute, unqualified enfranchisement of the colored people of the South."[12] Nothing else, he argued, would protect the freed people from the vengeance of their former masters.

12. *FDP*, ser. 1, vol. 4, pp. 25–30.

In January 1863 Douglass had said that the Emancipation Proclamation made the abolition of slavery inevitable—but not necessarily right away. One year later he reiterated his concern. The proclamation had been indispensable and praiseworthy, but by itself "it settles nothing." This was true, and no one understood the problem better than Lincoln himself. But Douglass also claimed to "detest the motive and principle" upon which the proclamation was based, for it implied that "the holding and flogging of Negroes is the exclusive luxury of loyal men." Douglass had not always been hostile to the "motive and principle" of the Emancipation Proclamation; once upon a time "military necessity" had struck him as a compelling rationale. Now he was confusing the legal basis of emancipation with the moral imperative behind it, a mistake he had accused others of making only a year earlier. He had his reasons: As 1864 opened, he was fighting another fight—this time to secure voting rights for emancipated slaves, a struggle that mattered a good deal more to Douglass than the intellectual consistency of his arguments from one year to the next.[13] He even revived his sarcasm about those who would carry on the war "within the limits of the Constitution."[14] This was not the rhetoric of someone who had taken an oath to uphold the Constitution. It was the polemical strategy of a reformer.

Yet Douglass was by now sufficiently attuned to political realities to tone down his criticism in public. There were no such restraints when he talked privately among his fellow abolitionists. Douglass outdid himself in an astonishing letter he sent to an English correspondent in June 1864. He denounced

13. Ibid., pp. 9, 12–13.
14. Ibid., p. 13.

Lincoln in the most vehement terms he had ever used. He complained once more about the unequal treatment of black soldiers. He assailed Lincoln's lenient plans for Reconstruction, especially his failure to support black voting rights in Louisiana. In an especially intemperate outburst Douglass characterized Lincoln's position as *"Do evil by choice, right from necessity."* None of his complaints had to do with emancipation as such; all of them had to do with racial equality. Blacks were good enough to fight for the government, Douglass wrote his friend, but not good enough to vote for the government. The government had invited slaves to rebel against their former masters, to take up arms against their former masters, thereby infuriating their former masters, and now the government expected the freed people to subject themselves to the political authority of their former masters. Lincoln's reconstruction policy was as good as sending sheep to their slaughter. *"No rebuke of it can be too strong from your side of the water,"* Douglass advised.[15]

Grant that this was a private letter with words Douglass would not have used in public. Grant also that this was one radical talking shop with another, saying things he would not dare put into print. Still, he said it. The question is why? What could possibly explain this sudden eruption of hostility on Douglass's part? Curiously enough, Douglass was playing politics.

THE ELECTION OF 1864

As the 1864 presidential election year got under way, a handful of radical Republicans began working behind the scenes to deny Lincoln their party's renomination and replace him with someone more firmly committed to their agenda. Lincoln's treasury secretary, Salmon P. Chase, trusted by the radicals for no good reason, was hoping to win the nomination for himself. Another candidate with even shakier radical credentials, John C. Frémont, ran openly against Lincoln. But Frémont's candidacy was designed chiefly to split the party's vote, thereby opening the way for Chase. Douglass took sides. He reopened his indictment of Lincoln's failures, hoping to replace the President with a more reliably radical Republican. In effect, Douglass had plunged himself into the nineteenth-century equivalent of a primary campaign. For the first time in his life Frederick Douglass was beginning to behave like a calculating politician, although not necessarily a skillful one.

Douglass knew perfectly well that Lincoln was not the most threatening political prospect of 1864. His real fear was the Democrats. They were gearing up for a campaign of unrelieved racial invective. They were claiming Lincoln's decision to free the slaves had unnecessarily prolonged the war. "Peace Democrats" in particular wanted to offer the South a restoration of the Union that would leave slavery in place wherever it still existed. Naturally Douglass was horrified by the prospect. "While the Democratic party is in existence," he said at the beginning of the year, "we are in danger of a slaveholding peace, and of Rebel rule."[16] Faced with the possibility of a Democratic victory, Douglass convinced himself that the Republicans had to nominate someone with a sturdier antislavery backbone. Notwithstanding the faith he had recently expressed in Lincoln's unwavering commitment to emancipation, Douglass now professed to fear "a slaveholding compromise" that would end the

16. *FDP*, ser I, vol. 4, p. 11.

war before the war ended slavery. To prevent that from happening he joined forces with those hoping to replace Abraham
Lincoln as the Republican Party's presidential nominee.

There was never much doubt that Lincoln would be that
party's candidate. He was widely popular among Republicans.
Leading party radicals like Charles Sumner supported Lincoln's
renomination, and even abolitionists were split over the move to
replace him. At the annual meeting of the Massachusetts Anti-
Slavery Society in early 1864, Wendell Phillips put forward a
resolution denouncing the government for pursuing a "sham
peace" that would leave the former slaves at the mercy of their
former masters. But William Lloyd Garrison argued that radicals had a moral obligation to support Lincoln's reelection.
Moreover, Lincoln was now popular even among black northerners. In 1860 they had been suspicious of the Republicans and
largely indifferent to Lincoln. Four years later Lincoln drew
strong support from black leaders and editors.

There was never any danger that Lincoln or the Republicans
would compromise with slavery, certainly not by 1864, if not
much sooner. Once Lincoln had skillfully lined up all the votes he
needed to flick away Chase's bungling challenge and secure his
renomination, the only active role Lincoln took in the Republican
Party's convention was to insist that the platform endorse a constitutional amendment abolishing slavery everywhere in the
United States. The convention assembled in Baltimore on June 7
and gave Lincoln what he asked for. A few weeks afterward
Lincoln accepted Chase's resignation, but later appointed him to
the Supreme Court, where he replaced the hated Roger B. Taney.
With two strokes Lincoln removed an irritant from his cabinet
and put him where he could do the most good by upholding the
constitutionality of wartime emancipation.

Douglass had to know from the start how quixotic the effort to remove Lincoln was. But even if he took the move seriously, there was something different about 1864: He was engaged in a struggle for power *within* the Republican Party. He renewed his criticism of Lincoln in January, when the effort to replace him first got under way. But after Lincoln had secured the Republican nomination and—even more important—after the Democrats had nominated George B. McClellan as their presidential candidate in late August, Douglass made it clear that he strongly favored Lincoln's reelection. This was a far cry from 1860, when Douglass had withdrawn his support for Lincoln and voted instead for a radical third-party candidate. For all the venom he spilled on Lincoln in the first six months of 1864, Douglass was now maneuvering within the Republican Party, something he had never done before.

But all such maneuvering was a minor distraction beside the very real threat Lincoln and the Republicans faced in 1864, the Democratic Party's ability to exploit rising war-weariness in the North. It was bad enough that the war went on and on. But in the spring and early summer of 1864 Grant and Lee had squared off in Virginia in a series of unspeakably bloody battles that shocked civilians and shook Lincoln terribly. Every day northerners opened their morning papers to find a long new list of the names of soldiers killed and wounded in action. But beyond the sheer volume of blood shed there was the apparent senselessness of it all. No real ground was taken; neither army seemed on the verge of surrender; the battles augured no new prospect of peace. Morale plummeted, and the Democrats jumped at their chance. They launched a relentless assault on Lincoln's handling of the war, in particular his decision to fuse the restoration of the Union to the emancipation of the slaves.

Frederick Douglass himself became a minor issue in the campaign when Democrats publicized the meeting he had with Lincoln the previous year. The American Anti-Slavery Society had printed the text of Douglass's December 3 address, with its brief but glowing account of his visit to the White House. The Democrats seized on Douglass's words, churning them back in a pamphlet entitled *Miscegenation Indorsed by the Republican Party*, published at the height of the presidential election campaign. Thus was coined a repulsive new word, *miscegenation*. The Democrats took particular note of Douglass's claim that the President had received him "as one gentlemen receives another." This kind of thing made a lot of Republicans cower in fear and their cowering made Douglass nervous. He still equated racial prejudice with the defense of slavery. "While a respectable colored man or woman can be kicked out of the commonest street car in New York—where any white ruffian may ride unquestioned—we are in danger of a compromise with slavery."[17] If the Republicans were soft on racism, Douglass reasoned, they had to be soft on slavery as well. It was something he always suspected about Abraham Lincoln.

But this time Lincoln did not flinch. At that very moment, when the Democrats were ruthlessly hounding him for having met with the notorious Frederick Douglass, Lincoln invited Douglass to the White House for a second meeting.

THE SECOND MEETING, AUGUST 25, 1864

Douglass found Lincoln in an "alarmed" state, disturbed by the calls for a negotiated peace sounded not only by Democrats but by moderates in Lincoln's own party. Even Horace Greeley, a

17. Ibid., p. 21.

strong advocate of emancipation, was calling on Lincoln to bro-
ker a speedy end of the war by sending emissaries to Niagara
Falls to meet with representatives of the Confederacy. Lincoln
had issued a public letter making it clear that he would not consider any restoration of the Union that did not also include the
complete emancipation of the slaves. That letter had provoked
another wave of Democratic denunciations of Lincoln, but even
skittish Republicans were pressuring the President to reverse
himself. That Lincoln would not do, but he was considering issuing a public statement clarifying his position. In it Lincoln suggested that it would be impossible for him to wage a war purely
for the purpose of abolition; the public would not stand for it,
and Congress would not authorize it. He showed Douglass a
draft of the statement and asked whether it should be publicized. No, Douglass said. It would be misconstrued, by friends
and enemies alike, as an indication that Lincoln was not as committed to emancipation as he actually was. Lincoln did not publish the letter.[18]

But there was another reason for asking Douglass to the
White House. Lincoln was afraid that if the Republicans lost the
election there would be no constitutional amendment abolishing
slavery in the United States. If the Democrats won, they would
swiftly negotiate a peace that might leave millions of blacks
enslaved. As of August 1864, the only legal basis for emancipation
in the Confederate states was Lincoln's proclamation, the force
of which rested on the willingness of the slaves to run for their
freedom to Union lines. Several hundred thousand slaves had
already done just that, but they constituted no more than 10 or
15 percent of all the slaves in the Confederate South. Lincoln was

18. *Life & Writings*, vol. 3, pp. 422–23.

fairly certain that slaves already freed could not be reenslaved, but he could not be sure about the millions still on farms and plantations across the South. Emancipation was not inevitable after all.

"The slaves are not coming so rapidly and so numerously to us as I had hoped," Lincoln told Douglass.[19]

The masters had ways to keep news of the proclamation away from slaves, Douglass pointed out.

"Well," Lincoln said, "I want you to set about devising some means of making them acquainted with it, and for bringing them into our lines." Douglass quickly agreed to organize a band of black scouts to move through the southern states, informing the slaves of their emancipation.

Douglass was bemused by Lincoln's request that he spread word of emancipation throughout the slave South. It reminded him of "the original plan of John Brown." Actually it was closer to the opposite. Disdainful of politics and politicians, Brown imagined that he could overthrow slavery by launching an attack on a federal arsenal. With no political or military support Brown's invasion was doomed before it began. Five years later it was the U.S. government that was attacking slavery. Lincoln was using his skills as a politician and his authority as commander in chief to impose emancipation on the rebel states. Douglass's group was supposed to move through the South acting on behalf of the U.S. government. They would spread the word among the slaves that the President had issued an Emancipation Proclamation and that their freedom would be guaranteed by the invading U.S. Army. Under those circumstances even John Brown might have succeeded in freeing a few slaves.

19. This and subsequent dialogue are from Douglass, *Life and Times*, pp. 358–59.

Twice during their conversation a secretary interrupted to remind the President that the governor of Connecticut was waiting, Lincoln sent the secretary away.

"Tell Governor Buckingham to wait," said Lincoln. "I wish to have a long talk with my friend Douglass." Lincoln and Douglass continued talking for "a full hour after this, while the Governor of Connecticut waited without for an interview."[20]

How could Douglass—how could anyone—not be flattered? "In his company I was never in any way reminded of my humble origin, or of my unpopular color." Once again Douglass was impressed by Lincoln's sincerity and lack of pretension. More important, he realized that all his ideas about reconstructing the defeated South would not mean much if the war ended with millions of blacks still enslaved. Douglass had already expressed concerns that the Emancipation Proclamation might not have freed all the slaves by the time the war ended. But once he saw how disturbed Lincoln was by the prospect of slavery's survival, Douglass's long-standing suspicions of the President's commitment to emancipation vanished. He saw in Lincoln "a deeper moral conviction against slavery than I had ever seen before in anything spoken or written by him." Only weeks earlier Douglass had denounced Lincoln as a man who did evil by choice and right by necessity. But he came away from his second meeting persuaded that Lincoln had issued the Emancipation Proclamation out of deep moral convictions, not "merely as a 'necessity.'"[21]

20. Draft of Speech by Frederick Douglass, June 5, 1865. Frederick Douglass Papers. Library of Congress.

21. There is strong documentation for the substance of the second meeting. Four days afterward Douglass wrote Lincoln responding to the President's request for help getting slaves to escape. Two months later Douglass described the meeting in a letter to Theodore Tilton on October 15, 1864. Both letters are printed in *Life & Writings*, vol.

The second meeting changed forever the way Frederick Douglass viewed Abraham Lincoln, beginning with his position on the upcoming presidential election. In some measure Douglass's revised sentiments had nothing to do with Lincoln. His Democratic opponent, McClellan, was committed to a military victory and the restoration of the Union, but he was not committed to emancipation. Worse still was the Democratic platform calling for immediate negotiations with the Confederacy with no stipulation that the South repudiate slavery as a precondition to truce. Here was the very nightmare that, Douglass now knew, he shared with Abraham Lincoln.

At about the same time the Democrats nominated McClellan, William Lloyd Garrison provided Douglass with an occasion to explain his views on Lincoln. Somehow Garrison had gotten his hands on the letter to an English correspondent that Douglass had written the previous June; he published excerpts from the letter as part of his own never-ending campaign to impugn the character of Douglass the apostate. Duly embarrassed, Douglass was compelled to explain himself. He wrote that letter a long time ago, he said. It was "flung off in haste." It was not intended for publication. In any case, the circumstances had changed. Since he wrote that letter three months earlier, the Democrats had nominated McClellan to run against Lincoln on a peace platform. He admitted that his earlier remarks were borne of a desire to spur the nomination of the most ardent antislavery man possible. "That

---

3, pp. 405–7. The following year, after Lincoln's assassination, Douglass drafted several speeches about Lincoln that include a few more details. These speeches are discussed more fully in the next chapter. The dialogue is taken from Douglass's third autobiography, first published in 1881 and, though it is plausible and consistent with earlier accounts, it must be read as the memory of a conversation that took place more than fifteen years earlier. Once again, Lincoln left no record of the meeting.

possibility is now no longer conceivable," Douglass wrote. A victory for McClellan and the Democrats "would be the heaviest
calamity of these years of war and blood." Accordingly "all hesitation ought to cease, and every man who wishes well to the slave
and to the country should at once rally with all the warmth and
earnestness of his nature to the support of Abraham Lincoln."[22]

Beneath Douglass's embarrassment lay genuine conviction.
He now knew, from firsthand knowledge, that Lincoln was resisting pressure to reach a slaveholding compromise and that the
pressure was coming not merely from the Democrats but from
Lincoln's fellow Republicans. In a lengthy October speech ana-
lyzing the upcoming election, Douglass repeated his now-familiar
charge that Lincoln should have moved against slavery at the outset of the war, that he was too slow in enlisting black soldiers, too
slow in issuing his Order of Retaliation, too indifferent to the discrimination against African Americans serving in the Union army.
But he mentioned such things only in passing, for the larger burden of his speech was to defend Lincoln by distinguishing him
from his nervous Republican allies. Lincoln was not the problem,
Douglass argued. The problem was the two-pronged threat coming from proslavery Democrats, on the one hand, and compromising Republicans, on the other. Indeed Douglass listed seriatim
the tremendous achievements of the previous four years—
everything from emancipation and the enlistment of black troops
to the diplomatic recognition of Haiti and Liberia and more—
every one of which could be reversed by a Democratic victory or
a Republican betrayal. Lincoln had to win this election, Douglass
insisted, not simply to squelch the Democrats but to strengthen
his hand against the appeasers in his own ranks.

22. *Life & Writings*, vol. 3, p. 407.

Douglass had other reasons to separate Lincoln from the general lot of Republican politicians. Republican leaders had asked Douglass to keep his mouth shut during the campaign despite his passionate conviction that Lincoln's reelection was a necessity. They "do not wish to expose themselves to the charge of being a 'N—r' party," Douglass complained a few weeks before election day. As far as most Republicans were concerned, "[t]he Negro is the deformed child, which is put out of the room when company comes."[23] Meanwhile Lincoln was inviting Douglass to tea. If Lincoln's lack of racial prejudice now stood out in sharp relief, so too did his honesty. Douglass always said that Lincoln was an honest man, but it took on added meaning after his second visit to Washington. He had revisted Secretary of War Edwin Stanton on the same trip, and as usual he found Stanton in a sour mood. "He thinks far less of the President's honesty than I do," Douglass wrote. "I have not yet come to think that honesty and politics are incompatible."[24]

After his second meeting with the President, Douglass wrote up a memo to Lincoln detailing his plans to spread word of emancipation as broadly as possible in the Confederate South. But the plans proved unnecessary when the fortunes of the war shifted decisively in favor of the Union. Weeks before election day the city of Atlanta was captured by Union forces after a successful siege by General William T. Sherman. Having taken Georgia's capital, he then turned his army eastward to begin its spectacularly destructive march to the sea. Farther north, the Union cavalry did further damage to the Confederacy by sweeping through the Shenandoah Valley, destroying the breadbasket

23. *Life & Writings*, vol. 3, p. 424.
24. Ibid.

that had been feeding Lee's army at Petersburg. By election day
the Union armies were no longer stalled; within months they
would be converging on the increasingly desperate Army of
Northern Virginia. The end of the war was in sight. Lincoln's
reelection was now assured, military and political power would
remain safely in antislavery hands.

Douglass breathed a gargantuan sigh of relief. The recent
presidential contest had been "the most momentous and
solemn" in the republic's history, he said. The question at issue
"was whether we should, with our own hands, scuttle the ship
and send her to the bottom."[25] All those who had labored so
long for the overthrow of human bondage should feel "the pro-
foundest gratitude . . . that he has not labored and prayed in
vain." 1864 was "the final test of our national fitness for self-
government . . . We have passed the test," Douglass rejoiced,
"and have come out of it like pure gold." Nevertheless, he cau-
tioned, "the war is still upon us, and is very properly the all
absorbing and all controlling thought of the nation." Douglass
was now echoing the sentiments Lincoln had expressed to him a
few months earlier.

But the danger soon passed. By early 1865 Sherman had
completed his devastating march through Georgia and was making hell in the Carolinas. In Virginia Grant broke through the
Petersburg defenses and had Lee's army on the run. There was
no more reason to fear that the war would end with a slaveholding compromise. Nor was there any reason to fear that the end
of the war would halt the emancipation process before it was
completed. Two border states at long last capitulated to the
inevitable. Maryland ratified a "Free Constitution." In Missouri

the state legislature abolished slavery. And in Washington, D.C., the Republicans, aided by Lincoln's strenuous arm-twisting, passed and sent to the states a Thirteenth Amendment to the Constitution, permanently abolishing slavery throughout the United States. "I was not among the first to give in that slavery was dead," Douglass said in January 1865. "But I believe," he added, "we may look upon it as certain to die by this great struggle in which we are engaged."[26] And he was now prepared to give Lincoln whatever credit he deserved for this turn of events.

Even as Douglass turned his attention to the future, campaigning tirelessly for black suffrage, his speeches contained no criticism of the recently reelected President. He was characteristically sharp in his condemnation of all proposals for southern reconstruction that did not include voting rights for the former slaves. His attacks on General Banks's repressive labor system in Louisiana were particularly ferocious. But Lincoln was spared any further assaults.

REDEMPTION

Shortly after their second meeting Lincoln invited Douglass to join him for tea at the Soldiers Home, a place where the President often went to relax, a bit removed from the immediate pressures of politics and the war. If the August summons to the White House had indicated the measure of Lincoln's respect for Douglass, the subsequent invitation to tea at the Soldier's Home hinted at something more. It seems that Lincoln really did think fondly of Douglass, that he genuinely enjoyed Douglass's company. They had a lot in common, after all, and

26. Ibid., p. 54.

they shared the rare capacity to admire each other without ever descending into flattery and without ever withholding their honest convictions. Both felt a deep hatred of slavery and an overriding concern for the outcome of the war, but they shared more than that. Both were uncommonly intelligent. Each was a brilliant orator whose greatest speeches fused razor-sharp logic to soaring idealism. Even their differences meshed. If Douglass was quick to take offense at even the smallest slight, Lincoln was instinctively sympathetic and careful not to give offense. And they seem to have felt a common bond in the fact that each had risen to greatness out of poverty and obscurity. They respected self-made men, and so each respected the other. But whatever the basis of their connection, there is every reason to believe that Lincoln invited Douglass to the Soldier's Home because he enjoyed Douglass's company as much as he valued Douglass's opinion. At least that is what Douglass believed when he recalled the invitation some years later. But we will never know, because Douglass had committed himself to speak somewhere else that evening and was unable to accept the President's offer.

Having turned down the invitation to the Soldier's Home, Douglass made a special effort to go to Washington for Lincoln's second inauguration. He was thus witness to one of the greatest speeches, perhaps the greatest speech, ever delivered by an American President. Even if Lincoln's words had been prosaic, the day itself would have been memorable. By then everyone knew that the war was almost over even though Lee had not yet surrendered. Four years earlier the President-elect had entered Washington, D.C., in stealth, his country collapsing and his life threatened. Now, in March 1865, the rebellion itself was collapsing, but the fears for Lincoln's life were more alive than ever. From the platform Lincoln spotted Douglass in the crowd and pointed him out to a scowling Andrew Johnson. Whatever impression Johnson had made upon him, Douglass's thoughts were soon riveted on Lincoln's remarkable words.

In its startling invocation of divine providence, the second inaugural was unlike any speech Lincoln had ever given. In 1862 he had undergone something like a spiritual conversion. It was not the rebirth experienced by so many American evangelicals, but a reversion to the sterner dogma of Lincoln's childhood. He had been reared in a strict Calvinist household. He knew his Bible well. But he had grown into something akin to an Enlightenment deist with a strong skeptical streak. As a young man Lincoln had earned a slightly scandalous reputation for the way he poked fun at biblical inconsistencies and the foibles of the ministry. He put such theological rebelliousness aside once he entered politics, and as a public speaker he developed a special talent for citing scripture in apt and eloquent ways. But an element of skepticism remained. The abolitionists often said that the slaveholders were sinners, but Lincoln doubted it. The slaveholders cited the Bible in their defense, but Lincoln scoffed at that idea as well. He wondered whether God would even bother to take sides in the struggle over slavery. But shortly after Willie's death, as he was making the decision to proclaim emancipation, Lincoln began searching for evidence of divine approbation. When Lee invaded the North in September 1862, Lincoln made a pact with himself: If the rebel army was turned back, he would take it as a sign from God that the time had come to issue the Emancipation Proclamation. Evidence of a deepening faith crept into Lincoln's words. But the tone of those words never smacked of triumphalism. It was Calvin's God who invaded Lincoln's thoughts, the God of his parents, the God who did not hesitate to dispense bloody justice to a sinful nation, the God who made his spectacular appearance in Lincoln's second inaugural address.

Douglass himself was receptive to the rhetoric of divine retribution. As a boy he had had no religious instruction to speak of, but as a teenager in Baltimore Douglass experienced a religious conversion. His initial enthusiasm waned, however, as he noticed that Christian conversion seemed to make slaveholders meaner rather than gentler, less disposed to question slavery and more inclined to defend it vigorously. The hypocrisy of slaveholding Christianity disgusted Douglass for the rest of his life, and although he never abandoned the church, he was never again a faithful churchgoer. Nevertheless, as the sectional crisis heated up during the 1850s, Douglass's words became tinged with the theme of divine retribution. The slaveholders would burn in hell for the sin of slavery. A just God would surely crush the life out of the Confederacy. During the war, whenever he fretted about weak-kneed politicians and untrustworthy generals, Douglass's faith in the inevitability of emancipation was sustained by his belief in a vengeful God who would smite the enemies of freedom. This wasn't quite the message Lincoln had to tell in his second inaugural address, but it bore a strong enough family resemblance for Lincoln's words to ring loudly in Douglass's sympathetic ears.

Lincoln did not try to review the details of the war that had consumed the nation for four years. Neither he nor anyone else had wanted this war, he said, and nobody could have imagined that once the war came it would be as enduring and destructive as it had been. Everyone did know, from the very beginning, that slavery was, "somehow, the cause of the war." But no one anticipated that the war would destroy the very thing that had caused it. "Each looked for an easier triumph," Lincoln said, "and a result less fundamental and astounding." Such were the mysteries of divine providence. Both sides read the same Bible, both prayed to the same God, "and each invokes His aid against the other." We may find it odd that southern men "ask a just God's assistance in wringing their bread from the sweat of other men's faces; but let us judge not that we be not judged." The Lord could not have answered the prayers of both sides, and the prayers of neither side had been answered fully. "The Almighty has His own purposes," not least of which is to punish men for their "offences." If we suppose slavery to be such an offense, perhaps the Lord had inflicted "this terrible war" as punishment on "both the North and the South." We can only hope and pray that "this mighty scourge of war" would come to a speedy end. "Yet, if God wills that it continue, until all the wealth piled by the bond-man's two hundred and fifty years of unrequited toil shall be sunk, and until every drop of blood drawn with the lash, shall be paid by another drawn with the sword, as was said three thousand years ago, so still it must be said, 'the judgments of the Lord, are true and righteous altogether.' "[27]

Douglass sensed immediately the greatness of Lincoln's second inaugural address. In the months and years to come he often quoted "these solemn words of our martyred President." But on that day he wanted to congratulate Lincoln personally. He decided to break all precedent by going to the inaugural reception at the White House, though no African American had ever dared such a thing. That evening he joined the procession heading toward the executive mansion, only to be stopped at the

27. *CW*, vol. 8, pp. 332–33.

door by guards claiming they had been instructed "to admit no persons of color." Douglass did not believe them.[28]

"No such order could have emanated from President Lincoln," Douglass believed. If Lincoln knew Douglass was there, he told the guards, Lincoln would certainly wish to see him. They then resorted to trickery, escorting Douglass through the door only to steer him toward the exit.

"You have deceived me," Douglass declared, "I shall not go out of this building till I see President Lincoln." Douglass then noticed someone he knew and asked him to convey a message. "Be so kind as to say to Mr. Lincoln that Frederick Douglass is detained by officers at the door." Within moments Douglass entered the East Room.

Lincoln, visible above all his guests, quickly spotted Douglass moving toward him. "Here comes my friend Douglass," he exclaimed to the crowded room. Lincoln took Douglass by the hand. "I am glad to see you," he said. "I saw you in the crowd today, listening to my inaugural address; how did you like it?"

"Mr. Lincoln," Douglass replied, "I must not detain you with my poor opinion, when there are thousands waiting to shake hands with you."

"No, no," Lincoln said. "You must stop a little[,] Douglass; there is no man in the country whose opinion I value more than yours. I want to know what you think of it."

"Mr. Lincoln," Douglass answered, "that was a sacred effort."

"I am glad you liked it!"

28. This account of the third meeting, the only full report available, is taken from Douglass's third autobiography, published more than fifteen years later. Unlike their first two meetings, Douglass left no contemporary or near-contemporary record of what happened on March 4, 1865. This, then, is an account of the third meeting as Douglass remembered it. Douglass, *Life and Times*, pp. 365–66.

Douglass wrote later that anybody, no matter how distinguished, would "regard himself honored by such expressions, from such a man." He went home to Rochester, honored.

Six weeks later, on April 15, 1865, a crowd of citizens called upon Douglass to deliver a spontaneous eulogy for Abraham Lincoln. The President had died early that morning, having been shot by John Wilkes Booth the previous evening at a theater in Washington, D.C. Douglass was stunned. "I have scarcely been able to say a word to any of those friends who have taken my hand and looked sadly in my eyes to-day." Daniel Moore, the mayor of Rochester, called a memorial service for three o'clock that afternoon in City Hall. So many people showed up that large numbers were turned away. But Douglass managed to get in and found a seat at the rear. The mayor spoke first, followed by several others, including a judge, the rector of St. Luke's Episcopal Church, and the president of the Rochester Theological Seminary. Douglass himself had not been invited to speak, but once he was noticed "his name burst upon the air from every side, and filled the house." Pressed by the crowd, Douglass rose to speak, and although he began his remarks by claiming that he found it "almost impossible to respond" to the invitation, by the time he had finished he had delivered a eulogy that was among the most heartfelt and moving speeches of his life.[29]

"A dreadful disaster has befallen the nation," Douglass said. "It is a day for silence and meditation; for grief and tears." No doubt the people of Rochester were shaken by the death of their President "and feel in it a stab at Republican institutions." There was some consolation in the fact that "though Abraham Lincoln dies, the

29. *FDP,* ser. I, vol. 4, pp. 74–79.

Republic lives; though that great and good man, one of the noblest men [to] trod God's earth, is struck down by the hand of the assassin, yet I know that the nation is saved and liberty is established forever." It was natural on such occasions, Douglass added, to struggle through "tears and anguish, to catch some gleam of hope—some good that may be born of the tremendous evil." For Douglass this desperate search through "the blinding mists that rise from this yawning gulf" gave him a glimpse of the great promise of freedom and "hope for all" that Lincoln had given them.

He then evoked Lincoln's second inaugural address to make a more salient point. He noted with dismay the recent impulse to lionize Robert E. Lee and to forget the crimes of "treason and slavery" for which Lee fought. He warned against rushing to reconcile with our southern foes while forgetting our southern friends, the freed people who had so recently proved their loyalty to the Union cause. Douglass suggested that Lincoln's martyrdom might serve to reawaken the nation to its true mission. "It may be in the inscrutable wisdom of Him who controls the destinies of Nations," Douglass said, "that this drawing of the Nation's most precious heart's blood was necessary to bring us back to that equilibrium which we must maintain if the Republic was to be permanently redeemed." He then quoted from memory the already familiar passage from the Second Inaugural in which Lincoln, though praying for a speedy end to the war, yet promised if need be to fight on until the blood shed by generations of slaves was at last repaid by the blood of thousands of soldiers in battle. "If it teaches us this lesson, it may be that the blood of our beloved martyred President will be the salvation of our country." Douglass had incorporated Lincoln's death into the redeeming bloodshed of the war and invoked it as a challenge to fulfill the promise of freedom for which the President had given his life. There was work to be done. It was the eulogy of a reformer.

But it was also the eulogy of a friend. Douglass felt Lincoln's death "as a personal as well as a national calamity." Personal because "of the race to which I belong and the deep interest which that good man ever took in its elevation." But personal also because of the genuine affection he had come to feel for Abraham Lincoln. How deeply he had this day mourned for "our noble President, I dare not attempt to tell. It was only a few weeks ago that I shook his brave, honest hand, and looked into his gentle eye and heard his kindly voice" as Lincoln delivered his second inaugural address, "words which will live in immortal history, and be read with increasing admiration from age to age." We called Lincoln a good man, Douglass said, and a "good man he was." But if "an honest man is the noblest work of God," he added, "we need have no fear for the soul of Abraham Lincoln."

A few months after the funeral a parcel arrived at Douglass's Rochester home along with a note from Mary Todd Lincoln. My husband considered you a special friend, she wrote, and before he died, he said he would like to do something to show his regard for you. She had decided, therefore, to send Douglass her late husband's walking stick as both a memento of the public man and an expression of Lincoln's personal regard. Douglass was moved by Mrs. Lincoln's gesture and told her that he would treasure the cane for as long as he lived. He accepted it not merely as a token of the "kind consideration" in which he knew Lincoln held him personally but also as "an indication of his humane interest in the welfare of my whole race."[30]

30. *Life & Writings*, vol. 4, p. 174.

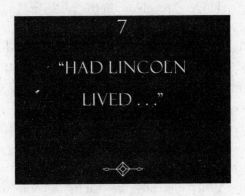

7

"HAD LINCOLN LIVED . . ."

"I Know That Damned Douglass"

On February 7, 1866, Frederick Douglass led a delegation of blacks to the White House hoping to convince President Andrew Johnson that voting was an urgent necessity for black men in the South. Douglass had been making this argument for more than two years. "Slavery is not abolished until the black man has the ballot," he insisted in May 1865.[1] Having armed the former slaves with guns, the Union had a moral obligation to arm them with the ballot. Emancipation had inflamed the slaveholders, and their fury was compounded when the Union

1. *FDP*, ser. 1, vol. 4, p. 83.

army enlisted over a hundred thousand freed blacks to help suppress the slaveholders' rebellion. In the weeks and months after Lee's surrender the freed people confronted a defeated but vindictive ruling class. Without the vote, Douglass warned, southern blacks would be left defenseless. Lincoln had begun to support voting rights for some blacks, but his assassination left the crucial early decisions to the new President.

Douglass was right. Through the summer and fall of 1865 southern whites showed just how angry they were. The Confederate government may have collapsed, but the ruling class did not easily surrender the habits of command. At the first sign of black resistance the former slaveholders—now landlords—instinctively reached for the whip and called for the sheriff, as though nothing had changed, as though slavery had ended in name only. Behind the landlords, stiffening their backs, were the state and local governments newly established under President Johnson's direction. Freedom would shortly be guaranteed by the Thirteenth Amendment, but it was already being circumscribed by a series of Black Codes, laws that limited the movement of the former slaves and all but required them to go to work for their former owners. Under the reestablished state governments the freed people had few civil and no political rights. They were arrested for "vagrancy" when they went out looking for better jobs. Their employers abused them. They were accosted on the streets. But if they turned for protection to the law, they confronted sheriffs who sided with the landlords, judges who would not allow blacks to testify, and all-white juries from which few blacks could expect justice. Those blacks who set out to test the strengths and limits of their freedom found themselves largely defenseless, just as Douglass had warned. Nevertheless, at the end of 1865

President Johnson proudly presented these new state governments to the returning Republican Congress. The reconstruction of the Union, he said, was largely complete. The delegation that Douglass led to the White House in early 1866 hoped to persuade the President otherwise.

The delegates had been appointed by the National Convention of Colored Men and included thirteen representatives from several different parts of the Union. George T. Downing, representing the New England states, spoke first. He was respectful, even deferential, but he was also clear and firm. He had come to ask Johnson's support for legislation enforcing the full meaning of the Thirteenth Amendment. As citizens of the United States, whose Constitution contains "no recognition of color or race," blacks should be guaranteed the same civil and political rights as whites. "[We] cherish the hope that we may be fully enfranchised," Downing told President Johnson, "not only here in this District but throughout the land." This was their "just due," and anything less would give "license" to those determined to "outrage" the rights of black men.[2]

Douglass spoke next, more briefly than Downing, no less respectfully but somewhat more firmly. Divine Providence had placed in Johnson's hands "the power to save or destroy us," Douglass said, "to bless or blast us. I mean our whole race." He then raised the specter of Abraham Lincoln. "Your noble and humane predecessor," Douglass pointed out, "placed in our hands the sword to assist in saving the Union." He was now asking Johnson to place "in our hands the ballot with which to save ourselves." Douglass claimed that he was not there to argue the point. As citizens of the United States and subjects of its government,

2. This account of the meeting is in *Life & Writings*, vol. 4, pp. 182–93.

blacks paid their taxes, volunteered their services to the nation, and enlisted in the military. Because they shared in the costs of maintaining the state, Douglass concluded, it was "not improper that we should ask to share in the privileges of this condition."

When Douglass finished, the President unburdened himself with a long and remarkable rant. His entire life, Johnson said, showed him to be "the friend of the colored man." It was true that he had owned slaves and had even bought slaves, "but I never sold one." This, Johnson said, showed that he had always been guided by humanity more than ambition. He had always treated his slaves well, and he dealt with his former slaves the same way; some of them had even come to Washington with him. So great were the sacrifices Johnson believed he had made for his slaves that for all practical purposes "I have been their slave instead of their being mine." Yet in spite of all this, after "my means, my time, my all has been perilled" for the sake of "the colored race," after he had given "tangible . . . practical" evidence of his concern for African Americans, Douglass and his colleagues still had the effrontery to ask Johnson to establish his credentials by supporting their demands. "I am free to say to you that I do not like to be arraigned by some who can get up handsomely rounded periods and deal in rhetoric," Johnson declared, "and talk about abstract ideas of liberty, who never periled life, liberty, or property. This kind of theoretical, hollow, unpractical friendship amounts to very little." So the answer was no, Johnson would not support black suffrage. That policy would lead to a race war that would "result in the extermination of one or the other. God forbid that I should be engaged in such a work!"

Johnson magnanimously offered to assume the position of a Moses for black people, leading them in the passage from bondage to freedom. But not at the expense of the ordinary white farmers who had suffered at the hands of the slaveholding monopoly and who, in consequence, had come to hate the slaves as much as their masters. A war fought primarily to suppress the slaveholding oligarchy had also, if only incidentally, liberated the slaves. Wasn't it enough that "there were two right ends accomplished in the accomplishment of one?" Besides, Johnson asked, what practical difference would it make if tomorrow every freed slave were suddenly endowed with the privilege of voting?

Douglass tried to speak. "Mr. President, do you wish . . ."

"I am not quite through yet," Johnson blurted out. He said that slaves themselves had helped sow the seeds of hatred that threatened to blossom into a full-scale race war. From behind the plantation gates, he claimed, the slaves had looked down upon their poor white neighbors. "Have you ever lived on a plantation?" Johnson asked.

"I have, your Excellency," Douglass said.

And did you not think "a great deal less" of the poor slaveless farmer "than you did of your own master?"

"Not I!" Douglass answered.

"Well," said the President, "I know such was the case with the large majority of you in those sections." Isn't that the reason the freed slaves preferred to work for their former owners because "they did not consider it quite as respectable to hire to a man who did not own negroes as the one who did?"

"Because," Douglass said, making a tactical mistake, "he wouldn't be treated as well."

That proved his point, Johnson shot back. "It shows that the colored man appreciated the slave owner more highly than he did the man who didn't own slaves. Hence the enmity between the colored man and the non-slaveholders."

Blacks who now demanded voting rights were mere ingrates, Johnson suggested. The Civil War had been a bonanza for the slaves. No one had intended to free them when the war first began. But whereas blacks had entered the conflict as slaves and come out as free men, poor whites had been dragged into the war against their will and then lost their lives and property in the bargain. It was unfair for those who had gained by the war to demand privileges that would alienate those who had lost by it. Moreover, Johnson continued, voting qualifications were left up to the states to decide. If the people of a state determined that blacks should not vote, that was the business of the majority in that state. It was not the business of the federal government.

"That was said before the war," Douglass replied, alluding to the belief that slavery was a state institution beyond the power of the federal government.

"I am now talking about a principle," Johnson shouted, "not what someone else said."

Downing spoke up. "Apply what you have said, Mr. President, to South Carolina." In that state blacks would have formed an electoral majority had they been allowed to vote.

"That doesn't change the principle at all," Johnson insisted. "Each community is better prepared to determine the depository of its political power than anybody else." It was undemocratic for the federal government to force voting privileges for blacks onto an unwilling white majority. "It is a fundamental tenet of my creed that the people must be obeyed," Johnson proudly declared. "Is there anything wrong or unfair in that?"

"A great deal wrong, Mr. President," Douglass replied, "with all respect."

"It is the people of the States that must for themselves determine this thing," Johnson insisted. If reconstruction were allowed to proceed from that assumption, and if all parties acquitted themselves well, the day might come when whites would see the justice of voting privileges for blacks. "But forced upon the people before they are prepared for it, it will . . . result in the injury of both races, and the ruin of one or the other." To deny this, the President concluded, was to reject the wisdom of Providence and the law of nature. At that point he abruptly tried to terminate the meeting by thanking his guests "for the compliment you have paid me."

"If the President will allow me," Douglass said, "I would like to say one or two words in reply." He was not sure that Johnson, having "taken strong ground in favor of a given policy," was of a mind to be persuaded differently. "But if your Excellency will be pleased to hear, I would like to say a word or two in regard to that one matter of the enfranchisement of the blacks as a means of preventing the very thing which your Excellency appears to apprehend—that is a conflict of races."

But as Douglass suspected, the President was not inclined to argue the point. "I repeat," Johnson said, "I merely wanted to indicate my views in reply to your address, and not to enter into any general controversy."

"Thank you, sir," said Douglass.

But Johnson would not take yes for an answer. Instead he revived the colonization schemes that Lincoln had already discarded. "I think you will find," the President said, "that the colored people can live and advance in civilization to better advantage elsewhere than crowded right down there in the South."

Douglass could not restrain himself. He alluded to the recently passed Black Codes that restricted the movement of the freed people. The masters, he said, "have the making of the laws, and we cannot get away from the plantations."

"What prevents you?" Johnson asked, apparently unaware of the labor and vagrancy statutes passed by the recently formed state legislatures of the South.

"We have not the simple right of locomotion through the Southern States now," Douglass said.

"Why not?" Johnson asked, "the Government furnishes you with every facility."

"There are six days in the year in which the negro is free in the South now," Douglass explained, "and his master then decides for him where he shall go, where he shall work, how much he shall work—in fact, he is divested of all political power. He is in the hands of those men."

"If the master controls him in his action," Johnson said, "would he not control him in his vote?"

"Let the negro once understand that he has an organic right to vote," said Douglass, "and he will raise up a party in the Southern states among the poor, who will rally with him. There is the conflict that you speak of between the wealthy slaveholder and the poor."

"You touch right upon the point there," Johnson said. "There is this conflict, and hence I suggest emigration. If he cannot get employment in the South, he has it in his power to go where he can get it."

By then Douglass was fed up. "The President sends us to the people," he said to his fellow delegates as they turned to leave, "and we will have to go and get the people right." It was an election year, and Douglass was making a political threat within earshot of Johnson.

"Yes, sir," Johnson shot back. "I have great faith in the people. I believe they will do what is right."

The interview was over. The delegation left. Johnson then

turned to his personal secretary and erupted in fury. "Those damned sons of bitches thought they had me in a trap," Johnson said. "I know that damned Douglass; he's just like any nigger, and he would sooner cut a white man's throat than not."[3]

Douglass meanwhile hurried from the White House and immediately wrote up a report of the meeting. The shocking transcript appeared in several major national newspapers.

"The Assassination and Its Lessons"

Douglass had had an inkling of how Andrew Johnson would treat him. His high hopes for the new President in the immediate aftermath of Lincoln's assassination had given way to a gloomy foreboding. He could not help making comparisons. In the year or so following the assassination Douglass drafted several versions of a lengthy speech about Abraham Lincoln. As the months passed and his opinion of Johnson sank, Lincoln's assassination loomed larger and larger in Douglass's thoughts.

In June 1865 Douglass was struck by a paradox of gleeful optimism amid grave national sorrow. The nation was still reeling from the recent murder of its beloved President, yet the future had never seemed so bright. African Americans felt these dueling sentiments with particular force. They sensed the loss of Lincoln more deeply, more personally than white Americans, Douglass said, yet "we find the prospect bright and glorious." This uncomfortable irony now gripped the nation at large. "The greatness and grandeur of the American Republic never appeared more conspicuously," Douglass believed, "than in connection with the death of Abraham Lincoln." Sustaining this optimism was none other than

---

3. Quoted in Hans Trefousse, *Andrew Johnson: A Biography* (New York, 1989), p. 242.

the new President. Andrew Johnson had come into office with a reputation for radicalism; he had repudiated his fellow slaveholders, remained loyal to the Union, and vowed that when the war was over, the treason of secession would be punished severely. "Already a strong hand is felt upon the helm of state," Douglass wrote less than two months into Johnson's presidency. "The word has gone forth that traitors and assassins, whether of low or high degree, whether male or female, are to be punished: that loyal and true men are to be rewarded and protected." Lincoln was dead, but the freed people were safe.[4]

In this mood of simultaneous exaltation and despair Douglass made one of his most startling observations about Lincoln. "No people or class of people in this country, have a better reason for lamenting the death of Abraham Lincoln, than have the colored people," Douglass wrote. He was protesting the exclusion of African Americans from many of the public memorials to the murdered President, insisting that blacks had as much right and far greater reason to participate than did white Americans. What, he asked, "was A. Lincoln to the colored people or they to him?" Compared with all his predecessors, Douglass answered, most of whom were "facile and servile instruments of the slave power, Abraham Lincoln, while unsurpassed in his devotion, to the welfare of the white race, was also in a sense hitherto without example, emphatically, the black man's President: the first to show any respect for their rights as men." Even hedged with qualifiers and comparisons, it was an astonishing thing for Frederick Douglass to label Abraham Lincoln "the black man's President."[5]

4. Draft speech, June 5, 1865, Frederick Douglass Papers, Library of Congress.
5. Ibid.

Such sentiments did not arise from any postwar disillusion. At the time he wrote those words Douglass was brimming with optimism and full of admiration for Andrew Johnson. Before the year was out, he felt very differently, though not so much about Lincoln as about the meaning of his assassination and the character of his successor. The freed people had needs, and Johnson proved oblivious of them. Without land most of the former slaves had little choice but to return to work for the same whites who had only recently owned them, and as the new year approached and new labor contracts were due to be signed, the freed people resisted. Encouraged by unreconstructed state and local officials, whites reacted to black resistance with fury and impunity. When Douglass returned to work on his Lincoln speech in December, he had a lot more to say.[6]

The new draft opened with a startling image. The year 1865 had witnessed two extraordinary events—the collapse of the Confederacy and the murder of Lincoln—and seemed about to witness a third, "one which shall be more striking, and revolting than either rebellion or assassination." What new event could possibly rise to such a dramatic level? Douglass indiscreetly named this third impending disruption, only to pull back by crossing out his own indictment: "~~The course of crimes to which I allude, and which I take to be impending over us, and which only needs that sanction of the Country and the Congress for its consummation: is the restoration policy of Andrew Johnson.~~" He had better not say that *before* he went to see the new President.

6. All quotations in the following account come from a draft speech, Frederick Douglass Papers, Library of Congress. Though internal evidence clearly establishes December 1865 as the time the bulk of it was drafted, some pages seem to have been drafted separately.

Still, the tactful deletion reveals how closely Douglass's first sustained postmortem on Lincoln's presidency was intertwined with his swiftly developing contempt for Andrew Johnson. How could Lincoln not look good by comparison?

The December draft was longer and more polished than its June predecessor, but it was still unfinished, a bit rambling. Nevertheless, Douglass had things to say about Lincoln that he had not said before, observations that reappeared in later years whenever he spoke of the former President. At a time when Douglass was redefining himself as the embodiment of the self-made American man, for example, he began to praise Lincoln for his own rise from obscurity to greatness. "He was the architect of his own fortune, a self-made man," Douglass wrote of Lincoln. He had "ascended high, but with hard hands and honest work built the ladder on which he climbed." They had this in common, Douglass often said, and from this shared experience of personal struggle their friendship had grown.

Lincoln's influence on Douglass was most clear in a second theme he developed in the December draft, the sanctity of the Union. What was at stake in the war, Lincoln had always argued, was the vindication of republicanism in the eyes of the world and the annals of history. He put it most beautifully at Gettysburg when he said the Civil War would determine whether "government of the people, by the people, and for the people" would perish from the earth. Lincoln's emphasis on the Union had been a source of frustration for Douglass during the war, but here he was in late 1865 bidding fair to catch up with Lincoln's eloquence. He now accepted the premise from which Lincoln himself started: that to defend the Union was to uphold the principle of universal liberty upon which the Union was based. When the South first seceded, Douglass wrote, European statesmen and philosophers rehearsed their old suspicions about the intrinsic weakness of the American Republic. It could survive perfectly well in calm waters, they predicted, but "would go down in the first great storm." With them, Douglass wrote, "there was nothing stable but thrones. Nothing powerful but Standing Armies. Nothing authoritative unsupported by the pretension of Divine Right." Even at home there had always been men who wondered if the nation could survive the storm over slavery. "Well, the trial has come," Douglass concluded triumphantly. "The experiment has been tried. The strength of the Republic has been tested. Tried by treason, by rebellion and by the assassination of its Chief, tried as few forms of Government were ever tried before." And what has been the result? Douglass asked. "This it is, the Country was never stronger than today. Certainty has taken the place of doubt. . . . We no longer tremble for the safety of the Ship of State." And for this glorious outcome they were indebted to no one so much as Abraham Lincoln.

"He never awed by his silence, nor silenced by the volubility or authority of his speech," Douglass wrote as he turned his attention from the Union to the character of the man who had given his life to save it. "He managed to leave his visitor not only free to utter his opinions, but by a wise reserve in the manner of insisting upon his own, he got even a little more from his visitor than his visitor got from him." Did Lincoln treat everyone this way? Douglass wondered. "What Mr. Lincoln was when in company with white men, of course, I cannot tell. I saw him mostly alone; but this much I can say of him." He wanted to be precise. Lincoln, he wrote, "was one of the very few ~~white men~~ Americans, who could entertain a negro and converse with ~~a negro~~ him without in anywise reminding him of the unpopularity of his color."

Lincoln's last days were his best, Douglass said, for he had grown in office. "If he did not control events he had the wisdom to be instructed by them. When he could no longer withstand the current he swam with it." Compare the first and second inaugural addresses, Douglass wrote, and notice the vast difference between them. "No two papers are in stronger contrast," Douglass said. "The first was intended to reconcile the rebels to the Government by argument and persuasion, the Second was a recognition of the operation of the inevitable and universal Laws." At the end of his life, Douglass concluded, Lincoln "was willing to let justice have its course.

"Had Mr. Lincoln lived . . ." With those words Douglass arrived at the theme toward which he had been building. With Lincoln still in command "we might have looked for still greater progress. Learning wisdom in war he would have learned more from Peace." Before he died, Lincoln had already "expressed himself" in favor of letting some black men vote, those who were educated and those who had fought in the Union army. This may have seemed like a small step, Douglass wrote, but it was the decisive one; it placed Lincoln in firm opposition to all those who opposed the idea that any blacks should vote. "It was like Abraham Lincoln," Douglass shrewdly observed. "He never shocked prejudices unnecessarily. Having learned Statesmanship while splitting rails, he always tested the thin edge of the wedge first, and the fact that he used this at all, meant that he would if need be, like the thick as well as the thin." There was every reason to believe that had he lived Lincoln would have moved still further. "He was a progressive man, a humane man, an honorable man, and at heart an antislavery man." The freed people could have reasonably hoped to vote, their lives would have been more secure, their futures brighter, had Mr. Lincoln lived. For that reason, Douglass concluded, "whosoever else have cause to mourn the loss of Abraham Lincoln, to the Colored people of the Country—his death is an unspeakable calamity."

When Douglass finally finished writing the speech a few weeks later, he titled it "The Assassination and Its Lessons." He delivered it a few times even before his February meeting with Andrew Johnson, and he was scheduled to give it again a few days later at the First Presbyterian Church in Washington, D.C. But after Douglass had allegedly shown his disrespect for the President by publishing the outrageous transcript of his delegation's visit to the White House, some of the church's trustees raised questions about Douglass's upcoming appearance on February 13. Would they get more of the same? Having just met with a President who could barely conceal his contempt, Douglass now proposed to speak about the consequences of Lincoln's untimely death. By then war had already broken out between Andrew Johnson and the Congress. Concerned by reports of abuse and violence against the freed people, congressional Republicans made it clear that they intended to exert some measure of control over the reconstruction of the defeated South. They refused to readmit the southern states that had been reorganized under the President's direction in 1865. They established a joint committee to investigate conditions in the South and develop a program of their own. Radical Republicans were already calling for black voting rights. This was the backdrop against which Douglass had gone to see President Johnson and the frame of reference for his first public address about the consequences of Lincoln's death.

The themes Douglass had been developing ever since the assassination were now polished and ready for public unveiling. There was Lincoln's strength of character, forged by his rise from humble origins. There were his appealing virtues: "his independence, his amiable temper, his devotion to his country, his temperance, his vigilance, his ability to bring together extremes and opposites in the cause of the nation." There was the "moral courage" Lincoln showed during the 1864 election campaign when, ignoring the demagogues, he not only went out of his way to "invite a black man to his house but also invited him to the Soldiers' Home to take tea with him." It was a legacy that Andrew Johnson could never match. When all of Lincoln's attributes were taken into consideration—his ascent from obscurity to greatness, his congenial temperament, his moral courage—it was easy for Douglass to imagine how much better things would be "had Mr. Lincoln been living today." He would have "stood with those who stood foremost, and gone with those who went farthest." Unlike Andrew Johnson, who had set himself up as Moses only to end up as Pharaoh, Lincoln was at heart "a progressive man" who had learned from the experience of war and would have continued to learn from the experience of peace.[7]

In the year since the assassination Douglass had come to appreciate aspects of Lincoln's record that had not especially struck him before 1864. Nevertheless, if "The Assassination and Its Lessons" stood as Douglass's final word on Lincoln, it would be a disappointing one. However graciously he now spoke of Lincoln's qualities, Douglass had yet to account for the crooked pathway by which he had arrived at his admiration. There had been too much mistrust, too many harsh words to be papered over with benign references to Lincoln's rise from obscurity and his ability to grow. There was a lot more Douglass could have said about Lincoln in February

7. *FDP*, ser. 1, vol. 4, pp. 110-12.

1866, but it would have to be said later, after the blinding contrast with Andrew Johnson had subsided.

Douglass's rising dissatisfaction with Andrew Johnson put him right in step with the Republican Party. Congress was already wary by late 1865. At first the Republican majority merely refused to accept the new state governments presented by Johnson. As winter gave way to spring and Johnson grew more intransigent, moderate Republicans helped override several of the President's vetoes. During the summer of 1866 whites in Memphis and New Orleans took to the streets in murderous riots against blacks attempting to secure the vote for themselves. Johnson blamed the Republican radicals. He had gone on the road hoping to drum up support for his own program, but his intemperate remarks had the opposite effect, and his campaign swing backfired. Shocked by events in the South and by the President's disgraceful behavior, northern voters gave their overwhelming support to the Republicans in the fall elections. By the time Congress returned to session in December the Republicans—moderates and radicals alike—had concluded that if the South were to be reconstructed, black men would have to be given the vote. Over Johnson's veto the Republicans first enfranchised black men in the District of Columbia and the federal territories. It took the congressional majority several months to agree on the broad outlines of its plan for dealing with the defeated South, but in March 1867 the Republicans passed their own Reconstruction Acts. They divided the South into ten military districts; they required every southern state to pass a new Fourteenth Amendment; they disenfranchised thousands of disloyal whites. And in its most revolutionary move, the thing that made Radical Reconstruction "radical," Congress required the former states of the Confederacy to let all black men vote before any of those states could be readmitted to the Union.

In 1866 reconstruction politics had shifted from the White House to Congress. In 1867 it shifted again, this time from Washington, D.C., to the South, where black voters began asserting themselves in every political arena from statehouses to county courthouses. From all walks of life a new class of black political leaders emerged. Some came from the North, some from the ranks of antebellum free blacks. They were teachers, ministers, businessmen, and craftsmen. But many hundreds of them had been slaves only months before, some barely literate, but nearly all of them inspired by the desire to build an equitable new democracy on the ashes of the defeated Confederacy. They were the backbone of the coalition with white Republicans that rewrote the southern state constitutions, elected thousands of new lawmakers and public officials, and began to confront the problems of equal justice, public education, fair taxes, and economic opportunity. As the Democrats feared, and as Frederick Douglass foresaw, the black vote revolutionized southern politics just as emancipation had revolutionized southern society.

"MEASURE HIM BY THE SENTIMENT OF HIS COUNTRY"

In 1872 Frederick Douglass's home in Rochester burned to the ground. His personal belongings were lost, including his library and his papers. It would cost him fifteen thousand dollars to rebuild. But not in Rochester. He had moved there more than two decades before, no doubt attracted by the city's reputation as a nerve center of antebellum reform. But he felt no strong ties to the city itself, and when his house was destroyed, he decided to go elsewhere. By then he was a prosperous lecturer, well paid and in great demand. For the first time in his life Douglass had the means to live anywhere he chose, and the place he chose was telling, Washington, D.C. From upstate New York, the district "burned over" with the flames of antebellum radical reform, Frederick Douglass moved to a place he now felt more comfortable, the center of American political power. If you had been paying close attention during the previous years, you could have predicted the move.

In 1868 Douglass had campaigned vigorously for Ulysses Grant, the Republican presidential nominee, more so than he had ever campaigned for Lincoln. By then his allegiance to the party was fixed, as much by his contempt for the Democrats as by the Republican record on emancipation, black troops, and now the black vote. For his unstinting support Douglass hoped for the proper reward, perhaps a job as postmaster in Rochester. But the patronage never came. Instead President Grant appointed Douglass to a commission sent to Santo Domingo to study the possibility of annexing the island to the United States. It was understood that the commission would produce a report favorable to annexation; Douglass's appointment was calculated to neutralize Senator Charles Sumner's opposition. But having done his duty, and risked undermining his friendship with Sumner, Douglass was rewarded with an insulting slight by the President. When the commissioners returned to Washington, Grant invited the three white members to the White House for dinner but conspicuously failed to invite Douglass. Rather than recoil from the affront Douglass relocated his family in the nation's capital and campaigned even more strenuously for Grant's reelection in 1872.

Throughout the 1870s, despite his party's waning support

for reconstruction, Douglass remained committed to the use of the ballot as a weapon for the advance of black interests in the South. It was not an unreasonable position to take. President Grant had effectively suppressed the Ku Klux Klan in the South, and as a result, blacks were voting and even winning elections throughout much of the former Confederacy. As sheriffs, justices of the peace, marshals, city councilmen, judges, and state legislators, black public officials were able to provide some measure of security against whites who might otherwise have been unrestrained in their vengeance. This was precisely the sort of protection Douglass had predicted the vote would give blacks. Beside these crucial gains, he concluded, the petty insults and shortcomings of party politics could be borne. It was from this perspective that Douglass formulated his most complex and compelling evaluation of Abraham Lincoln.

On April 14, 1876, Douglass delivered the keynote speech at the unveiling of an emancipation monument in Washington, D.C. Paid for with small donations accumulated over a decade from freed men and women across the South, mostly black veterans, the monument was placed in Lincoln Park, where it still stands. Douglass later said he disliked the statue. It depicted a slave on bended knee rising to freedom beside Abraham Lincoln, who stood with one hand on the slave and the other clutching a copy of the Emancipation Proclamation. But on the day of its unveiling Douglass was more concerned with Lincoln's record than with the statue's demeaning symbolism. The dedication ceremony attracted a host of dignitaries, including President Grant, Chief Justice Salmon P. Chase, and a number of congressmen, diplomats, and members of the clergy. They must have squirmed in their seats as Douglass began speaking.

He gently warned his listeners that it was only proper to

speak the truth as he and his fellow African Americans saw it. As
he had in his great Fourth of July speech years before, Douglass
set himself up as the spokesman for black Americans by speaking
in the first person plural—"we"—while provocatively distinguishing himself from "you," the largely white audience.
"Abraham Lincoln was not, in the fullest sense of the word,
either our man or our model," Douglass declared. "In his interests, in his associations, in his habits of thought, and in his prejudices, he was a white man." A decade before, Douglass had
written that Lincoln was "emphatically the black man's president." Ten years later he was to call Lincoln a "leader of the colored people, far greater than I." But on this occasion, in 1876,
Douglass opted for an opening shocker to set up the more profound argument that was to follow. Lincoln, Douglass told his
listeners, "was preeminently the white man's President, entirely
devoted to the welfare of white men."[8]

This startling pronouncement was immediately followed by
a scandalous rehearsal of all the criticisms Douglass had hurled
at Lincoln during his presidency. Until the very last years of the
war Lincoln had been willing to sacrifice the interests of blacks
for the sake of whites. He had taken office committed to halting
the extension of slavery and nothing more. His arguments
against slavery's extension had been framed, Douglass said, in
"the interest of his own race." He had entered the presidency
vowing to "draw the sword" in defense of slavery wherever it
already existed. He would enforce the "supposed constitutional
guarantees" of slavery, not least the notorious Fugitive Slave Act
of 1850. "You and yours," Douglass told his white listeners,
"were the object of his deepest affection and his most earnest

8. Ibid., p. 431.

solicitude. You are the children of Abraham Lincoln. We are at best only his step-children." It is therefore you, the whites, who should be hanging pictures and dedicating monuments to the memory of Abraham Lincoln.[9]

How inappropriate. The audience had come to sing Lincoln's praises and instead Douglass subjected them to a caustic summary of his old abolitionist indictment.

Then, almost imperceptibly, Douglass shifted his ground. Having rolled out his indictment, he proceeded to roll it back up and put it away. Having reminded his listeners of how Lincoln's presidency had once appeared to a committed abolitionist, he proceeded to argue that there were other points of view to consider. Radical abolitionists may have had nothing good to say about the President, but in the eyes of most black Americans Lincoln's record was a good deal more complicated. Maybe he had been the white man's President, but if so, Douglass hoped that whites would nevertheless accept "the humble offering" that African Americans were that day unveiling. For although white Americans had every reason to honor the memory of Lincoln, African Americans had good reasons of their own. "Abraham Lincoln saved for you a country," Douglass said, but "he delivered us from a bondage, according to Jefferson, one hour of which was worse than ages of the oppression your fathers rose in rebellion to oppose."[10] From the beginning of the Civil War blacks understood this, Douglass said, and for this reason they had never lost faith in Lincoln. Whether the war was going badly or well, whether northern morale soared or sank, blacks remained faithful to Lincoln—even when he himself "taxed" their faith. And tax it he did. He was slow to move against slavery,

9. Ibid., pp. 431–32.
10. Ibid., p. 432.

he told them they were the cause of the war, he invited them "to leave the land in which we were born," he resisted making them soldiers, and when he relented, he resisted retaliating "when we were murdered as colored prisoners." He said he would save the Union with slavery; he rebuked General Frémont but stayed too long with General McClellan. "When we saw this, and more, we were at times stunned, grieved, and greatly bewildered." And yet they remained faithful. In the face of all of Lincoln's apparent failings, "our hearts believed." Why? Because despite the tumult and confusion of the war, "we were able to take a comprehensive view of Abraham Lincoln, and to make reasonable allowance for the circumstances of his position."[11]

Each of the criticisms that Douglass had earlier specified he now dismissed, for each was based on "partial and imperfect glimpses" of Lincoln—on his "stray utterances" rather than long-standing commitments, on "isolated facts torn from their connection." Blacks, Douglass said, were able to look beyond these to see the "broad survey, in the light of the stern logic of great events." To "us," he said, it mattered little what language Lincoln chose to use on any particular occasion. What mattered was that he sympathized with the great movement he found himself leading, the complete destruction of slavery in the United States. When considered in the light of his irreducible greatness, all of Lincoln's failings were but minor irritations rather than fundamental flaws. "We came to the conclusion that the hour and the man of our redemption had met in the person of Abraham Lincoln."[12]

Lincoln may have loved the Union more than he hated slavery, Douglass continued, but he always hated slavery. It was by

11. Ibid., p. 433.
12. Ibid., pp. 433–34.

no means an accident that it was abolished "under his wise and beneficent rule, and by measures approved and vigorously pressed by him." Under Lincoln's rule "we saw our brave sons and brothers laying off the rags of bondage." Under his rule two hundred thousand blacks fought as soldiers in the U.S. military. Under his rule the republic of Haiti was finally recognized, and its minister, a black man, was "duly received" in Washington. Under his rule slavery was abolished in the nation's capital, and the illegal Atlantic slave trade was effectively suppressed. Under his rule, the Confederacy—"based upon the idea that our race must be slaves, and slaves forever"—was utterly destroyed. Lincoln's great proclamation, "though special in its language, was general in its principles and effect, making slavery forever impossible in the United States. Though we waited long, we saw all this and more." Once that proclamation was issued, "we forgot all delay, and forgot all tardiness . . . and we were thenceforward willing to allow the President all the latitude of time, phraseology, and every honorable device that statesmanship might require."[13] The flaws that were inexcusable to an impatient radical seemed more like forgivable lapses to most black Americans.

Broader and more generous than that of radical abolitionists, the African American perspective on Lincoln was still a limited one. A great statesman must have a wider field of vision. So Douglass shifted perspective again, this time to see events from Lincoln's point of view, that of a democratically elected official with legitimate obligations to all the people. When Douglass looked at events in that light, Abraham Lincoln's record soared to greatness. Lincoln, he said, brought to his politics extraordinary personal qualities. "Though high in position, the humblest

13. Ibid., pp. 434–36.

could approach him and feel at home in his presence. Though deep, he was transparent; though strong, he was gentle; though decided and pronounced in his convictions, he was tolerant toward those who differed from him, and patient under reproaches." This was high praise, but it was nothing new. Even at his most critical moments during the Civil War Douglass was usually careful to note Lincoln's unimpeachable character even as he scolded the President for his policies. What was new in Douglass's speech was his final evaluation of those policies.[14]

"I have said that President Lincoln was a white man," Douglass said, "and shared the prejudices common to his countrymen towards the colored race." But appealing to those prejudices may have been necessary if Lincoln was to crush the rebellion and end slavery. "Looking back to his times and to the condition of the country," Douglass now saw that Lincoln's ability to mobilize loyal Americans for a long and painful conflict depended on his sensitivity to popular opinion, and to popular prejudice. Lincoln's "great mission" was to accomplish two things: restore the Union and "free his country from the great crime of slavery. To do one or the other, or both," Douglass acknowledged, Lincoln "must have the earnest sympathy and the powerful cooperation of his loyal fellow-countrymen." That sympathy would have been lost "had he put the abolition of slavery before the salvation of the Union." It would have "rendered resistance to rebellion impossible." It may be that Lincoln shared the prejudices of his fellow whites, but "it is hardly necessary to say that in his heart of hearts he loathed and hated slavery."[15]

By the time Douglass reached his conclusion he had long

14. Ibid., p. 436.
15. Ibid.

since retreated from the provocative claims with which he had opened his speech. It was certainly true that from the perspective of the abolitionists "Lincoln seemed tardy, cold, dull, and indifferent," Douglass admitted. But Lincoln was a statesmen, the elected President of the nation at large, and it was by the standards of the nation at large that he should be judged. "Measure him by the sentiment of his country," Douglass finally said, "a sentiment he was bound as a statesman to consult." By that measure, Lincoln "was swift, zealous, radical, and determined." Never before had Douglass so clearly distinguished the role of a reformer from that of a politician. He did not claim that the abolitionist perspective was invalid, only that it was partial and therefore inadequate. Lincoln was an elected official, a politician, not a reformer; he was responsible to a broad public that no abolitionist crusader had to worry about.

In a sense Douglass's speech mimicked his own shifting perspective, from the unyielding abolitionist to the leading voice of black America to the loyal member of the Republican Party. By the 1870s Douglass could shift from one voice to the other with remarkable ease, but never did he manipulate those voices as brilliantly as he did at the dedication of the emancipation memorial. It gave his evaluation of Lincoln a depth that has rarely been matched and that not even Douglass reproduced. He saw how tempting it was for elected officials to lapse into cynicism and demagoguery, but he also recognized that the political independence of the abolitionist reformer could lead to irresponsible criticism and contempt for democracy itself. African Americans were more forgiving, but theirs was inevitably a view of the world too partial for a President elected to serve all the people. The great politician was the one who could sustain the highest principles of the reformer and acknowledge the legitimate grievances of minorities—without losing the trust of the whole people. The finest statesmen could hold the people's trust without becoming a cynic or a demagogue. By this standard Lincoln was one of the great politicians of all time.

Douglass's speech is often read as a devastating critique of Lincoln, but it is far more interesting for its undertone of self-criticism. Douglass had many virtues, but introspection was not one of them. Yet here he was carefully and sensitively distancing himself from a part of himself. Few great men, he said, have ever been subjected to "fiercer denunciation" than was Abraham Lincoln during his administration. Reproached by his fellow Republicans, Lincoln was often "wounded in the house of his friends." He was "assailed by abolitionists; he was assailed by slaveholders; he was assailed by men who were for peace at any price; he was assailed by those who were for a more vigorous prosecution of the war; he was assailed for not making the war an abolition war; and he was most bitterly assailed for making the war an abolition war." No one knew better than Douglass that he himself had been one of those assailants. But this was 1876. Lincoln's work was done. Douglass had made his peace with American democracy. He understood the limits of what a statesman like Lincoln could do and so appreciated all the more deeply how much Lincoln had actually done.[16]

In the very act of criticizing himself Douglass was also identifying with Lincoln, and this added yet another layer to his already remarkable speech. He had begun to develop this theme shortly after the assassination, but never more elaborately than on this occasion. Lincoln had been the object of ferocious criticism, but Douglass too had been assailed from every side, sub-

16. Ibid., p. 437.

jected to the vengeful gossip of the Garrisonians and the vicious race-baiting of proslavery Democrats. Both Lincoln and Douglass were able to withstand the assaults because each had been toughened by youthful deprivation and a determined rise from obscurity. By the 1870s, famous and prosperous, Douglass liked to give speeches about the self-made man. His own life was his most compelling example, but in the popular imagination it stood well behind that of Abraham Lincoln. And so Douglass closed his speech by evoking Lincoln's rise to greatness in terms he could as easily have applied to himself: "Born and reared among the lowly, a stranger to wealth and luxury, compelled to grapple single-handed with the flintiest hardships from tender youth to sturdy manhood, he grew strong in the manly and heroic qualities demanded by the great mission to which he was called by the votes of his countrymen. The hard condition of his early life, which would have depressed and broken down weaker men, only gave greater life, vigor and buoyancy to the heroic spirit of Abraham Lincoln." By day the young Lincoln performed the most arduous physical labor while by night he studied his English grammar. "A son of toil himself he was linked in brotherly sympathy with the sons of toil in every loyal part of the Republic." It went without saying that Douglass saw himself in precisely the same way. [17]

The inner strength that enabled Lincoln to rise above his impoverished origins later steeled him against all efforts to compromise with the forces of disunion. When others suggested that a war against the Confederacy could not be won, Lincoln resisted. "He calmly and bravely heard the voice of doubt and fear all around him, but he had an oath in heaven, and there was not

17. Ibid., pp. 437–38.

power enough on the earth to make this honest boatman, back-woodsman and broad-handed splitter of rails evade or violate that sacred oath. He had not been schooled in the ethics of slavery; his plain life favored his love of truth. . . . His moral training was against saying one thing when he meant another. The trust which Abraham Lincoln had of himself and in the people was surprising and grand, but it was also enlightened and well founded. He knew the American people better than they knew themselves, and his truth was based on that knowledge."[18]

There it was, Douglass's longest and most considered evaluation of Lincoln. By the time he delivered the address, in 1876, Douglass was living in Washington, D.C., in close quarters with the Republican Party establishment. The perspective on Lincoln at which he arrived mirrored Douglass's own journey from slave to alienated outsider and then from skeptical engagement to a full embrace of the American political system. From that final perspective Lincoln now struck Douglass as a principled statesman, a man who always hated slavery, a politician with a keen sense of how far the American people could be pushed in an antislavery direction, and a leader willing to push them when the time came.

The Life and Times of Frederick Douglass

In 1877 the patronage Douglass had waited for finally came. He had not been made postmaster of Rochester, and he had been passed over as ambassador to Haiti. But upon taking office after the disputed election of 1876, the Republican President,

18. Ibid., p. 439.

Rutherford B. Hayes, appointed Douglass marshal of the District of Columbia. Douglass accepted the position gladly and fulfilled his responsibilities professionally. He was nearly sixty years old and much in demand as the elder statesman of American blacks and a leading fixture in the Republican Party. The steady job in Washington allowed him to cut down on his grueling lecture schedule without diminishing his now-substantial income. In keeping with his status, Douglass moved to a new home just across the Anacostia Bridge. Cedar Hill was a large, comfortable house that sat atop a hill overlooking the river and the nation's capital beyond. It had a library large enough to hold his two thousand volumes and grounds ample enough to entertain his growing family of grandchildren. Douglass enjoyed his status as America's most influential black man, but he also seemed to enjoy—perhaps for the first time in his life—the steady company of his children and grandchildren.

As he settled into a life of public acclaim and private contentment, Douglass took up his pen once more to produce the last, and least compelling, of his three autobiographies. Published in 1881 and updated ten years later, *Life and Times of Frederick Douglass* lacks the hard Garrisonian edge of the 1845 *Narrative* and the analytical depth of the 1855 *My Bondage and My Freedom*. Douglass was a proud man, and *Life and Times* was a proud book, but unlike his earlier autobiographies, this one tended to slip into self-satisfaction. Douglass's theme was his rise to prominence as a self-made man in a nation of self-made men. However compelling this was in his own case, it sat uncomfortably amid the desperate struggles of most black Americans in the late nineteenth century. But it did provide Douglass with another opportunity to reexamine his relationship with Abraham Lincoln.

Nothing in *Life and Times* conflicted with the views Douglass had expressed in his earlier retrospectives of Lincoln. Indeed, he reprinted both of them—"The Assassination and Its Lessons" of 1866 and the brilliant 1876 memorial—in an appendix to the 1881 autobiography. Like those earlier speeches, *Life and Times* evaluated Lincoln in terms far more glowing than anything he had offered during the President's lifetime. But because this was an autobiography, Douglass had to be specific about how he had responded to Lincoln beginning with his first campaign for the presidency. How would Douglass handle the disjunction between the way he felt in 1881 and what he had said back in 1861? The unflattering answer is: He backed away from the burden of candor, rewriting his own history to cleanse it of his earlier criticism of Lincoln. He softened his once harsh attacks. He omitted crucial events that reflected his earlier feelings. He even rearranged the sequence of events to leave the impression that his criticism had ended earlier than it had.

Mostly, however, *Life and Times* relied on the distinction between a reformer and a politician that Douglass developed after the war. Lincoln first appeared as the Republican candidate for the U.S. Senate from Illinois in 1858. At the time Douglass had mixed feelings about the moderate position Lincoln was articulating, but in 1881 he was more understanding. Lincoln's words were not those "of an abolitionist—branded a fanatic, and carried away by an enthusiastic devotion to the Negro—but the calm, cool, deliberate utterance of a statesman, comprehensive enough to take in the welfare of the whole country."[19] This was the same point Douglass had been making for some time: that the obligations of a statesman were different from those of a

19. Frederick Douglass, *Life and Times of Frederick Douglass*, intro. Rayford Logan (New York, 1881; rev. ed., 1892; repr., New York, 1962), p. 29.

reformer and that by the standards of statesmanship Lincoln's record was impeccable.[20]

Douglass elaborated on this theme in his discussion of the Emancipation Proclamation, singling out Lincoln's skillful navigation of public opinion. The proclamation, he wrote in *Life and Times*, was "framed with a view to the least harm and the most good possible in the circumstances. . . . While he [Lincoln] hated slavery, and really desired its destruction, he always proceeded against it in a manner the least likely to shock or drive from him any who were truly in sympathy with the preservation of the Union." Douglass still allowed himself to wonder if Lincoln's concern with the border states had earned as much as it had cost. But as for the "wisdom and moderation" of Lincoln's general policy, Douglass now had nothing but the highest praise.[21]

Even so, the memory of Douglass's wartime rancor haunts the passages on Lincoln in *Life and Times,* especially his concluding observations about the former President. He was "a man so amiable, so kind, humane, and honest," Douglass wrote, "that one is at a loss to know how he could have had an enemy on earth." Lincoln certainly had his accusers, "in whose opinion he was always too fast or too slow, too weak or too strong, too conciliatory or too aggressive," but "they would soon become his admirers," Douglass pointed out. They would realize that Lincoln "had conducted the affairs of the nation with singular wisdom, and with absolute fidelity to the great trust confided in him."[22] Douglass had been one of those accusers, soon to become one of

20. Ibid., p. 327.
21. Ibid., p. 355.
22. Ibid., pp. 370–71.

those admirers. In saying so, he was not merely paying his respects to Abraham Lincoln but offering his apologies.

"IT WAS NOT SO MEANT BY
ABRAHAM LINCOLN"

Scrounge through the heap of Douglass's postwar writings and it is possible to find scraps of evidence which, carefully arranged, suggest an aging lion unable to find either the cause or the words to reanimate his roar. When the Civil War ended, he recalled, "I felt that I had reached the end of the noblest and best part of my life." Douglass had been an abolitionist since the day he learned what the word meant. The abolitionist movement had been his base of operations for most of his adult life. But now "my school was broken up, my church disbanded, and the beloved congregation dispersed, never to come together again."[23] He found a new home, a new loyalty, in the Republican Party. Too much loyalty, critics said. Worse, he had taken up the nostalgic cult of the martyred Lincoln.

But Douglass had experienced no sudden postwar conversion; his drift into politics was a long time in the making. He had begun his public career as a protégé of William Lloyd Garrison's, repudiating the U.S. Constitution and with it all attempts to end slavery by political means. In the early 1850s he changed his mind about the Constitution and became a convert to antislavery politics. He had mixed feelings about the new Republican Party, but those feelings actually reflected his growing attraction to the political mainstream. During the Civil War, as Lincoln and the Republicans

23. Ibid., p. 373.

became the party of emancipation, Douglass allied himself with its radical wing. By the fall of 1864 he was hoping and praying for Lincoln's reelection. Radical reconstruction cemented his party allegiance. Once the Republicans committed themselves to the black vote, Douglass's political conversion was irrevocable. Looking backward from 1885, Douglass had little trouble tracing the roots of his commitment to the "great Republican party." It had emancipated the slaves, saved the Union, reconstructed the South, and enfranchised black men. It had carried the country through a terrible and costly war, yet it had raised the nation's credit, backed up the nation's currency, and lowered the nation's debt. In all this the Republican Party had enhanced "the honor, prosperity, and glory of the American people" as no party had ever done before. Now his party was in trouble. The Republicans had lost the 1884 presidential election, and for the first time in twenty-four years a Democrat occupied the White House.[24]

As in 1864 so in 1884. The threat of an overtly racist Democratic Party anchored Douglass firmly among the Republicans, notwithstanding their retreat from reconstruction, notwithstanding their personal slights. "If the colored man does not depend upon the Republican party, he will depend upon the Democratic party," Douglass explained, "and if he does neither, he becomes a nonentity in American politics." For him, he added, "I must say that the Democratic party has as yet [not] given me sufficient reasons for doing it any such service, nor has the Republican party sunk so low that I must abandon it for its great rival. With all its faults it is the best party now in existence."[25] To withhold sup-

24. *FDP*, ser. 1, vol. 5, p. 176.
25. Ibid., p. 235.

port from the Republicans was to hand power over to the Democratic Party, the declared enemy of all African Americans. Douglass could see no alternative. And unlike his critics, then and now, Douglass was not equipped with the exquisite moral calculus that apparently enables them to determine the precise moment at which his allegiance to the Republican Party became disgraceful.

The only thing remarkable about Douglass's position was that it made sense. Compared with where he and the Republicans had begun thirty years earlier, in 1856, it was as if Douglass had stepped through a looking glass into a world of reversed images. Before the war he was a radical first, increasingly committed to politics but always in the service of reform. After the war he was a Republican, still committed to equal justice but always by means of party politics. He was surely right to point out that black voters had solid reasons to support the Republicans and oppose the Democrats. But the Republicans of the postreconstruction years did not repay African American voters for their unswerving fidelity. The party lost its radical edge, its idealism withered away, and it settled into the easy corruptions of entrenched political power. The Republicans held Douglass at arm's length, alternately embracing, using, and insulting him for his unstinting efforts. Through it all he remained loyal.

Loyal but critical. Douglass was not blind, and he was not stupid. He knew when he was being treated shabbily by his own party. He saw how Republicans began to look away as white southerners did all they could to deprive blacks of the full measure of their freedom. "I am a Republican," Douglass openly declared in 1888. "I believe in the Republican party." But there were limits, he warned; his loyalty was not unconditional. He was a Republican in large measure because of the party's great history, but it "can no longer repose on the history of its grand and magnificent achievements." Much of what the Republicans had accomplished was now being nullified all across the South; the party had a moral and political obligation to stop that nullification. "It must make the path of the black citizen to the ballot box as safe and smooth as that of the white citizen." If the Republican Party failed to do this, Douglass declared, "I for one shall welcome the bolt which shall scatter it into a thousand pieces."[26]

Douglass was becoming angry again. By the early 1880s he had sensed a great white reaction beginning to sweep across the South. African Americans were being lynched in growing numbers, their homes burned, their families terrorized—just because they went looking for work, just because they tried to vote, just because they were black. By 1890 the spearhead of reaction was passing from vigilante mobs to state legislatures. Meanwhile the U.S. Supreme Court was whittling the Civil War amendments to the Constitution down to almost nothing. The Fifteenth Amendment prohibited the use of race as qualification for voting, but white officials in the South were devising devilishly ingenious means to circumvent it. Grandfather clauses, literacy tests, poll taxes, and even the much-heralded secret ballot were successfully eliminating black men from voter registration rolls across the South. This was "disfranchisement." Enlightened southerners thought of it as a progressive reform necessary for good government. What it produced was white government. As black voters disappeared so did black state legislators, black sheriffs, black justices of the peace, and black jurors. When the war ended, Douglass had said that black men needed the vote

26. Ibid., vol. 5, pp. 370–71.

because they needed political power to protect themselves. Now black political power was being destroyed, and southern blacks were losing their defenses. It was reconstruction in reverse.

Watching in horror, Douglass raised his voice in furious indignation. There was no justice for blacks in southern courtrooms, he shouted. Mob violence passed without rebuke from the press. And all the while the northern people said they were growing tired of the Negro's demands. The fire had returned to Douglass's speeches, and so had the old themes. Back in the 1850s Douglass used to argue that slavery was as much a threat to northern whites as to southern slaves. In the 1890s he made a similar argument about disfranchisement. What was happening to southern blacks, he said, was neither a "southern problem" nor a "negro problem." The "suppression of the legal vote in the south," he insisted, "is as much a question for Maine and Massachusetts as it is for the Carolinas and Georgia."[27] It was a "national problem," he said, demanding action from a seemingly paralyzed Republican Party.

Then he invoked Lincoln's famous metaphor of the house divided. "What Abraham Lincoln said in respect of the United States is as true of the colored people as of the relations of those States. They cannot remain half slave and half free."[28] He used the same metaphor several times in the 1880s and 1890s, but not as often as he played off the Gettysburg Address, which itself played off the Declaration of Independence. "We hold it to be self-evident that no class or color should be the exclusive rulers of this country," Douglass snapped in September 1883. "If there is such a ruling class, there must of course be a subject class, and

27. Ibid., p. 400.
28. Ibid., pp. 67, 100. For similar examples of Douglass's use of the Gettysburg Address, see also pp. 48, 218, 262.

when this condition is once established this Government of the people, by the people and for the people, will have perished from the earth."[29] So went the lineage: from Thomas Jefferson to Abraham Lincoln to Frederick Douglass.

Echoes of Lincoln reappeared over and over in Douglass's words. More than once Lincoln had associated slavery with the divine right of kings or with predatory aristocrats who lived off the fruits of other men's labor. In 1894 Douglass used nearly identical language to rebuke those who favored stripping black men of their voting privileges. Those who now denounced black suffrage as "a blunder and a failure" thought they were saying something new, Douglass noted. In fact the argument "is as old as despotism and about as narrow and selfish. . . . It is the argument of the crowned heads and privileged classes of the world. . . . It does away with that noble and just idea of Abraham Lincoln, that our government should be a government of the people, by the people, and for the people, and for *all* the people."[30]

This was Lincoln without tears, Lincoln with a purpose. Douglass the politician was enlisting the former President in the cause of reform. He did it quite consciously. For years he had been taunting listeners with the suggestion that John Brown and Abraham Lincoln were two of a kind. By the 1880s Douglass often recited a litany of the great men he had known, not only John Brown but William Lloyd Garrison, Wendell Phillips, Charles Sumner, and Gerrit Smith. Sometimes the names on the list changed, but Lincoln's was always there, right beside the radical reformers he had worked so hard to distance himself

29. Ibid., p. 110. See also pp. 218, 262.
30. Ibid., p. 593.

from. Lincoln had become the model for the public person Douglass was now trying to be, the loyal party man who somehow remained a steadfast reformer. Those two identities, once so incompatible, might be reconciled after all. But it would not be easy, for the politician's job was to make friends, and the reformer's fate was to make enemies. "The reformer," Douglass explained in 1883, had "a difficult and disagreeable task before him. He has to part with old friends; break away from the beaten paths of society, and advance against the vehement protests of the most sacred sentiments of the human heart." It was a path strewn with victims. "Garrison was mobbed and haltered," Douglass recalled, and "Lovejoy shot down like a felon . . . John Brown hanged, and Lincoln murdered."[31]

Having conscripted Lincoln into the company of radical reformers, Douglass began to speak of him in the same heroic terms he had once reserved for the likes of John Brown. Lincoln's name, he said, "should never be spoken of without reverence." In 1883 he called Lincoln "the greatest statesman that ever presided over the destinies of this Republic." Five years later he was "one of the greatest and best men ever produced by his country, if not ever produced by the world at large." When Lincoln died, Douglass suggested, he went before his Maker "with four millions of broken fetters in his arms as evidence of a life well spent. Glorious man!" Douglass now claimed to have seen in their very first meeting "real . . . saintliness" in Lincoln's face. It is hard to imagine that Douglass's estimation could go any higher, but it did. He had known men "who stood only a little lower than the angels," Douglass exclaimed in 1893, but he

31. Ibid., p. 136.

had met with no man "possessing a more godlike nature than did Abraham Lincoln."[32] A great statesman was one thing. But a saint? Godlike? What was going on? There was method to this hero-worshiping madness. As the condition of southern blacks grew increasingly desperate, Douglass raised up Lincoln as the standard of justice against which he measured his contemporaries.

In 1888 Douglass's anger and frustration boiled over into one of the most shocking pronouncements of his entire career—with Lincoln figuring as a dramatic coda. Notwithstanding all the disadvantages of their condition and the obstacles thrown in their way, Douglass had always been optimistic about the prospects for the former slaves. Now he was not so sure. He felt "compelled to admit" that the Negro in the South "is worse off, in many respects, than when he was a slave." He had been swindled, his energy paralyzed, his ambitions suppressed, his hopes blasted. Nominally free, "he is actually a slave." Here and now, Douglass shouted, I "denounce his so-called emancipation as a stupendous fraud—a fraud upon him, a fraud upon the world." This was not what freedom was supposed to be. It was not what emancipation was supposed to be. "It was not so meant by Abraham Lincoln."[33]

Here was the old Frederick Douglass—scathing, sarcastic, and urgently angry—still able to denounce injustice with all the contempt of an unreconstructed Garrisonian but with all the wounded patriotism of a Lincoln Republican. His critical edge was as sharp as ever. The difference was that Douglass had revived his lifelong struggle for equality from within the political mainstream, and in his search for an ally he had turned to the

32. Ibid., pp. 77–78, 339, 536, 537.
33. Ibid., pp. 362–63.

memory of Abraham Lincoln. Black Americans "look to you as a leader," a reporter for the *Washington Post* said to Douglass during an interview in 1884. "I do not presume to be a leader," Douglass said. He was being disingenuous—of course he presumed to be a black leader—but he wanted to make a point. "Mr. Lincoln and Mr. Sumner were leaders of the colored people, far greater than I, an humble citizen, can ever hope to be."[34] Douglass was puffing up Lincoln for a reason. If he was going to do battle under the protective shadow of Abraham Lincoln, he wanted that shadow to be an imposing one.

When Douglass said to an audience of Brooklyn Republicans in 1893 that Lincoln was the most "godlike" person he had ever known, he was setting his listeners up for a jolt at the end of the speech. He lured them in with exalted words about their party's founding hero, only to regale them at the end with a chanting refrain of possibilities, all of them implying the same hypothetical question: What if Lincoln were alive today? "Did his firm hand now hold the helm of state; did his brave spirit now animate the Nation; did his wisdom now shape and control the destiny of this otherwise great republic; did he now lead the once great republican party . . ." If Lincoln were still with us, if he were still in command, Douglass charged, officials in Washington would not be spouting the "weak and helpless" claim that "there is no power under the United States Constitution to protect the lives and liberties of American citizens in any one of our own Southern states from barbarous, inhuman and lawless violence."[35] It was nearly thirty years since Douglass had first laid the same trap, when his disillusionment

34. Ibid., p. 146.
35. Ibid., p. 545.

with Andrew Johnson led him to emphasize the greatness of the murdered President so that he could speculate more freely about what might have happened "had Mr. Lincoln lived."

For northern whites at the end of the nineteenth century the memory of Lincoln was becoming an empty artifact, an exercise in nostalgia. For Frederick Douglass the memory was something else entirely: Lincoln was his bludgeon, his sledgehammer, the destructive weapon Douglass wielded as he charged back into battle against the regrouping forces of injustice and inequality.

He never abandoned the fight. On February 10, 1895, he drove down into Washington from his home atop Cedar Hill to join his old friend Susan B. Anthony at a rally for women's rights. Douglass had been committed to her cause from the beginning, but after the war they had quarreled over whether black men should get the vote before women did. That was all behind them now, and as Douglass entered the hall, the two great reformers locked arms and proceeded to the platform amid wild applause. Late in the afternoon Douglass went back to Cedar Hill for dinner all full of enthusiasm. He started to tell his wife, Helen, about the day's events, mimicking one of the speakers in a way that only he could. Midway through the performance he rose from his chair, fell to his knees, then to the floor. The old warrior was dead. Just then the carriage arrived to take Douglass back to the rally, where he was scheduled to deliver his own speech for women's rights. Three days later they took his body back to Rochester and buried him at Mount Hope.

FOR FURTHER READING

I've made no attempt to write a dual biography of Frederick Douglass and Abraham Lincoln, much less a study of their lives and times. Nor have I introduced readers to a newly unearthed stash of documents. At its heart this book is a close reading of the things Lincoln and Douglass had to say about slavery and race, about politics and war, and about each other. To get at their words I relied primarily on the sources whose abbreviations are listed at the front of the book. After weeks at the microfilm reels reading the newspapers Douglass published under different titles between 1848 and 1863—first *The North Star*, then *Frederick Douglass' Paper*, and finally *Frederick Douglass' Monthly*—I initially intended to cite only those articles and editorials that were most readily accessible in Philip Foner's edition of Douglass's writings. By the time I finished writing, however, the digital age outpaced me by making the actual newspapers more readily available than anything in print. Accessible Archives Inc. is well along the way toward putting online all the Douglass newspapers in searchable form. See www.accessible.com. The Abraham Lincoln Association has done the same for the Lincoln papers. See www.hti.umich.edu/l/lincoln. Finally, the important collections of Lincoln and Douglass papers at the Library of Congress are available at its American Memory website: http://memory.loc.gov/ammem/index.html.

Needless to say, I could not have begun to understand what either man had to say had I not also consulted the work of other scholars. But because this book is so fundamentally an examination of two men's words, I have restricted my citations to the sources from which the words were taken and have cited secondary works only sparingly. To compensate somewhat for my minimalist notes, this essay is designed to give readers some sense of my relationship to the scholarship on which this book is based, and guide them to further explorations of the subject.

FREDERICK DOUGLASS

Biographies of Douglass began appearing shortly after his death in 1895, yet despite his standing as the leading African American of the nineteenth century, no one has produced a life of Douglass comparable in scope to the distinguished multivolume biographies of Booker T. Washington by Louis Harlan or W. E. B. DuBois by David Levering Lewis. The starting place for modern biographies of Douglass is Benjamin Quarles, *Frederick Douglass* (1948). Philip Foner's extensive introductions to each of the four volumes of *The Life and Writings of Frederick Douglass* constitute a valuable political biography in their own right. Dickson J. Preston, *Young Frederick Douglass: The Maryland Years* (1980) is excellent, for both its intrepid research and its balanced judgment. Nathan Irvin Huggins, *Slave and Citizen: The Life of Frederick Douglass* (1980), a good short biography, puts Douglass in the context of African American activism in the nineteenth century. Waldo E. Martin, *The Mind of Frederick Douglass* (1984) is an intellectual biography that highlights what Martin sees as Douglass's lifelong struggle with his own racial identity. David W. Blight, *Frederick Douglass's Civil War: Keeping Faith in Jubilee* (1989) ranges more broadly than its title suggests and offers the best coverage of Douglass's growing Christian millennialism and his corresponding commitment to revolutionary violence. The only full-length biography is William S. McFeely, *Frederick Douglass* (1991), which probes Douglass's inscrutable interior life more deeply than any other biography and is well written besides.

Douglass's meetings with Lincoln are covered in Benjamin Quarles, *Lincoln and the Negro* (1963). Two good articles focus on Lincoln and Douglass: Christopher N. Breiseth, "Lincoln and Frederick Douglass: Another Debate," *Illinois State Historical Society Journal*, vol. 68 (1975), and David W. Blight, "Race and Rebirth: The Relationship between Abraham Lincoln and Frederick Douglass in Language, War, and Memory," in his *Beyond the Battlefield: Race, Memory, and the American Civil War* (2002), pp. 76–90. For a brief, accessible summation of the Lincoln and Douglass meetings, see John Stauffer, "Across the Great Divide," *Time* (July 4, 2005).

Several specialized studies help locate Douglass's ambivalent views about race, but precisely because of his ambivalence different writers see different facets of Douglass's thought. For the broad context, see Mia Bay, *The White Image in the Black Mind: African American Ideas about White People, 1830–1925* (2000). Where Bay focuses on popular ideas, Bruce Dain, *A Hideous Monster of the Mind: American Race Theory in the Early Republic* (2002) explores the scientific ideas about race within and against which Douglass struggled. But sometimes Douglass rejected the category of race altogether, and this aspect of Douglass's thought is the focus of John Stauffer, *The Black Hearts of Men: Radical Abolitionists and the Transformation of Race* (2002), which traces Douglass's relationship with three like-minded radical abolitionists.

The recent emphasis on race and racial identity stands in contrast to the relative dearth of scholarship on the emergence of black politics before the Civil War. African American leaders debated fiercely among themselves about how best to wage political struggles against racial discrimination in the North and slavery in the South, but there is no full-length scholarly study of this internal debate. A good place to begin is Benjamin Quarles, *Black Abolitionists* (1969), one of his many path-breaking books. Two prolific communists, both committed to the primacy of the party, saw from the outset the importance of the political struggle: Philip Foner's biographical introductions to his own edition of the Douglass papers zeroed in on the political question, prodding Douglass along his path toward the Republican Party. The first volume of Herbert Aptheker's monumental *Documentary History of the Negro People in the United States* (1951) traced the wider debate among northern blacks. The question of political engagement was central to Douglass's development as an activist and goes far toward explaining the difficulty he had in staking out a stable position.

Douglass often changed his mind, he exaggerated, and he wasn't always reliable. For an impatient historian in search of steady ideas and hard facts, this sometimes makes Douglass a frustrating subject. But for literary scholars, it makes him a rich vein to be mined for penetrating insights. More comfortable than most historians with the inconsistencies, absences, and hyperbole in his texts, literary scholars have produced some of the best work on Douglass. They read his polemics for what they were—polemical texts—not to evaluate their

truth claims but to discern their rhetorical strategies. This puts literary scholars well ahead of everybody else in their sophisticated
approach to the way Douglass constructed his own public image.
Some of the range and depth of this scholarship can be gleaned in two
impressive collections of essays: William Andrews, ed., *Critical Essays
on Frederick Douglass* (1991) and Eric Sundquist, ed., *Frederick Douglass:
New Literary and Historical Essays* (1990). A high point of this body of
work is Sundquist's own book, *To Wake the Nations: Race in the Making of
American Literature* (1993). Here is an example: To validate Douglass's
autobiographical account of his years as a slave, historians and biographers have tended to emphasize the factual consistency between the
1845 *Narrative* and the 1855 *My Bondage and My Freedom*. But Sundquist
noticed the profound (and profoundly important) rhetorical shift
from alienation to a troubled American identity between Douglass's
first and second autobiographies. Philosophers also have taken up
Douglass in another useful collection of essays, Bill E. Lawson and
Frank M. Kirkland, eds., *Frederick Douglass: A Critical Reader* (1999).
Of special note is the contribution by Charles Mills, "Whose Fourth of
July? Frederick Douglass and 'Original Intent.'" Mills is critical of
Douglass's premise about an egalitarian founding (although the same
principle of fundamental human equality is the unacknowledged
premise of Mills's own essay). For a more sympathetic account of
Douglass's most famous speech, see James A. Colaiaco, *Frederick
Douglass and the Fourth of July Oration* (2006).

ABRAHAM LINCOLN

There are dozens of Lincoln biographies, but the standard for our
time has been set by David Herbert Donald's *Lincoln* (1995). Of the
many shorter biographies, *Abraham Lincoln and Civil War America* by
William E. Gienapp is noteworthy for its grasp of the political culture

within which Lincoln emerged. Richard J. Carwardine's *Lincoln* (2003) is a political biography, especially good on Lincoln's sensitivity to public opinion. Allen Guelzo, *Abraham Lincoln: Redeemer President* is an erudite and well-written intellectual biography. Two collections of essays show how much is still to be gained by mining hitherto neglected sources on Lincoln's life. Douglass Wilson, *Lincoln before Washington* (1997) traces critical aspects of Lincoln's life prior to his presidency. Michael Burlingame, *The Inner World of Abraham Lincoln* (1994) reflects the author's unparalleled mastery of the sources. Two sympathetic books cover the White House years: Philip Shaw Paludan, *The Presidency of Abraham Lincoln* (1994) and Mark E. Neely, Jr., *The Last Best Hope of Earth: Abraham Lincoln and the Promise of America* (1995).

During the 1960s Lincoln's remarks on race (as opposed to slavery) left him open to some overly harsh criticism, which has in turn provoked some overly defensive rejoinders. The subject was broached in a measured, scholarly way by Benjamin Quarles, *Lincoln and the Negro* (1962). An uncompromising assault was launched by Lerone Bennett, Jr., first in a provocative essay in 1968 and more recently in *Forced into Glory* (2000). More balanced assessments came from Don E. Fehrenbacher, "Only His Stepchildren," written in 1973 and reprinted in his *Lincoln in Text and Context: Collected Essays* (1987); George Frederickson, "A Man but Not a Brother: Abraham Lincoln and Racial Equality," *Journal of Southern History* (1975). Two important essays touch on Lincoln, although they focus on prevailing racial attitudes in the North and the Republican Party: C. Vann Woodward, "The Northern Crusade Against Slavery," in his *American Counterpoint* (1971); and a rejoinder of sorts in Kenneth M. Stampp, "Race, Slavery, and the Republican Party," in his *The Imperiled Union: Essays on the Background of the Civil War* (1980). LaWanda Cox, *Lincoln and Black Freedom: A Study in Presidential Leadership* (1981) was the first book-length attempt to salvage Lincoln's reputation on matters of race.

When the focus shifted from race to slavery, and from racial ideology to political thought, the case for Lincoln was easier to make and the literature is more balanced. A turning point in this regard was Eric Foner, *Free Soil, Free Labor, Free Men* (1970), followed several years later by Gabor S. Boritt, *Lincoln and the Economics of the American Dream* (1978). Some of the most important defenses of Lincoln have come in analyses of his speeches. The catalyst for this approach was Garry Wills's outstanding study *Lincoln at Gettysburg: The Words That Remade America* (1992). See also Ronald C. White, *Lincoln's Greatest Speech: The Second Inaugural* (2003) and Harold Holzer, *Lincoln at Cooper Union: The Speech That Made Abraham Lincoln President* (2004).

Lincoln was first and foremost a politician, and the skill with which he pursued his craft has long been at the center of Lincoln scholarship. Here some of the older works are still essential. David Donald, *Lincoln Reconsidered: Essays on the Civil War Era* (1961) highlighted Lincoln's roots in the Whig Party. Don E. Fehrenbacher, *Prelude to Greatness: Lincoln in the 1850's* (1962) traced, with characteristic precision, Lincoln's reentry into politics in the 1850s. A useful collection by a group of master historians is Gabor S. Boritt, ed., *Lincoln the War President: The Gettysburg Lectures* (1992). Until the end of his life Lincoln thought of himself as a Whig, and that background is covered extensively in Michael Holt, *The Rise and Fall of the American Whig Party* (1999). Most of the biographies mentioned earlier speak to Lincoln's political savvy. The most recent entry into this seemingly well-plowed field is Doris Kearns Goodwin's engaging *Team of Rivals: The Political Genius of Abraham Lincoln* (2005).

The political crisis of the 1850s brought both Lincoln and Douglass into antislavery politics. David Potter, *The Impending Crisis, 1848–1861* (1976) is a subtle political history of the decade. Michael F. Holt, *The Political Crisis of the 1850s* (1978) is a clever restatement of the older "revisionist" interpretation that held politicians, rather than slavery itself, responsible for the sectional crisis. For a critique of Holt, see Eric Foner, *Politics and Ideology in the Age of the Civil War* (1980). Kenneth M. Stampp, *America in 1857: A Nation on the Brink* (1990) is an excellent account of the *Dred Scott* decision and the climactic events in Kansas. Bruce Levine, *Half Slave and Half Free: The Roots of Civil War* (1992) is a good brief survey stressing the conflict over slavery.

ABOLITIONISM AND ANTISLAVERY POLITICS

The 1830s and 1840s were the heroic years of the abolitionist movement, when skilled organizers succeeded in provoking a raging political discussion of slavery at a time when most politicians wanted the subject suppressed. These were also the years of William Lloyd Garrison's greatest influence and most important contribution. But because Lincoln was never an abolitionist, and because Frederick Douglass only entered the movement after it had already done its most important work and had splintered into competing factions, the importance of the abolitionist movement itself is somewhat slighted in this book. Readers seeking a broader view can begin with several good surveys. Gilbert Hobbs Barnes, *The Antislavery Impulse, 1830–1844* (1933) was eccentric and unbalanced even when it was published, but it was also shrewd, lively, and well-researched, and it has an excellent account of the campaign to flood Congress with antislavery petitions. Barnes deliberately understated Garrison's importance to the early movement, and he paid no attention at all to black abolitionists. Benjamin Quarles, *Black Abolitionists* (1969) corrected for this deficiency. Subsequent surveys are friendlier to Garrison and more attuned to the role of African Americans. See in particular two books by Merton Dillon, *The Abolitionists: The Growth of a Dissenting Minority* (1973) and *Slavery Attacked: Southern Slaves and their Allies, 1619–1865*

(1990). The best brief analysis of abolitionism is James Brewer Stewart, *Holy Warriors: The Abolitionists and American Slavery*, 2d. ed. (1996). An earlier work, James M. McPherson, *The Struggle for Equality: The Abolitionists and the Negro in the Civil War and Reconstruction* (1963) showed that abolitionists remained active during and after the Civil War. McPherson's book was one indication of how the civil rights movement of the sixties inspired a new generation of scholarship on abolitionism. Three anthologies demonstrate what has and has not changed since then: Martin Duberman, ed., *The Antislavery Vanguard: New Essays on the Abolitionists* (1965); Lewis Perry and Michael Fellman, eds., *Antislavery Reconsidered: New Perspectives on Abolitionists* (1979); and Timothy Patrick McCarthy and John Stauffer, eds., *Prophets of Protest: Reconsidering the History of American Abolitionism* (2006).

The trips Garrison and Douglass took to Great Britain as emissaries of American abolitionism are only one indication of the transatlantic aspect of antebellum reform. As far back as the 1930s, Barnes, *The Antislavery Impulse* was attuned to the significance of British developments. But the level of discussion rose several notches with the publication of David Brion Davis, *The Problem of Slavery in the Age of Revolution* (1974) and the subsequent debate it provoked. For the debate, see Thomas Bender, ed., *The Antislavery Debate: Capitalism and Abolitionism as a Problem in Historical Interpretation* (1992). The most thorough comparative treatment, with a similar theme, is Robin Blackburn, *The Overthrow of Colonial Slavery: 1776–1848* (1988). The emphasis on the bourgeois origins of the antislavery movement is one indication of a wider shift toward a broader study of middle-class reform. An exemplar of this literature is Stuart M. Blumin, *The Emergence of the Middle Class: Social Experience in the American City, 1760–1900* (1989). Two fine surveys of the reform movement are Ronald Walters, *American Reformers* (1978) and Robert Abzug, *Cosmos Crumbling* (1994).

Garrison and the Garrisonian wing of the abolitionist movement were a force unto themselves and so demand some consideration of their own. John L. Thomas, *The Liberator, William Lloyd Garrison: A Biography* (1963) set a very high standard for subsequent work. Thomas was sympathetic to abolitionism but critical of Garrison's arrogance and disdain for politics. Aileen Kraditor, *Means and Ends in American Abolitionism: Garrison and His Critics on Strategy and Tactics, 1834–1850* (1969), responded with a sharply reasoned, well-researched, but not entirely persuasive defense of Garrison. His stance, Kraditor said, made sense given the thoroughly proslavery and racist consensus of American society. At issue is whether that stance, which made a great deal of sense in 1835, was still viable in 1855. James Brewer Stewart's brief *William Lloyd Garrison and the Challenge of Emancipation* (1992) gives full credit to Garrison's role in bringing about a change that he himself had trouble adapting to until the very eve of the Civil War. Henry Mayer, *All on Fire: William Lloyd Garrison and the Abolition of Slavery* (1998) is a work of prodigious research but limited critical distance.

One of the dilemmas facing historians of abolitionism is the fact that by the middle of the 1850s most abolitionists were Republicans. Because the antislavery movement merged into antislavery politics it is not easy to trace a continuous history of abolitionism as such up to the Civil War. Because Garrison resisted active political engagement for so long, he stands out in the 1850s and students of the movement find it hard to take their eyes off him, even as they acknowledge how marginal he had become. There is a tendency to equate "abolitionism" with "Garrison," especially in later years. It's a difficult trap to avoid and I don't think I myself have completely avoided it. At times I speak of "abolitionists" when I mean only Garrison and his followers, losing sight of the fact that most abolitionists had moved into the Republican Party. All the more reason, then, to balance the history of abolitionists with the history of antislavery politics.

The outstanding study of the rise of antislavery politics is Richard Sewall, *Ballots for Freedom: Antislavery Politics in the United States* (1976). Eric Foner, *Free Soil, Free Labor, Free Men* (1970), gives full attention to the place of abolitionists within the new Republican Party. On the origins of antislavery politics, William M. Wiecek, *The Sources of Antislavery Constitutionalism in America, 1760–1848* (1977) is superb. More recently Jonathan H. Earle upgrades the reputation of the Free Soilers in *Jacksonian Antislavery & the Politics of Free Soil, 1824–1854* (2004). Sean Wilentz, *The Rise of American Democracy: Jefferson to Lincoln* (2005) develops a similar theme by way of a magisterial survey of early American political history. William E. Gienapp, *The Origins of the Republican Party, 1852–1856* (1987) is comprehensive. On the Democratic Party nothing has yet replaced Roy Nichols, *The Disruption of American Democracy* (1962). Two essential monographs are Jean Baker, *Affairs of Party: The Political Culture of Northern Democrats in the Mid-Nineteenth Century* (1983) and Wallace Hettle, *The Peculiar Democracy: Southern Democrats in Peace and Civil War* (2001). The standard biography of Lincoln's great rival is Robert W. Johannsen, *Steven A. Douglas* (1973).

CIVIL WAR AND EMANCIPATION

Because emancipation was so closely tied to the fortunes of the Union Army, the military history of the Civil War is an essential starting point. Long ago Bruce Catton made slavery and emancipation the central theme of his masterful three-volume history of the Civil War: *The Coming Fury* (1961), *Terrible Swift Sword* (1963), and *Never Call Retreat* (1965) collectively trace the process by which the Civil War became a social revolution and the goal of restoring the Union gave way to the goal of recreating a Union without slavery. Besides being a first-rate stylist, Catton was as astute an observer of politics and politicians as he was of soldiers and battles. But for the purely military history of the war, the battles and the generals, there is nothing quite like Shelby Foote, *The Civil War: A Narrative* (1958–1974). Foote's broad interpretive framework is a reiteration of the discredited "Lost Cause" explanation for Confederate defeat—the South was doomed from the start by overwhelming northern numbers—and he simply could not take slavery and African Americans seriously. But Foote was a master storyteller more than an analyst, and in the details of his battle narrative he is lucid, witty and shrewd. Those seeking a better balance of narrative and analysis, of social, political, and military history, are fortunate to have James McPherson's modern classic, *Battle Cry of Freedom* (1988).

The most recent generation of military historians has proven remarkably adept at incorporating political and social history into the study of the war. The tip of this impressive iceberg is Herman Hattaway and Archer Jones, *How the North Won: A Military History of the Civil War* (1983) and, to a lesser but still impressive extent, a companion volume by Richard E. Beringer, Herman Hattaway, Archer Jones, and William N. Still, Jr., *Why the South Lost the Civil War* (1986). A sense of how sophisticated the military history of the Civil War has become, as well as the lively debates that have ensued, can be gleaned from the following, a mere sample of the best literature: Richard M. McMurry, *Two Great Rebel Armies: An Essay in Confederate Military History* (1989) is a well-reasoned intervention in, and introduction to, the debates over Robert E. Lee and the strategy and tactics of the Confederate armies. Gabor S. Boritt, ed., *Why the Confederacy Lost* (1992) has several powerful essays. Mark Grimsley, *The Hard Hand of War: Union Military Policy toward Southern Civilians, 1861–1865* (1995), is an erudite intellectual history of northern military policy, with full attention to the way emancipation unfolded. Gary Gallagher, *The Confederate War* (1997) is a spirited argument that white Confederates were united in their commitment to the southern nation. A rejoinder of sorts—though the two interpretations are ultimately compatible—is William W. Freehling's brilliant *The South vs. The South: How Anti-Confederate Southerners Shaped the Course of the Civil War* (2001). Jeffry D. Wert, *The Sword of Lincoln: The Army of the Potomac* (2005) updates Bruce Catton's older pioneering history of the Union's troubled army in the eastern theater. For further reading, several of the essays in James M. McPherson and William J. Cooper, Jr., *Writing the Civil War: The Quest to Understand* (1998) are exceptional.

On emancipation itself, the pioneer was John Hope Franklin, *The Emancipation Proclamation* (1963), which foreshadowed the social historians' emphasis on the role the slaves themselves played in securing their freedom. Leon Litwack, *Been in the Storm So Long* (1979) is a beautifully evocative re-creation of the way slaves and masters experienced the transition from slavery to freedom. Litwack played down the importance of the Emancipation Proclamation and at the same time highlighted the actions the slaves themselves took to gain their freedom. This aspect of the argument soon became popular. A version of it appears, for example, in the Freehling book mentioned above. My own slant was published as James Oakes, "The Political Significance of Slave Resistance," *History Workshop* (1986). Carried to one possible conclusion, the argument might suggest that the slaves freed themselves. For this tendency, see Ira Berlin et al., *Slaves No More: Three Essays on Emancipation and the Civil War* (1992); Steven Hahn, *A Nation under Our Feet* (2003). On the surface, Armstead L. Robinson, *Bitter Fruits of Bondage: The Demise of Slavery and the Collapse of the Confederacy, 1861–1865* (2005) is a sophisticated reworking of an interpretation made famous long ago by Frank W. Owsley. But where Owsley claimed that "states' rights" killed the Confederacy, Robinson adds that states' rights was born of the southern elite's need to protect slavery at the local level. Robinson goes on to argue that various policies aimed at protecting slavery embittered southern yeomen, turned them against the war, and caused the Confederacy to collapse from within. It is this emphasis on class conflict by Robinson and others that Gallagher, cited above, seeks to rebut.

Most historians agree that black troops, largely recruited from the slave South, played an important role in Union victory and thus emancipation. On black troops, see Benjamin Quarles, *The Negro in the Civil War* (1953); Dudley Taylor Cornish, *The Sable Arm: Negro Troops in the Union Army* (1956); Joseph T. Glatthaar, *Forged in Battle: The Civil War Alliance of Black Soldiers and White Officers* (1990). Particularly important is Glatthaar's essay "Black Glory: The African American Role in Union Victory," in Boritt, ed., *Why the Confederacy Lost*. See also the chapter on "Black Liberators" in Litwack, *Been in the Storm So Long*.

With the recent emphasis on the slaves' role in emancipation has come a reassertion of the criticism, first aired in late 1862, that the Emancipation Proclamation freed no slaves at all because it applied only to areas beyond Union control. Richard Hofstadter's brilliant essay "Abraham Lincoln and the Self-Made Myth," in his *American Political Tradition, and the Men Who Made It* (1948) gave this old argument a new respectability. But even Hofstadter seemed to appreciate what a dead end this line of reasoning came to, since he later claimed in the very same essay that the proclamation probably made the abolition of slavery inevitable. Thus Hofstadter ended up exaggerating the proclamation's importance almost as much as he first underestimated it. More recently the proclamation is sometimes discounted because by the time Lincoln announced it in September 1862 the slaves had allegedly sealed slavery's fate. But claiming that the proclamation meant nothing is no more balanced than claiming it meant everything. In fact, it was a crucial turning point in a process that began perhaps two years before it was issued and did not end for two or three years after it was issued.

Dismissal of the proclamation is part of a larger critique of

Lincoln for his allegedly "slow" and "grudging" acquiescence in emancipation. "Fast" and "slow" are, of course, relative terms, and as
Frederick Douglass came to realize, by the standards of the American
people as a whole Lincoln's pace toward emancipation was radical and
swift. That pace was set first by military events, then by political considerations, but also—and to a degree that Lincoln's critics often lose
sight of—by profound constitutional constraints. For a critical examination of the legal issues, see Louis Gerteis, *From Contraband to
Freedman: Federal Policy Toward Southern Blacks, 1861–1865* (1973). A
shift in favor of Lincoln and the Republicans is evident in two
very intelligent books by Herman J. Belz, *A New Birth of Freedom:
The Republican Party and Freedmen's Rights, 1861–1866* (1976) and
Emancipation and Civil Rights (1978). See also Donald J. Nieman,
Promises to Keep: African Americans and the Constitutional Order (1991) and
Michael Vorenberg, *Final Freedom: The Civil War, the Abolition of Slavery,
and the Thirteenth Amendment* (2001). Much more favorable to Lincoln
are James M. McPherson, *Abraham Lincoln and the Second American
Revolution* (1991), an insightful collection of essays, and Allen Guelzo,
Lincoln's Emancipation Proclamation: The End of Slavery in America (2004),
which summarizes the legal and constitutional issues surrounding the
proclamation. The title of Richard Striner's *Father Abraham: Lincoln's
Relentless Struggle to End Slavery* (2006) speaks for itself.

The Postwar Years

Eric Foner's magisterial *Reconstruction: America's Unfinished Revolution,
1863–1877* (1988) traces the movement of the freed slaves into the
social and political mainstream where they entered into contracts as
free laborers and entered into politics as engaged citizens. In sharp
contrast to Foner's emphasis on revolutionary transformation, Steven
Hahn, *A Nation Under Our Feet: Black Political Struggles in the Rural South*

from Slavery to the Great Migration (2003) sees the freed people as a pre-capitalist peasantry whose strong national identity and potent separatist impulses developed during slavery and continued long after emancipation. For those who, like Frederick Douglass, believed that the enfranchisement of the former slaves was the crowning achievement of Reconstruction, the later disfranchisement of black southerners was nothing less than counterrevolution. On the destruction of the black vote in the postwar South see J. Morgan Kousser's classic, *The Shaping of Southern Politics: Suffrage Restriction and the Establishment of the One-Party South, 1880–1910* (1974) and Michael Perman, *Struggle for Mastery: Disfranchisement in the South, 1888–1908* (2001).

ACKNOWLEDGEMENTS

This book was nurtured by a great publishing house and a great editor. Were it not for the patience of W. W. Norton and the confidence of Steve Forman there would be no book. For their e-mails, conversations, readings, insights, citations, documents, and sometimes just for listening to me, I must also thank David Abraham, Evan Friss, Allen Guelzo, Don Herzog, Bill Kelly, Jan Lewis, Michael McGerr, John R. McKivigan, Jim McPherson, David Nasaw, Rita Roberts, Judith Stein, Sean Wilentz, the students in my Spring 2006 graduate seminar and, of course, my wife, Deborah. Several of these folks had no idea what I was up to when I bombarded them with my questions, so they cannot possibly be held responsible if anything is wrong with this book. But they all helped me get it done, and for that I'm grateful.

INDEX

❖ ❖